I0892420

The Art of Ballet Accompaniment

GERALD R. LISHKA

The Art of Ballet Accompaniment

A Comprehensive Guide

INDIANA UNIVERSITY PRESS

This book is a publication of

Indiana University Press
Office of Scholarly Publishing
Herman B Wells Library 350
1320 East 10th Street
Bloomington, Indiana 47405 USA

iupress.org

© 2022 by Gerald R. Lishka

All rights reserved
No part of this book may be reproduced or utilized in any form or by any means, electronic or mechanical, including photocopying and recording, or by any information storage and retrieval system, without permission in writing from the publisher. The paper used in this publication meets the minimum requirements of the American National Standard for Information Sciences—Permanence of Paper for Printed Library Materials, ANSI Z39.48-1992.

Manufactured in the United States of America

First Printing 2022

Library of Congress Cataloging-in-Publication Data

Names: Lishka, Gerald R., author.
Title: The art of ballet accompaniment : a comprehensive guide / Gerald R. Lishka.
Description: Bloomington : Indiana University Press, 2022. | Includes index.
Identifiers: LCCN 2022014765 (print) | LCCN 2022014766 (ebook) |
ISBN 9780253063342 (cloth) | ISBN 9780253063359 (ebook)
Subjects: LCSH: Musical accompaniment. | Ballet dancing. | Ballet.
Classification: LCC MT68 .L47 2022 (print) | LCC MT68
(ebook) | DDC 781.47—dc23/eng/20220404
LC record available at https://lccn.loc.gov/2022014765
LC ebook record available at https://lccn.loc.gov/2022014766

This book is dedicated to the memory of

Marina Svetlova,

a great dancer and former Professor of Ballet and Chairwoman of the Ballet Department at Indiana University, where I was her ballet accompanist for a time. Her encouragement and assistance were key to the successful publication by Indiana University Press of my earlier book, A Handbook for the Ballet Accompanist. *Madame Svetlova passed away in Bloomington, Indiana, in 2009.*

Contents

Foreword

Foreword by Kyra Nichols

Like most dancers, I did not give much thought to the skills required to be the person in the corner of ballet class playing the piano. The accompanists were always a quiet presence, and certainly I was aware of those fundamental people—both the ones who brought a special energy to a class, and the ones who didn't.

But it was not until I began teaching ballet later in my career that the importance of a skilled accompanist became clear to me. It is not simply a matter of preferring the contributions of a live person to the hassle of using recordings. It is about the unique skills that the accompanist brings to the room. The ability to intuit what the teacher is wanting to hear, how the tempos and mood of the piece might be reflected in the steps. About how quickly the accompanist comes up with the right music and keeps it varied to help students maintain focus.

Only when I began teaching did I truly understand how spoiled I had been, especially at New York City Ballet. I can only imagine the degree of intimidation a pianist must have felt playing class for Mr. Balanchine, himself a pianist. Now I can truly appreciate the varied skill set of our accompanists, people like Gordon Boelzner and Jerry Zimmerman, who played company class for ninety minutes in the morning, played again for a few hours of rehearsal in the afternoon, and then might perform the complete Goldberg Variations that same evening. And the skills are different for each.

Among the things that so greatly appeal to me about this book are the clarity with which it explains the range of skills required to be a good accompanist and the way it delineates how those skills differ from the ones required to be a concert pianist. People commonly make the mistake of assuming that because someone can play the piano, that person inherently has the skills necessary to play for ballet class. I truly admire Gerald's honest explanation of the deer-in-the-headlights confusion he experienced in his initial efforts to play for dance class.

Memorizing a score or perfecting your keyboard technique are not sufficient when you play for class. A ballet teacher might appear to be doing random steps in the front of the room, but they expect you to come up with music in the correct tempo without hesitation.

The necessary skills are highly valued in some cultures. For example, at the School of American Ballet, the official school of the New York City Ballet, we had many accompanists of Russian heritage. Playing for class was something that was clearly respected and valued in that culture, and pianists trained for the role. In my experience outside New York, finding pianists anxious to embrace the role of class accompanist and do the work required to excel is a rarity.

In my career, and especially during my years working for Mr. Balanchine, dancing was always about the music. When all goes well, a relationship develops between the dancer and the music. As Mr. Balanchine said, "Come see the music." For Mr. Balanchine, the music always came first, and we were trained to dance to the music as it was played, whatever the tempo. I was amazed when I'd visit other companies and see dancers instructing the accompanists and conductors where they wanted them to slow down or speed up. For Mr. Balanchine, we danced what they played.

But you are not likely to develop either ability—to dance to the music as played, or to ask for the tempos you want—if you don't get to train to live music.

A partnership evolves between the teacher and the accompanist. Ideally, the accompanist learns the teacher's habits, their preferences, and yet keeps things fresh and inspiring. Being an accompanist for dance is both a specific set of skills developed on one's own, and a group experience shared with a roomful of dancers who probably don't truly appreciate all the work required to make their classes move smoothly.

I am hopeful that this book will help build the ranks of excellent accompanists and help those in and around the dance world to understand the importance of the live accompanist in training dancers who are capable of performing to live music with spontaneity, flair, and confidence. Schools and companies that consider using only recorded music in their classes and rehearsals, likely due to budgetary constraints, must also consider the limitations that this presents for the training they are providing. Paying live accompanists may have a monetary cost, but denying your dancers this necessary experience hinders their training.

It is similar to requiring dancers to take class in pointe shoes. At New York City Ballet, we took class every day in pointe shoes, rehearsed in them, and performed in them as well. There were costs to this, but it also ensured that we were the best we could be on pointe. I firmly believe that using recorded music is like letting dancers take all their classes in ballet slippers and then expecting them to look comfortable and confident on pointe.

As long as we expect excellence from dancers, we will need similar excellence in accompanists. This book provides a road map to turn a good pianist into an excellent accompanist. I hope you will pursue this path. We in the dance world need you!

Kyra Nichols
Violette Verdy and Kathy Ziliak Anderson Chair in Ballet;
Professor of Music (Ballet)
Indiana University, Jacobs School of Music

Preface

This book, *The Art of Ballet Accompaniment: A Comprehensive Guide*, is the evolutionary outgrowth of its predecessor, *A Handbook for the Ballet Accompanist*, which was published by Indiana University Press in 1979. The *Handbook*, which has been a steady seller for more than four decades and which has been described as the first comprehensive book of its kind, has continued to be a valuable reference work both for pianists who aspire to be ballet accompanists and for anyone who is already working in the profession.

While preserving the wealth of relevant material contained in the *Handbook*, the *Guide* provides rich, new detail in the form of updates, enhancements, and new topics. Chapters 1 and 2 of the *Guide* offer all of the essential information and advice that a pianist inexperienced in ballet work would need in order to embark on this journey in an informed manner. These sections of the book will also provide valuable support and insight for the more seasoned practitioners of the art, since many of the dynamics of playing for ballet class remain challenges throughout one's career.

Since many technical aspects of playing for ballet remain unchanged through the years, Chapters 3, 4, and 5 of the *Guide* retain all of the valuable information formerly included in the *Handbook* regarding descriptions of dance steps and combinations, suggested musical repertory, and preparing and arranging music for class. In the new *Guide*, however, this core material has been significantly enhanced through the advanced treatment of earlier subjects and the introduction of invaluable new knowledge and guidance. Areas now covered include finding the proper balance between existing repertory, musical arranging, memorization, and—significantly—improvisation; developing an in-depth understanding of ballet instructors and how to work with them; feeling empathy for the dancers; researching the wealth of music scores available online, many of which can be downloaded at no charge; finding a true balance between the discipline of dance accompaniment and the preservation of artistic integrity; and tapping the potentially unlimited expansion in musical consciousness available to accompanists who have imagination and drive.

The *Guide* provides a sample list of composers whose music can be used in class; it also provides a provocative list of music terrain to be explored—ranging from the traditional, relatively accessible repertory to repertory that is challenging both technically and musically. This second grouping will especially interest the intrepid pianist who seeks to distinguish herself among the instructors and dancers with whom she works. Of high importance are the detailed analyses of compositions by Bach and, in contrast, Prokofiev, in order to orient the accompanist to the often highly challenging work of transforming the music into components of logical, aesthetically acceptable phrasing that are absolutely indispensable for dance class.

Serious dance instructors and dance students are strongly encouraged to study this book, and thereby to gain insight into how the accompanist perceives dancers and what are the thought processes that a musician experiences in her desire to support work in the studio. Because of their continued relevance today, and their relevance to this new *Guide*, a few thoughts are excerpted from the preface to the *Handbook* and paraphrased here:

> The purpose of this book is to advise and instruct pianists in the art of ballet accompaniment. Accompanying the ballet, and doing it well, is a unique skill that requires a great deal of experience, a resourceful and flexible musical imagination, and a special sensitivity to dance movements. It would be extremely difficult for the ordinary pianist to imagine all of the problems that are inherent in dance accompaniment. Succinctly stated, the challenge of the dance accompanist is to provide the quality of musical support and inspiration that is absolutely necessary for the dancer, while maintaining her own sense of musical individuality and integrity.

To this, only the following needs to be added:

> Working with and inspiring dancers is an art. It must be pursued while maintaining high aesthetic standards, and while balancing a respect for the traditional with an appetite for the new and exciting. The challenge is, at all costs, not to let oneself become dull or to dull the dancers. Vigilance, and the perfection of the craft, are paramount.

Special acknowledgment is warmly expressed here to Alison Hennessey, Chair of Dance at the California School of the Arts—San Gabriel Valley, in Duarte, California, for her careful review of and enhancements to the terminology for the dance steps and related information contained in this book. She holds a master's degree in dance education, ABT Ballet Pedagogy, from New York University, and she is also a graduate of Loyola Marymount University and Orange County School of the Arts. Ms. Hennessey was the director of a dance school in the New York metropolitan area and has taught, choreographed, and adjudicated for over a decade throughout the United States and Canada. She has won numerous awards for her choreography on both the regional and the national levels. Her students have found placement with Beyoncé, Pacific Northwest Ballet, Ballet Idaho, Nashville Ballet, and Dana Foglia Dance, as well as with numerous other companies and artists. Heartfelt appreciation and gratitude are also extended here to David E. Farrell, DM, Assistant Professor of Music at Metropolitan State University of Denver, for his superb work in preparing all of the musical engravings in this book, which he accomplished with precision, efficiency, timeliness, and great attention to detail, while offering ready solutions to a number of challenges.

The Art of Ballet Accompaniment

Introduction

I wrote the following in 2019 as part of my ballet accompaniment résumé and strategy for capturing the interest of various dance institutions. I include it here to share my beliefs and practices regarding ballet accompaniment.

Gerald R. Lishka

How I View the Art of Ballet Accompaniment

My professional training as a concert pianist and my experience in playing for all levels of dancers, including professionals, would, I believe, make me an asset to any dance conservatory or university environment. Here are some of my thoughts on how I view the art of ballet accompaniment.

When I play for ballet classes, I draw on hundreds of scores—or generally, excerpts of scores—that I have selected over the years for their beauty, energy, interest, variety, and applicability to dance steps. My repertory comprises an extensive list of composers, many of whom are well known and some that are not. It spans from Bach and Scarlatti to a wealth of twentieth-century composers including Ravel, Debussy, Satie, Gershwin, Poulenc, Bartok, Milhaud, and many others; and it also includes judiciously selected popular pieces for spice, when applicable to the dance steps.

Only a small percentage of my repertory is aired in class in its original, pristine form. There is an element of improvisation in most of my offerings, sometimes to the extent that the original composition, however familiar, might not be easily recognized, if at all. In my experience, dance accompanists who rely solely on improvisation can get into deep ruts just like pianists who do not improvise at all. I find, at least in my own playing, that a rich, fluid blend of existing repertory and the infusion of improvisation avert repetitive, deadening playing.

Some dancers with whom I have worked have been highly intelligent, musically. Others, even stars, have occasionally shocked me regarding how little they know about music. Nevertheless, I do not believe that any dancer needs to be played down to. Dancers of all levels need to develop an ability to listen to the music being played in class, not to tune it out. If musical offerings are played clearly and intelligently, and with a sensitivity to the dance combination being executed, an incredible variety of music of can be utilized, ranging from simple to highly sophisticated, without confusing even young, inexperienced dancers.

My worst nightmare would be that my music might become monotonous to dancers. I am always looking for new sources. Recently, I added "Kitten on the Keys" to my repertory. I recently heard a heartbreakingly beautiful piece on the radio and immediately researched it—the Eclogue for Piano and String Orchestra by the twentieth-century English composer, Gerald Finzi. I obtained both the recording and the score and developed an arrangement for pliés and adagios. I also recently added an Elegy of Rachmaninoff, and an excerpt from the Variations on a Theme of Paganini; also the Pavane Pour une Infante Défunte of Ravel, which, as is sometimes the case, required expert surgery to shape it into the "square" numbers of measures required for ballet class, while preserving its grace and logic. I have been generously incorporating Poulenc, because his lyricism and colorful harmonies serve for me as a refreshing antidote to the monotonous drone that I often hear in ballet classes.

I avoid playing almost all traditional ballet music.

Music for ballet class can range from meltingly lyrical to percussive and dissonant, as long as it is rendered by an intelligent pianist who understands context and who performs in a manner that infuses energy and inspiration into a dance class.

1 The Ballet Class

The Ballet Studio

Wide Variations in Characteristics. The physical and aesthetic qualities of dance studios, whether for ballet, modern dance, or other styles, vary dramatically. The ballet accompanist will encounter an enormous range in characteristics, such as studio dimensions, acoustics, lighting (both artificial and natural), ventilation, and overall maintenance. Dimensions range widely from studio to studio, depending on the type of institution (e.g., university, community college, public or charter high school, or private academy) and the levels of funding and operating budgets. Some studios are comparable in size to large living rooms; on the upper end, they can be vast and magnificent, with high ceilings, and can occupy several thousand square feet.

Mirrors. Mirrors are a feature of virtually all ballet studios and enable the dancers to observe their own body positions and movements—and those of other dancers. Mirrors are about eight feet in height and cover at least one studio wall, or sometimes two adjacent walls.

Barres. Ballet studios always feature horizontal bars—"barres"—that provide support and balance to the dancers while they are doing their barre exercises during the first ("barre") portion of the class. Barres, made of wood or metal, may be permanently affixed to various walls in the studio—except those walls with mirrors—or may be portable so that they can be placed out on the dance floor during the barre portion of the class and then set aside during the center portion. Whether the barres are attached to the wall or are portable, they consist typically of two parallel barres, one bar directly underneath the other, in order accommodate various dancer heights and age levels and various types of exercises, including stretches. The height of the upper barre is generally about forty to forty-two inches from the floor to the center of the barre. The lower barre is usually ten to twelve inches below the upper barre.

Dance Floors. Traditionally, dance floors have been sprung floors with a hardwood surface. "Sprung" floors absorb shocks and have a softer feel, and they are regarded as the best for dance because they enhance performance and significantly reduce injuries. Modern sprung floors are supported by foam backing or rubber feet—as opposed to traditional flooring, which provides spring through bending, woven wooden battens. Currently, the popular alternative to the traditional hardwood surface is sheet vinyl, commonly referred to as "marley" (or marley-type flooring), a term derived from an extremely popular reversible vinyl flooring manufactured for many years (until around 1978) by Marley Floors Ltd.

Pianos. The ballet accompanist will encounter every make and size of piano, from spinets to concert grands—and in every condition imaginable, from out of tune and decrepit to immaculately maintained. Electronic keyboards are not uncommon, and they can serve quite well. The issue of pianos will be discussed in more detail elsewhere in the book, including the advantages, in some cases, of electronic pianos.

Class Size. Dance class enrollments can range from a handful—four or five—to twenty, forty, up to seventy-five or above.

Caliber. Depending on the institution where one accompanies, the caliber of dancers and dance instructors comprises a very broad spectrum—from demanding, fastidious, and professional artists to the rankest amateurs.

Class Length. Class lengths vary significantly, depending on the institution and its scheduling constraints, but primary determinants are age and proficiency levels. Ballet technique classes range from forty-five minutes to two hours or more. A typical length is eighty to ninety minutes. Pointe classes generally last about an hour.

Effects on Accompanist. Some of the topics touched on above may have an effect on the ballet accompanist and can influence her approach to playing in the studio. These effects will be discussed later in more detail.

The Major Technical Methods of Ballet Instruction

A short overview of the six internationally recognized methods of ballet instruction is offered here, although this information will have little to no bearing on how the accompanist works in the ballet studio. These methods of instruction are the French school, the Vaganova method, the Cecchetti method, the Bournonville method, the Royal Academy of Dance (RAD) method (English style), and the Balanchine method (American style). Other schools exist in various countries. Generally, the three schools that the ballet accompanist will hear referred to in class most frequently are Vaganova, Cecchetti, and RAD.

French. This method is the basis of all ballet training, codified under Louis XIV and his Académie Royale de Danse. This technique prevails today, irrespective of the specific method employed. Rudolf Nureyev (1938–1993) revitalized it, and it is therefore sometimes referred to as "Nureyev school." Central to this method are technical precision, gracefulness, and clean lines.

Vaganova. This method, originated by Agrippina Vaganova (1879–1951), grew out of Russian ballet and was codified in 1934 in her book *The Fundamentals of Classical Dance*. The Vaganova method combines elements from the classical French style, the Italian method, and the Russian ballet. Vaganova's precise teaching methods, which are age specific, appeared in her 1948 book *Basic Principles of Russian Classical Dance*. Her books and teaching methods remain influential.

Cecchetti. This method, developed by Enrico Cecchetti (1850–1928), is based on the understanding of anatomy in relation to classical ballet. Important elements of this method include balance, poise, and strength. It promotes the idea that all parts of the body move together to create graceful lines, and it de-emphasizes the concept idea of arms, legs, and neck, and torso as separate parts. This method is well known for its eight distinctive port de bras movements.

Bournonville. This Danish method was conceived by August Bournonville (1805–1879), who was strongly influenced by early French ballet technique. It is distinct from other ballet methods currently taught, and it develops dancers with "ballon"—an illusion of profound lightness.

Royal Academy of Dance (RAD). This method, known also as the English style, was established in 1920 by the dancers and teachers Adeline Genée, Tamara Karsavina, Phyllis Bedells, Eduardo Espinosa, Philip Richardson, and Lucia Cormani. It focuses on academic training in classical ballet in Great Britain. Now used extensively in the United States, it employs specific grade levels to be completed by dance students to complete the training. This method emphasizes that ballet training must be developed very slowly in terms of difficulty—that is, that significant effort in perfecting basic steps enables a student to assimilate more challenging steps at an easier rate.

Balanchine. This method was developed by George Balanchine (1904–1983) at the New York City Ballet. Based heavily on Balanchine's Russian training, this technique is characterized by extreme speed, emphasis on lines, and deep pliés. It features an unorthodox positioning of the body, often with flexed hands and feet, and off-balance positions. The Balanchine method is utilized at the Miami City Ballet, the Ballet Chicago Studio Company, and the School of American Ballet.

Understanding Ballet Terminology

Always in French. In many respects, ballet is an art that embodies a broad universality in its basic nature. Still, ballet originated in France, and the basic terminology of ballet and the names of the ballet steps have consistently remained in the French language, regardless of where the ballet classes are being given—whether, for example, in the United States, Russia, or Brazil. Furthermore, the general ballet vocabulary has remained very stable over a long period of time; a plié is always a plié, a tendu is always a tendu.

Many Reference Sources Available. Although it is acknowledged that the pianist who understands ballet terminology is in a more secure position as a ballet accompanist than one who does not, the aspiring or inexperienced ballet accompanist need not feel unduly discouraged if she is relatively or even totally unfamiliar with ballet terminology. Numerous dictionaries of ballet terms can be freely accessed online, and there are ample printed dance dictionaries available if the accompanist prefers a hard copy that she can study and also refer to quickly. The *Technical Manual and Dictionary of Classical Ballet*, by Gail Grant, first published in 1950, is considered by many professionals to be an outstanding reference guide. The book's third revised edition, published by Dover Publications in 1982, includes over 1,100 ballet steps, poses, and related concepts, and a pictorial supplement.

Observe Carefully. Knowing the names of the various dance steps and having an idea of the physical mechanics associated with them will help the accompanist feel more at ease and better prepared in the ballet studio. One of the advantages of knowing the names of dance steps is that, as soon as the instructor announces one, the ballet accompanist can immediately give thought to what kind of music is needed. However, such knowledge will likely be gained gradually, over time and with experience. The essential matter of concern for the new dance accompanist is to carefully observe the movements of the dancers, sensitizing herself to their maneuvers. Generally, the dance instructor will demonstrate at least part of any dance combination to the students prior to their undertaking it, and having gained a little experience, the accompanist will be able to grasp the essential idea behind each step and will become more adept at selecting music that is suitable in feeling and tempo. Many dance instructors will assist the accompanist by indicating in some way the kind of music they want.

Indeed, the experienced ballet accompanist will have little problem functioning in a dance class in which the language that is spoken—with the exception of the universal French terms for the steps—is totally foreign to her, since she will have developed the essential ability to empathize with the dance instructor's movements. By watching the instructor demonstrate the combinations, she can easily ascertain pretty much all she needs to know in order to choose appropriate music.

Same Combinations for Successive Classes. The accompanist will occasionally encounter situations in which the instructor expects dancers to perform certain combinations the same way class after class, or at least for a number of classes. Mostly, this would apply to foundational combinations at the barre, such as pliés, tendus, or stretches. In such cases, an accompanist who is new to the class will need to be especially aware and responsive in order to respond quickly, since making the class wait for music is not desirable. This will be addressed in much greater detail elsewhere in this book.

Observing Other Accompanists. Observing other pianists in class—a topic fully explored elsewhere in this book—will be very instructive to novice ballet accompanists who are learning to associate specific dance terms with a few examples of appropriate music, while bearing in mind that innumerable compositions in various styles could be successfully adapted to the same step.

Uniform Musical Phrases

The Absolute Rule of Square Phrasing. Any dance combination given by an instructor in a classical ballet technique class will, virtually without exception, be structured to accommodate musical phrases that are square and even. In ballet technique instruction, this can be regarded as an absolute rule, and breaking it would not be worth even considering. The ballet accompanist will want to note, however, that this does not necessarily hold true in a class for modern dance—an environment in which considerably more flexibility in phrasing and counting is enthusiastically embraced, but which is addressed in this book only occasionally.

Even Phrases. In a ballet technique class, the sequence of dance steps will always fall into four-, eight-, sixteen-, and—if the combination is a longer one—thirty-two-bar phrases. The *occasional* exception is a combination that, for example, is a twelve- or twenty-four-bar-phrase, but this is uncommon and may actually be an oversight on the part of the dance instructor. Even if the instructor gives a dance combination that has an unusual meter, such as 5/8 or 7/8—which is extremely rare, and in most classes is unheard of—the phrases will, with virtually no exceptions, be square and even.

Cadencing After Three Equal Phrases Instead of Four. Although it is not common, an entire dance combination may consist, for example, of three sixteen-measure phrases, rather than four sixteen-measure phrases. In other words, the combination may end after forty-eight measures rather than sixty-four, or at twenty-four measures rather than thirty-two. This will not, by any means, always be clear to the accompanist ahead of time. In fact, it is not always apparent to the instructor until the end of the combination. If the accompanist is alert, there will be no serious difficulty. Since the accompanist knows that the musical phrase will be a square one, she does not need to worry from measure to measure exactly when the music will end. By watching the dancers or by receiving an indication from the instructor, she will quickly discern whether it is time to cadence at the end of a particular phrase. The accompanist should finish any dance combination in a musical fashion that sounds natural and graceful. The music should not be chopped off abruptly or unexpectedly in a manner that leaves the dancers hanging in the air, so to speak.

Explore the Possibilities. Bearing all of the above in mind, the ballet accompanist should prepare and program herself and her music so that she always plays in even musical phrases, that she cadences—or is prepared to cadence—in the proper measure of music, and that she ends combinations with the dancers. This is not to say—ever—that the accompanist should not explore and investigate music that is unsquare in its phrase structure (for example, music originally written in phrases of perhaps seven or eleven bars), because in many cases she can easily—or with some degree of thought and work—perform some kind of musical surgery that will render the music suitable for ballet accompaniment purposes (that is to say, making it into phrases of eight bars), while leaving the musical sense of the altered piece intact in its own right, logical, and acceptable to the ears. In fact, if the accompanist is *not* open to looking into music that can be revamped for ballet technique classes, she will be turning her back on a universe of rich possibilities.

Uneven Phrasing Can Be Fixed. Later in this book, various methods will be discussed for arranging music with uneven phrasing to make it suitable for ballet technique accompaniment. As was stated just above, when considering music for the ballet class, the pianist who walks away from a nice piece of music solely because it is not square or not immediately usable is depriving herself. She may lift only a phrase or two from the original score, or she may appropriate a particular harmonic progression that she can expand on her own into an entirely independent musical idea. Exercising this kind of imagination, flexibility, and creativity is essential for anyone who wants to accompany for ballet class and do it well.

Musical Preparations and Their Functions

Preparations Are Universal and Indispensable. The ballet accompanist provides a musical introduction—referred to as a *preparation*—for each and every dance combination given in a ballet technique class, whether at the barre or in the center. Although different ballet instructors have their own preferences and idiosyncrasies regarding how to conduct their classes, preparations are universal. Since giving preparations is a basic, indispensable function, the ballet accompanist must understand how to offer them and the many ways in which this can be done. Preparations, including musical examples, will be discussed in chapter 5, Preparing and Arranging Piano Repertory for Ballet Class.

Communicating Mood and Tempo. The purpose of the preparation is to enable the dancers to prepare and position themselves appropriately for the combination. The preparation may provide some indication of the general character—and ideally, even the mood—of the music to follow and, *of absolutely central importance*, what the tempo for the combination will be.

Types of Preparations. Preparations can be of many types, especially depending on the skill of the accompanist, but generally they are short—or, to state this another way, they are no longer than necessary for the dancers' orientation. The length of a preparation, and probably other features of it as well, will vary a bit depending on the types of dance steps involved and the associated tempo. A preparation may consist simply of two chords—for example, a dominant chord followed by a tonic chord, or a ii chord followed by a dominant seventh chord—or perhaps an arpeggio in the tonic or dominant. Alternatively, it may be a two- or four-bar phrase, or eight beats of a left-hand ostinato.

A further comment and clarification: although used by accompanists, preparations that consist of a couple of chords or an arpeggio are not ideal, since they are not an effective means of communicating tempo. If they are used at all, it should probably be for slow pliés, adagios, or stretches. Ostinato-type preparations are fine for medium- to faster-paced steps. The only caveat is that the dancers may have some doubt as to when the combination begins. Perhaps the best preparations are those that offer a complete musical phrase or part of a phrase, with a clear beat, and some type of cadence that signals that the combination is going to begin.

Generally at the Accompanist's Discretion. It is highly unlikely that the dance instructor will tell the accompanist how to play the preparation. However, the instructor may indicate to the accompanist the desired tempo and, in some instances, the general character of the music desired—for example, a tango, a waltz, or an adagio. Otherwise, it will be left up to the accompanist, more or less, what the all-important preparation is to be. If the accompanist plays the preparation at one tempo and then plays the combination at a different tempo, there will, at a minimum, be confusion. He must therefore make certain to give the preparation in a tempo that is clear and in uniformity with the tempo of the combination that follows.

When the Preparation Does Not Work. Because the all-important and always-required preparation will almost always be of a character determined by the accompanist, it follows that if the preparation the accompanist offers is or seems to be misleading, confusing, or otherwise inappropriate, the instructor will stop him and provide some kind of feedback. The most common issue, by far, will be that the tempo is not right—especially when the instructor has not indicated to the accompanist what it is to be. Because time in a ballet class is generally limited and therefore is a precious commodity, having to restart a combination because the preparation was "off" can elicit a slight tension on the part of the instructor and a corresponding discomfort on the part of the accompanist. However, this is life in the ballet class. Such things will happen on occasion. The accompanist's goal is to minimize these occurrences by being as alert as possible—and to trust, when there is an issue, that the instructor will be diplomatic.

Preparations for Fast Combinations. When a dance combination is exceptionally fast, the accompanist may be uncertain about the best length for the preparation. A preparation that is too short may leave the dancers unprepared. On the other hand, if the accompanist attempts to play a combination that is twice as long—for example, four bars instead of two—the dancers may be confused and start prematurely. Interestingly, with really bright combinations, the line between playing a short preparation and playing one twice the length—there is no in-between—can be blurry, which can make the accompanist uncomfortable. In these cases, if the accompanist "takes his best shot" but the dancers end up confused, the instructor and the accompanist may pause and then agree that the length of the preparation should remain the same, or be doubled, or perhaps be reduced by half.

Confidence with Experience. Experience is a good teacher, and over time the ballet accompanist will become more adept at getting everything right the first time—including preparations. However, the ballet technique class, being the dynamic environment that it is, will not fail to slip some occasional stumbling blocks in front of him, and he should not be unduly discouraged by them. "Pitching a perfect game" in a dance class is a great goal, but it is rare.

Ending Combinations with the Dancers

Not an Insignificant Challenge. The ability of the ballet accompanist to consistently end her music to coincide with the end of a dance combination requires a high level of alertness and is a skill that takes time to develop. Consistent perfection is perhaps not a realistic goal. When an instructor demonstrates or explains a dance combination to the dancers, the instructor may appear—to the accompanist, at least—to do it somewhat hastily. The dancers will generally understand what the instructor has in mind, whereas the accompanist may find herself in considerable doubt as to exactly how many bars of music a given combination will require. In such cases, the accompanist need not feel totally confused. At the least, she may rely on the assumption that the combination will be designed to fit into even, square phrases of music, as was discussed earlier in this chapter under "Uniform Musical Phrases." At any rate, her challenge will always be to not end her music until the combination has finished, and to not have her music spill over after the dancers have finished. If the accompanist remains poised and is as prepared as possible to cadence at the end of each major musical phrase, while keeping an eye on the instructor for potential instructive signals (many instructors will appreciate and respond meaningfully to this, especially when eye contact is made), she will generally, and with practice, be able to end at the appropriate time.

Exceptional Communication. Rarely, the accompanist may have the pleasure of working with a dance instructor who will actually give the accompanist a verbal heads-up when, for example, the last eight counts or bars of a combination commence, thereby giving clear, courteous notice about when the music should conclude. Again, it is a rare instructor who offers this, and the accompanist should appreciate and be responsive to it.

Recovery Methods. Occasionally, the accompanist will end a combination, only to realize that the class is still dancing. There are several possible reasons for this. Perhaps she has been too absorbed in her own playing to be aware of what is going on with the dancers. Perhaps she has failed to calculate the amount of music required and has stopped too soon, or perhaps the instructor has decided unexpectedly to have the combination repeated without interruption and has indicated this to the dancers without giving clear or ample notice to the accompanist. One effective technique the accompanist can use to ameliorate this situation—especially with faster combinations—is to continue counting beats after the combination appears to have ended. By doing this, the accompanist will know exactly where she is in terms of the beats in a measure and, with a little practice, can jump back into the music quite readily and at the right place. In such a tight spot she will have no time to grope around mentally for the right beat but will have to react almost instantaneously in order not to confound the dancers and disrupt the combination. The accompanist can be even more in control of the situation not only by counting silently after she assumes that the combination has ended, but also by continuing to play silently on the surface of the keyboard. This method is nearly infallible, and it will bail the accompanist out of the situation outlined above every time: she has only to begin depressing the keys again, and she will be exactly where she should be in the music.

Balancing at the End of a Barre Combination. One issue that has the potential to complicate the accompanist's life a bit is that, after various combinations at the barre, the instructor may expect the dancers to balance in one pose or another for a certain number of counts or measures. Although the accompanist will generally be alerted to this instructor preference in advance, she may not always be aware of it immediately beforehand. She will likely become better accustomed to how this practice is employed—and therefore be better prepared—as she gets to know how particular instructors work, since their preferences will vary. When balancing work is being added, after the combination has ended, the music should not stop, but should continue until the balancing portion has been completed. The challenge, again, is to end the music when the dancers have completely finished. Some instructors seem not to mind if there is no music during the balancing, but generally music is desired. A point of refinement: if the music has been especially driving during the combination itself, it is not inappropriate to soften and otherwise modify it for the balancing portion, although the tempo should not change.

Center Work. After the dancers have completed the barre portion of the class and are working out on the dance floor during the second phase of the class, the accompanist's responsibility to end with them presents essentially the same challenges as it did during the barre work. In addition, and especially toward the end of the ballet class, the dancers will likely be involved in steps and combinations for which they start at one corner and dance diagonally to the opposite corner, or they may simply dance from one side of the studio to the other. They may do this singly, in pairs, four at a time, or in larger groups. In such cases, the accompanist, after giving an appropriate introduction (preparation) for the first dancer or group of dancers, will simply continue to play, while each succeeding dancer or group of dancers prepares and then begins at each new four, eight, or sixteen measures of music (whatever the instructor wishes). Occasionally, the instructor may ask the accompanist to insert a preparation into the music—for example, every sixteen bars—to prepare the next dancer or group of dancers. In this case, the music will not stop between each group of dancers; instead, two or, more likely, four introductory measures will be inserted at regular, appropriate intervals. The accompanist will likely finish playing after all dancers have completed the combination from one corner or side of the room. However, the instructor may have the dancers circle around the room and perform the combination again, without a pause in the music. In some cases, the instructor will even have dancers who have completed the combination assemble at the opposite corner or side of the room, to prepare to do the combination from the new starting point, without any break in the music. Various aspects of this kind of accompanying will be discussed in greater detail elsewhere in this book.

Changing Sides and Reversing Combinations

Two practices—performing combinations on both sides and reversing combinations—are basic elements of the ballet technique class.

Changing Sides. All combinations given in the ballet class should be executed on *both sides*. This means that, during barre work, the first side is traditionally performed with the left hand on the barre; the left side of the body is the supporting side and the right side of the body is the working side. Then the dancers *change sides*, meaning that the second time the combination is performed, the dancers turn and face the opposite direction so that the right hand is on the barre; the right side of the body is now the supporting side and the left side of the body is now the working side. Again, the order set forth above is considered traditional, but some instructors may do the opposite, either consistently or whenever they choose. However, to have dancers do combinations on only one side would be considered a deficient practice. During the center portion of the class, combinations are also performed on both sides.

Reason for Changing Sides. Whether at the barre or during center work, although changing sides affords the dancers the opportunity to execute a combination twice, so to speak, the foundational reason is so that each side of the body—and the brain—can be trained and developed uniformly, in a balanced manner that distributes strength and coordination throughout the entire body.

The Accompanist's Role in Changing Sides. Pursuant to the practices described above, the ballet accompanist should expect to play for each dance combination at least twice—once for the left side and once for the right side—during the barre and center portions of the class, subject to the comments below. (Combinations may always be repeated, at the discretion of the instructor, especially if she feels that the dancers need to improve their execution of the combination.)

The Accompanist, Changing Sides at the Barre. During barre, there may be a full break between the performance of one side of a combination and the other, during which time the instructor may give some corrections. The instructor may also ask the accompanist not to end the music between sides but to play continuously, thereby requiring the dancers to execute an immediate and sometimes rapid about-face. Alternatively, the instructor may ask the accompanist not to stop playing between sides but to insert a musical bridge of, for example, four or eight beats, to give the dancers just enough time to do their about-face and have an extra second or two to get positioned. The accompanist should not be surprised if it is during the actual execution of the first side that the instructor calls out her decision to have the dancers perform both sides of a combination continuously or with a break.

The Accompanist, Changing Sides in the Center. During center work, generally there will be a full break between the execution on the left side and the execution on the right side. In this case, the accompanist will stop, and will begin again when the dancers are prepared and the instructor indicates.

Reversing Combinations. During the barre or the center, the instructor may ask the dancers to *reverse* a combination. When a dance combination is reversed, the dancer's working leg moves in the direction opposite the direction in which it moved in the original combination. A simple illustration: if a dancer is doing a tendu exercise in which his working leg is extended in front of him, when the dance combination is done in reverse, his working leg will be extended behind him.

Accompanist's Role in Reversing Combinations. When a combination is reversed, the accompanist will use the same music as was used for the original combination, unless the instructor asks for something new (very rare). There will be a break before a combination is reversed, whether the work being done is at the barre or in the center. The instructor may go over the entire reversed combination with the dancers before its execution, possibly by having them mark it, that is to say, do a walkthrough, probably at a slower tempo.

Thinking Ahead

Anticipating the Next Combination. As the ballet accompanist becomes more experienced in playing for classes, both in general and for specific instructors, she will become increasingly able to anticipate, in a general way and with fair accuracy, what the next dance combination will be or is likely to be. This is particularly true with respect to the order of combinations in the barre work. Here, while still taking into account normal variation and varying class levels, the sequence of steps is fairly well established or at least reasonably predicable.

Strategies for Being Prepared. Different instructors have different approaches to teaching a class, and as the accompanist becomes more familiar with individual instructors, she will be in a fairly good position to anticipate their routines. But if the accompanist does not readily improvise (a very desirable skill) or does not have many of her musical scores memorized, it is very wise to think ahead a combination or two and to be prepared for what may come. For example, if the class has just finished their plié combination, or combinations, at the barre, the accompanist may anticipate with reasonable certainty that the following combination will be tendus. The tendus will probably be slow or possibly moderate in tempo. After the tendus will probably come battements tendus dégagés. If these are omitted, the next exercise is likely to be either fondus or ronds de jambe. By thinking ahead in this manner and knowing what kind of music is suitable for each step, the accompanist will be able to prepare herself mentally about what to improvise or play from memory, or she will take this opportunity (perhaps while the instructor is giving a correction to the class) to locate appropriate scores and position them where they will be immediately available when she requires them.

Helpful Sections in This Book. By studying chapter 3, Barre and Center Combinations, and also the section of chapter 2 entitled "Organizing Music for Ballet Class," the accompanist can become thoroughly knowledgeable about the sequence of dance steps in a ballet technique class and the strategies for preparing for them musically. When combined, these two sections will enable her to be well positioned for quick and appropriate responses to anticipated combinations.

Maintaining Musical Options. It is appropriate to reiterate here that it is very wise, whenever possible, for the accompanist to be prepared—*poised* is perhaps the best word—to play on demand, and instantly, any one of three or four different pieces for the same dance combination, since one piece or another may turn out to be most suitable for some reason or other—possibly just because the instructor takes a liking to it. Being prepared in this way, the accompanist will save valuable class time, which is always at a premium. Instructors do not like to stand by and wait, even for a moment, for the accompanist to come up with music, and the dancers will start to feel uncomfortable when the flow of the class is disrupted.

Prerecorded Music for Ballet Technique Class

Live Accompaniment Invaluable. Good accompanists are more than an asset to the ballet class. Some instructors and dancers would argue that they are practically indispensable—certainly with regard to advanced instruction. If the class does not have the advantage of a good accompanist, there are two alternatives, neither of which is usually preferred or even desirable.

No Music. The instructor may elect to teach the class without music. To say the least, this is not a desirable or uplifting prospect. Aside from being totally uninspiring for both the dancers and the instructor, such an environment does nothing to expand the musicality of the dancers. The instructor is left to her own resources—singing, counting, clapping her hands, snapping her fingers, or stamping on the floor. The only outcome can be a tired instructor, with sore hands or a raw throat, unable to devote full attention to the class.

Prerecorded Music. As a second alternative, the instructor may elect to use some type of prerecorded music. Years ago, this meant using a record player or a tape machine. Later, there were compact discs. Today, the preferred method is to download the music to the instructor's mobile phone and play it from there. This latter alternative allows the instructor to move around the studio, at least, with the music in hand.

Downsides of Prerecorded Music. Although prerecorded music is much better than no music at all, it has significant downsides. First, it imposes serious limitations on the spontaneity and creativity of the instructor. It is a relatively limited and nonflexible source from which to draw. Its inherent drawbacks are magnified by the fact that the same recorded music is often used over and over again, for the same classes, possibly for a very long period of time. Second, having to use prerecorded music disrupts—unquestionably—the flow, momentum, and spontaneity of the dance class. After teaching a particular dance combination to a class, the instructor must then locate a suitable prerecorded musical selection. This wastes time and disrupts her train of thought and focus.

Lack of Flexibility. Although any ballet class will reflect a certain format and order that is fairly universal, there remains ample opportunity for the instructor to modify, embellish, and improvise on the relatively established routines. Such avenues may be taken in order to devote more time to specific weaknesses of the dancers, to address certain individual needs, or to emphasize a particular point in that class. With prerecorded music, the instructor may be faced with locating suitable music for each of these situations—which most instructors consider a nuisance. It is also time-consuming, as well as unsatisfactory for dealing with many impromptu situations that arise during class. With prerecorded music, all of the scenarios outlined above make for a relatively rigid class. Another example: if unforeseen issues arise, precious time may be consumed when the instructor must find music to accommodate a routine that is temporarily suspended for the purposes of a teaching moment.

Tempos. Using prerecorded music may mean that the tempo for any particular dance combination is preestablished, or it may mean that if an alteration is needed, the instructor has to find different music, taking more of her time and focus. Given the many variables during ballet technique instruction—such as the abilities of the dancers, the technical difficulty of any given step, or the condition of the dancers' muscles—the relative inflexibility and inconvenience of prerecorded music can significantly diminish the possibilities that might otherwise be easily explored during the dance class.

Some Specific Examples of the Advantages of Live Accompaniment

Quick Tempo Changes. If the instructor needs to adjust the tempo of a combination while it is in progress, a good accompanist can respond to this need on the spot—virtually instantaneously.

Connecting Music Between the Right and Left Sides. In the ballet technique class, all combinations are performed on both the right side and the left side—generally in that order. Instead of giving a combination—either at the barre or in the center—that is performed on the right, then stopped, and then performed on the left, the instructor may decide, either before the combination is executed or even during its actual execution, that she wants the combination to be performed on the right and then *immediately*—that is to say, without interruption—on the left, with no interruption to the music. Alternatively, she may want the music to be continuous but with a four- or eight-bar musical interlude inserted between the right side and the left side. A word or two to a good accompanist, either prior to or in the midst of a combination, can make this happen smoothly and effortlessly.

Variety in Music Repertory. The presence of live accompaniment, with all of its benefits for the ballet technique class, exposes the dancers—and the instructor—to a much wider and richer universe of music. It keeps them stimulated and challenged, while encouraging them to listen actively to what is being offered. This is discussed in detail later in the book.

Life in the Dance Studio Much Easier. Finally, the best response to the challenges inherent in the use of prerecorded music is a live accompanist (provided that she is a good one). The presence of an accompanist who is attentive, responsive, and experienced will alleviate these difficulties and make life in the dance studio much easier and far more enjoyable for both the instructor and the students.

Open Classes

Many private dance schools offer "open" ballet classes to the public. Generally, anyone who walks in and pays the fee can participate in an open class—largely irrespective of ability, physical conditioning, training, proficiency, or age (generally early high school to senior adult). Open classes are sometimes referred to as "adult" classes.

It is not uncommon for an open class to be made up of a combination of professional or semiprofessional dancers, trained high school students, young adults to seniors of varying skill, and even individuals who appear to have had very little—if any—formal training. Sometimes an individual with apparent but not debilitating physical challenges may take an open class—at least the barre and possibly a portion of the center. Since each combination given by the instructor must be "one size fits all," or nearly that, some of the dancers will execute the steps with a high degree of proficiency, while others often "fake it."

Because of the wide variance in the dancers' abilities, open classes often resemble what amounts to little more than a workout routine—a "cardio" class—in which most participants get little to no correction or training, except if the instructor chooses to focus on one or two dancers who can actually benefit from and absorb corrections. The rest of the class may be passed over.

The Accompanist's Perspective. Playing for open classes usually offers little reward (and it can be assumed that the same applies to the instructor). The problem for the accompanist is that, since the instructor takes little time to train or correct most of the students, open classes often proceed at a fast or sometimes almost breakneck speed—so that, if nothing else, the class can perspire and burn calories. The accompanist plays almost constantly, with very little time between combinations, in an environment in which pianistic concerns about aesthetics and beauty easily become almost irrelevant. During the center portion of the class, the across-the-floor and diagonal combinations are often performed in a highly repetitive manner, with infrequent breaks, if any. Even in an open class in which the dancers share some comparability in training and ability, the pace is intense, especially with higher levels of training, since these dancers are there primarily for the workout.

For the accompanist, an open class can amount to a marathon—exhausting and, especially during the latter portion of the class, conducive to muscle and tendon strains in the hands or forearms. The accompanist may find that playing for this kind of class, where his major focus becomes watching the clock, is just not worth it.

2 Advice and Guidance

The Attitude of the Accompanist

A Vital Role. The accompanist plays a vital role in the ballet technique class. Her effect on the dancers and the instructor is immediate and continuous. Depending on her ability, experience, sensitivity, and temperament, she may be a great inspiration, or she may drag a class down and drain its momentum. Both the instructor and the dancers, if they are at all sensitive to music, will be impacted by the accompanist, her music, and her attitude. The accompanist should strive to project an interested, uplifting, collaborative attitude, and be sensitive to and actively engaged in what the dancers are going.

Repertory and Interest. Of great importance, she can succeed in her work by offering an inspiring repertory that embraces many styles and that grows and changes over time, so that her playing will not become stale or hackneyed; by learning to improvise freely and often, summoning from her own creativity fresh, new musical ideas; and by maintaining an active interest in the mechanics of the ballet class—being attentive and alert to the dialogue between instructor and dancers, and to the corrections given.

The Purpose of the Guide. All of the technical information and advice contained in this *Guide* is aimed at helping the accompanist to develop and maintain a healthy, professional attitude toward her work; to understand dance; to avoid potential pitfalls; and to deliver a scope and quality of music that will earn her the respect and affection of teachers and dancers.

The Accompanist as Music Educator

For Better or for Worse. Whether she realizes it or not, the ballet technique class accompanist is a music educator. This may be for better or for worse, depending on the professionalism that she brings to her work. She is—consciously or not, and conscientiously or not—a kind of dietitian: responsible for what the dancers in a technique class consume musically, and responsible for whether it is rich, varied, and nurturing, or uninteresting and nutritionless.

A Primary Source. Sometimes, the music the accompanist plays in the dance studio is one of the primary sources, if not the only source, of serious, high-quality music literature to which a dance student is exposed. Those dance students who have had the opportunity to study music theory or literature, or who are able to learn to play a musical instrument, are very fortunate. They are bound to be better and better-informed artists as a result of this exposure and training. However, since many dancers do not have these opportunities, their musical horizons and tastes likely suffer. The ballet accompanist may be someone to whom the dancers are exposed regularly, over a substantial period of time, and therefore her own musical training, knowledge, tastes, and experience are potentially an impactful source of musical exposure and knowledge for the dance students—and many times, for the instructor.

The Unlimited Body of Music Literature. Although a lot of piano music is definitely unsuitable for a ballet technique class—experience will inform the accompanist about this—the body of keyboard literature from which the accompanist has to draw is practically infinite. The accompanist who has improvisation skills has even greater—virtually unlimited—horizons; and those pianists with some knowledge of orchestral, operatic, and vocal literature have yet another immense source of material that they can adapt and arrange, if they are motivated to do so.

Not Just Classical Music. In order to have a truly rich musical repertory for ballet technique class (also discussed in great detail later in this book), the accompanist needs to be open-minded regarding the wealth of high-quality, *nonclassical* music that is more than serviceable—that can supply refreshing variety, and should be embraced enthusiastically—for ballet classes, including, for example, pop, rock, Broadway, Latin, and jazz.

Take note here that, at least in the context of this book, "classical" does not just mean compositions from Bach to Tchaikovsky. Rather, it includes a huge body of works from the pre-Baroque and early Baroque periods, and virtually the entire twentieth century, with all of its neoclassical and other styles.

Staying Fresh. The ballet accompanist will find it a real challenge to avoid having her playing become stale—to herself (especially herself, since she will likely hear it more than anyone else), to the dancers, and to the instructor. She should put continual effort into expanding her own dance music repertory, for everyone's sake. By doing so, she will be introducing more and more music literature to the dancers and familiarizing them with new musical styles. Not only will this offer stimulation and intellectual challenge to the dancers, but also it will help to prepare them for working with a great variety of music to which they will likely be exposed while they are dancing professionally. For those dance students who intend at some point to become dance teachers themselves, the musical exposure that has been provided by motivated dance accompanists will be invaluable.

Avoid Cliché Ballet Music

The introduction "How I View the Art of Ballet Accompaniment" is a brief statement of the author's philosophy regarding playing for ballet classes: "I avoid playing almost all traditional ballet music." Accordingly, the accompanist is encouraged to avoid the use of "cliché" ballet music for ballet classes—that is to say, well-known tunes (at least well known by many ballet instructors) from ballets such as Tchaikovsky's *Sleeping Beauty* and *Swan Lake*, Adam's *Giselle* (or *The*

Wilis), *Les Sylphides* (music of Chopin, arranged by Glazunov and originally choreographed by Fokine), or Catel's opera *Les Bayadères*. An exception might be the occasional use of a piece like the *Coda* from the ballet *Don Quixote* (music by Minkus).

Although Tchaikovsky's ballet scores are brilliant, as are those of, for example, Bartók, Prokofiev, and Stravinsky, many other traditional ballet scores are not. Some are, in fact, little more than musical wallpaper written to enable the dancers to show off their virtuosity. On the other hand, many of the truly interesting and challenging ballet scores are not suitable, as written, for the ballet class, and to perform the musical surgery necessary to make them usable would render them unacceptable, and justifiably so, to many dance instructors.

There are too many musical resources—thousands of pieces—available for the accompanist's exploration that offer support and inspiration, as well as challenge, to a ballet class, without having to resort to the "hit tunes" of the ballet world. In addition, although professional dancers and those students aspiring to become professionals may smile at an occasional, familiar favorite, they may on some occasions experience a slight cognitive dissonance in doing combinations in the ballet studio to music that they may be familiar with in relation to other specific choreography.

A final point may be made: most of those dance students who do make it into the professional world of dance will not be part of a corps de ballet in a large, international ballet company that performs traditional works. They will be picked up by smaller, regional or local companies in which they likely will have the opportunity to perform to new and original music or to music that is less commonly heard. It will have been to the advantage of such dancers to be provided, during their training, with a rich and varied musical diet.

The position taken in this book is that the accompanist has an opportunity and an obligation to infuse ballet classes, at least at times, with music that is new, original, and interesting, while offering the support necessary for the development of ballet technique.

Observing Other Accompanists

Observing Other Accompanists Strongly Recommended. It is strongly recommended that aspiring or beginning accompanists and those with a few months of experience seek opportunities to observe other accompanists playing for ballet classes: to see how they operate; how they organize themselves, if at all; and what mix of improvised and printed music they draw on. If the observer is playing or wants to play at a large institution where several ballet pianists are in service, then the main issue will likely be whether to observe discreetly or to do so openly, perhaps even in the studio, seated near the accompanist. The same issues apply, with potential additional complications, to schools where the observer is an outsider. Another option is to search the internet, especially YouTube, where accompanists can sometimes be observed—at least heard, if not seen—playing for classes.

The Unobserved Observer. Whatever conditions or limitations may apply in various settings, the most instructive environments will be those in which the accompanists who are being observed are unaware of it, for then they will, so to speak, be themselves—for better or worse. It follows that it will also be instructive to observe both good accompanists and those who are not so good. Lessons can be learned either way. At any rate, watching other accompanists play, under any conditions that can be accessed, should be a valuable learning experience.

Modern Dance Classes. It is highly recommended that all ballet accompanists—aspiring, beginning, and advanced—observe at least a few modern dance classes, especially if a pianist is used, but also where the accompaniment is percussion. Even if the ballet accompanist feels that she is largely or exclusively interested in playing just for ballet technique classes, these experiences will be highly informative and instructive to her, both in and of themselves and as a way of informing her about her approach to ballet accompaniment. These experiences may even arouse aspirations to expand into modern dance work. Having the ability to accompany both for ballet technique and for modern dance is very desirable.

Avoid Sounding like Wallpaper

Becoming a Superior Dance Accompanist. This section is offered to both aspiring and experienced ballet accompanists in the same spirit as that of "How I View the Art of Ballet Accompaniment" and the section "Avoid Cliché Ballet Music," earlier in this chapter. In fact, were it not for the proscriptive, if not downright negative, tone of a phrase like "Avoid Sounding like Wallpaper," it could be the title of this book. This general admonition, taken with the strong viewpoints mentioned above, amounts to a *credo*—a statement of beliefs and aims intended to guide pianists in becoming superior dance accompanists. Everything else in the book offers techniques and disciplines to achieve this—to excite and challenge dancers, and to avoid mediocrity, which dulls the accompanist, the dancers, and the instructor.

Observing Other Accompanists. Any pianist who desires to become a ballet accompanist—or a better ballet accompanist—is advised that one of the most instructive and informing things they can do is observe and listen to other ballet accompanists while they work in class. Whether or not direct observation is possible, recommended alternative or complementary ways to get exposure to other ballet accompanists and the quality of their work include the following:

- Spending some time seeking ballet class and ballet company videos online—most especially on YouTube,
- Sampling some recordings that accompanists have made for instructors to use in the ballet class when live accompaniment is unavailable or too expensive, and
- Reviewing or obtaining a couple of anthologies of music for ballet class that other pianists have composed and published.

The latter two options will, of course, guarantee that the accompanists recording and publishing are presenting themselves in the very best light possible—at least to their way of thinking and insofar as they are able. The first option will likely ensure the same, at least most of the time.

Therefore, it is stressed again that opportunities to observe and listen to other accompanists firsthand, when they are not expecting it or at least when they have had little preparation, are very desirable. However, the most revealing insights of all will be for the observer to listen and watch *outside the door or window* of the ballet studio while accompanists are playing for classes and are unaware that they are being observed.

Evaluating Other Accompanists. Regardless of the dynamic, there are a number of questions that the observer can ask himself, especially when he is in a position to hear several accompanists over a period of time.

For each accompanist observed:

- Is the accompanist a good pianist?
- Is he playing musically or like a robot?
- Does he distinguish himself in any way from other accompanists (if there is an opportunity to compare)?
- Is he using printed music or playing from memory?
- Does the music being played support the dance steps?
- Does the music appear to energize and uplift the dancers?
- Do the dancers seem more or less oblivious to the music, except as a metronomic device?
- DOES THE MUSIC SEEM JUST TO FUNCTION LIKE WALLPAPER?

After observing a number of accompanists:

- Do most of the accompanists sound more or less the same?
- Does it seem like they are all working from the same model?
- If the accompanists differ from each other, how?
- HOW MUCH OF THE PLAYING SOUNDS LIKE WALLPAPER?

The Value of Repeated Observations. Finally, but of key importance, is this: one of the most instructive things the observer can do is *to listen to the same accompanist more than once*—if possible, at least three times. This will enable the observer to get a much more detailed impression of the scope of that accompanist's capabilities. Thus, if the observer is working as an accompanist in an institution with more than one pianist, he may be able to catch the beginning or end of someone else's playing on many occasions, in a back-to-back ballet class situation.

The observer's conclusions will become more discerning as he gains experience, and the information gleaned should help him significantly in his development as an artist.

Organizing Music for Ballet Class

Three-Ring Binders. The best way for the accompanist to organize music for ballet class is to store it in three-ring binders with a capacity to comfortably hold about two to three inches of music. It is recommended, however, that the "rings" not be the circular kind; instead, the type that features the straight diagonal bar on each ring tends to impose less wear and tear on the manuscripts—especially the three-hole-punches in the paper. Binders should not be bulging with music. This wears out manuscripts more quickly and makes page-turning cumbersome.

Backup Set. The accompanist must always strictly maintain a complete and up-to-date set of backup binders in a secure place, in case any of the original binders currently in use is lost or stolen. In addition, the accompanist may choose to maintain electronic copies of all music, organized in the same manner as the binders.

Music Manuscript Paper. The music manuscripts contained in the binders should always be 8½" × 11" and should be reproductions on either heavy card stock or sturdy divider tabs. The heavy card stock can be three-hole-punched and then reinforced with tape. Divider tabs generally come three-hole-punched and reinforced.

One-Sided Only. The music manuscripts in the binders should always be printed on one side only—never on both sides—to reflect the following guidelines and the reasoning behind them:

- If the music comprises two pages, the pages should be laid out so that the first page can be read on the left side of the binder and the second page on the right side.
- If the music comprises more than two pages, the additional pages should be laid out with the same easy readability in mind.
- If the music is more than two pages long, the end of the second page should accommodate a logical stopping or breaking point.
- Music comprised of only one page can be three-hole punched so the page lies on either side of the binder, whichever side is more convenient for the accompanist.
- One-sided copying enables the easy insertion of new selections without disrupting the existing order of music.

Organization by Composer. Most binders should be organized in alphabetical order, by composer. Organizing by types of dance steps or combinations (e.g., plié, tendu, grand battement, petit allegro) is definitely not recommended, since—at least for accompanists with any flexibility and imagination (which are not only desirable, but necessary)—one piece of music could, hopefully, be modified to accommodate a wide variety of dance combinations.

Organizing the music of a specific composer can be accomplished in various ways, according to the preferences of the accompanist. For example, compositions can be arranged as follows:

- Alphabetically, by title; or
- By type of composition—for example, with Chopin, by selected mazurkas, nocturnes, preludes, waltzes, etc.; or
- By likelihood of where a composition will best or most likely be used in the class sequence—for example, barre first and then center, and further subdivided for barre work by plié, tendu, rond de jambe, grand battement, etc. (This is not the ideal method, however, since, as stated above, one composition can generally be used for many different steps.)

Supplementary Binders. In addition to organizing the contents of binders by composer, accompanists are encouraged to assemble supplementary binders, with contents organized, for example, by

- Broadway tunes
- Ragtime
- Tango

Finally, having a couple of binders that focus on national character dances and folk dances adds spice to the accompanist's repertory.

Reproduction and Backup of Manuscripts. Hauling around original publications of music for use in a ballet class is cumbersome and impractical, and it produces wear and tear—and risk of loss—on expensive manuscripts. Originals should be reproduced and adjusted to 8½" × 11" to fit uniformly in binders. Applying the guidance in the section of this chapter entitled "Free Online Music Scores"—which deals with the Petrucci Music Library and other free online sources of printed music—should free the accompanist from needing to carry around published music from his own collection.

An excellent practice for the ballet accompanist would be to maintain a hard copy library or an electronic library of downloaded music (1) in its original form, for reference and for future use, and (2) most especially, for storing music that the accompanist has edited to use in the ballet class. In the latter case, if a score that the accompanist has edited and regularly uses is worn out or lost, it can easily be replaced with a copy that includes all the work the accompanist performed in preparing the selection for use in the ballet class.

Editing Musical Scores. Editing and arranging musical scores for ballet class can entail varying levels of detail and documentation. The amount of detail the accompanist desires in order to address his needs and satisfy his comfort level determines the amount of work involved. In general, however, spending more time and effort preparing the score means there will be less or no guesswork and doubt when the accompanist is under pressure playing for a dance combination. The payoff is well worth the up-front effort.

Generally, it is advisable that the finished version of the manuscript, which incorporates the accompanist's editorial work, include clearly executed notations of most, if not all, of the following:

- All necessary fingering
- If desired, the portion of the score to be used as an introduction
- Measure numbers—if not at all measures, then at least at key points of phrasing: measures 4, 8, 12, and 16, and if applicable, measures 24 and 32, and possibly 64
- Additional identification of bar lines at the end of measures 8, 16, 24, 32, etc.—shown by a colored marking superimposed over the printed bar lines
- Notations at the end of appropriate bar lines, indicating efficient harmonic resolutions that accommodate anticipated or unexpected endings of combinations at those points (For example, if the resolution is G major or G minor, then a simple "G" or "g," respectively, with a circle around it and dabbed with a transparent color like green or orange, is simple and sufficient.)
- The clear identification of any measures that need to be artfully repeated, skipped over or eliminated, or otherwise addressed or altered in order to maintain the square phrasing (four, eight, sixteen bars, etc.) that is always required for dance combinations in ballet (In the midst of playing for a dance combination, the accompanist might otherwise forget to execute such necessary accommodations.)
- Measures requiring repetition can be identified by repeat signs, brackets, and/or additional measure numbers.
- Measures to be eliminated (skipped over) can be identified by a complete blackout or a prominent "X" drawn through that section.

In chapter 6, Adapting Piano Repertory with Complex Phrasing Challenges, three preludes from Johann Sebastian Bach's *Well-Tempered Clavier* and the first movement of Prokofiev's Piano Concerto no. 2, are presented as detailed examples of how to arrive at square phrasing in order to make a piece of music usable for ballet technique class.

Improvisation. The ability to improvise skillfully—and on the spot—in ballet class is touched upon here, although it is discussed in much greater detail elsewhere. That is to say, although improvisation should be approached as a worthy and comprehensive art in itself, with no further justification needed, it is referenced here because it is the key backup for the ballet accompanist who, on some occasions, suddenly finds himself without a handy manuscript and under pressure to produce some music immediately.

Memorizing Music

Easy Advice, But Possibly Problematic. It is easy enough to advise the ballet accompanist to prepare and maintain himself for dance class by memorizing as much of his musical repertory as possible. And, although it is not bad advice, theoretically, it may not really be desirable, practical, or even possible.

Obstacles to Memorization. First of all, not all pianists memorize music with the same proficiency. While some may do it with relative ease, others accomplish it only through significant mental labor. Significant labor means the expenditure of a significant amount of time. Second, once the accompanist has memorized a piece of music, he will need to use it with some frequency—perhaps too much frequency—in order to retain the memory of it. The problem is compounded, ironically, when the ballet accompanist follows the very sound advice of having a large repertory for ballet technique class, since this places further demands on his memory and, at the same time, reduces the likelihood that he will access all or most of his repertory frequently enough to maintain it in his head. Finally, it follows that committing music to memory for use in ballet technique class means—with very, very rare exceptions—that it is usable in *only* that setting. In other words, no one performs or entertains in a serious setting in which he plays only sixteen, thirty-two, or sixty-four bar fragments of something. Thus, a potentially enormous expenditure of energy used in memorization can pay off in only one setting—the ballet technique class.

Advantages to Memorization—Sudden, Unanticipated Changes. Even when the accompanist maintains his music in a well-organized fashion (refer to the section of this chapter entitled "Organizing Music for Ballet Class"), he will find that there are times in the ballet technique class (e.g., when the instructor unexpectedly asks him to change to another piece of music, or when the accompanist himself realizes that the music he is using does not work at the tempo required) when it will be greatly to his advantage to be able to jump as quickly as possible to another musical selection without having to locate the score. If, for whatever reason, improvisation does not seem to be an option in a particular setting, then being able to recall some music from memory will save the day.

Long, Repetitive Combinations. The accompanist will also frequently find himself in situations in which he must play virtually without interruption for relatively long periods of time (perhaps as long as ten to fifteen minutes), in which case a change or changes in music (as in a medley of pieces) are advisable, both for the accompanist and for the dancers. This happens most often in more advanced classes, during the latter portion of center work—with combinations being performed by a single dancer or a small group of dancers moving diagonally across the floor, from one corner to the other, in sequence and without interruption. Being able to change music appropriately and seamlessly during such long, continuous combinations will actually help the accompanist conserve his energy, and it will enable him to eliminate or at least mitigate the exhausting drudgery of pounding out the same measures over and over again—especially when the studios are big and a large number of dancers are involved.

Dramatic Transitions Possible. As long as a transition is executed skillfully and smoothly—and definitely without a change in tempo—the accompanist can accomplish even a dramatic transition from one piece of music to another, for example, by shifting to another key—or, if the combination is in duple time (4/4 or 2/4), by moving back and forth between a classical coda and a polka. Injecting such musical variety in this kind of setting will also have a positive effect on the dancers and the instructor (although it is unlikely that the instructor will actually complain under these circumstances if the music is excessively redundant, because everyone in the class will be aware—or should be aware—that the accompanist is working very hard under what can be described as marathon conditions). Again, if the accompanist does not have a piece or two music in front of him for such fairly common occasions, or if he is not confident about improvising under this kind of pressure, memorized music is the alternative.

Finding a Compromise. A good compromise, and an obvious one, between having no music memorized and memorizing a large body of music is to have a modest selection of repertory committed to memory. Although this is a nice goal for any type of combination, whether for barre or center—and is encouraged, as far as practicable—the focus should, as suggested above, be on the powerful, all-out combinations that occur during the final portion of center work—large waltzes, grands jetés en tournant, cabrioles, and so forth—that is to say, big 3/4, 2/4, and 4/4 offerings. (See also chap. 3, Barre and Center Combinations.)

Degrees of Memorization. Finally, it should be stressed that *memorizing* a piece of music for ballet technique class does not necessarily mean the literal, precise, note-for-note memorization that would be required for a piano recital; rather, it means the accompanist is able to retain music mentally to the degree that he can substantively reproduce it without needing to have the score in front of him. After all, the more experienced the dance accompanist becomes, the more likely he will be to experiment with, embellish, and improvise upon original music—rarely, if ever, reproducing it exactly as it was originally written.

Practicing Repertory at Varying Tempos

Tempo Adjustment During Combinations. In the course of accompanying for ballet technique classes, the accompanist will find it not uncommon for the instructor to ask him—sometimes unexpectedly—to either decrease or increase the tempo of the music while a combination is actually being performed. The instructor may adjust the tempo of a combination anytime he feels that it is out of sync with the intent or character of a combination.

Faster Repeats, Presets. There will also be times—especially at the barre—when the dance instructor announces during the actual execution of a combination that it is to be *repeated* without pause at a faster tempo—sometimes significantly faster, or even at double the original tempo. Instructors will occasionally choreograph a combination with a *preset* tempo change (usually an increase), so that the dancers and the accompanist will be prepared ahead of time for the adjustment. In addition to switching gears for the new tempo, a good accompanist may quickly discern that, for instance, a lighter musical texture may be more appropriate and so will implement this as well.

Implications for the Accompanist. In making announcements regarding tempo changes, especially impromptu ones, the instructor is not likely to have specifically taken into account any *technical* implications for the accompanist—who will have to figure out what, if anything, this means for him. If the accompanist is performing technically demanding music, perhaps with a lot of fast note patterns or octaves, he may not have much "wiggle room" to speed up without getting tripped up. If increasing the tempo is pushing his technical boundaries too far, he has the option of immediately simplifying the music—a kind of improvisation—or even "ditching" entirely what he is playing and improvising something entirely new and easier to play.

Where Tempo Changes Commonly Occur. Marked tempo changes tend to arise more commonly with certain combinations at the barre, involving steps like tendus or frappés, rather than ronds de jambe; such changes almost never arise with slow combinations like pliés or adagios, where adjustments to tempo would likely be minor anyway. With such slow combinations, however, more sophisticated accompanists may appropriately embellish, or thicken, the texture of the music so that it provides more support for the dancers' movements. Tempo adjustments also commonly occur during center work—for instance, with petit allegro.

Men versus Women. It also bears pointing out that, for big combinations during the latter portion of center work, although the male and female dancers often perform a combination together, there will be occasions where the instructor has the men go separately—probably last. In these cases, the accompanist will be expected to slow the music down appropriately, so that the men can execute higher jumps or more extended leaps.

Preparing for the Unexpected. Since the tempos of combinations do get changed, and sometimes unexpectedly, for various reasons in technique class, it is recommended that the accompanist find opportunities to practice at least some of his repertory, particularly the more technically demanding portions of it, at various tempos—especially faster tempos—while striving to make the material sound musically acceptable and natural. The accompanist can further develop flexibility and comfort by taking particular pieces in his repertory and switching tempos, both up and down, in the midst of the music, without pause or interruption, while making any technical adjustments that may be necessary for him.

The essential point here is that, in the ballet technique class, tempos can be adjusted at any time, and sometimes changed with very short notice. The accompanist should always be alert for such changes and be prepared, mentally and technically, to accommodate the needs of the dance class.

Asking When in Doubt

Either Guess or Ask. Occasionally, even a seasoned ballet technique accompanist will be challenged when it comes to being precisely clear regarding what a dance instructor is conveying to the class and, therefore, exactly what kind of music will be suitable for a combination. If clarifying information is not forthcoming from the instructor, then the accompanist will either have to take a chance by guessing about the right music or have to ask the instructor for a little help. This situation tends to be more common during center work than with combinations given during barre.

Arriving at a Quick Resolution. In general, the accompanist should not feel embarrassed or overly reluctant about asking an instructor for clarification.

If done quickly, the accompanist can offer a couple measures of music that he thinks might work in order to get a buyoff from the instructor. Such interruptions, however brief, should be kept to a minimum, but an empathetic instructor will likely appreciate the accompanist's desire to get it right the first time.

As an accompanist gains experience, he will have to ask questions only infrequently, which is desirable, since class time is at a premium and disruptions tend to impact momentum. But it is challenging to learn to become a good ballet accompanist and, one hopes, the dance instructor will be able to exercise a bit of understanding and patience when working with an inexperienced accompanist. After all, asking an occasional question should be preferable to disrupting a combination in progress because the music is not right, resulting in the instructor and dancers having to backtrack, find more suitable music, and start again.

More Detailed Guidance. The guess-or-ask dilemma is briefly introduced here to acknowledge to new or relatively inexperienced accompanists that it will inevitably come up. The section of this chapter entitled "Working with Dance Instructors" offers more detailed information and guidance on this subject, as it relates to various instructor–accompanist dynamics in the ballet technique class.

Looking Up and Developing Empathy

Pianists Naturally Self-Focused. Pianists with little or no experience in accompanying for dance classes will likely not adjust automatically to watching the dancers while playing. Generally, pianists are used to focusing only on themselves, in their practice routines and in solo work—a tendency that is perhaps somewhat ameliorated if they have been involved in chamber work or vocal accompaniment. But even with chamber work, the pianist's attention on the other members of the ensemble is largely auditory, as opposed to visual.

Looking Up—The Exoteric Aspect. An important part of the dance accompanist's growth is to be able to partially separate himself from his own music and motor functions and to keep some part of his attention on the dancers (never to the point of relinquishing appropriate self-awareness and control, of course). This facility can be thought of as the *exoteric* aspect of the accompanist's interactive role in the technique class. It means looking up from his music or around it at least part of the time, or being aware of the dancers out of the corner of his eye—habits that should become automatic and intuitive, especially as the accompanist comes to know his repertory better, or at least parts of it, so that he does not need to keep his eyes glued to it all of the time. Developing this dual focus will help prevent him from falling victim to problems that confront inexperienced dance accompanists, such as running on after the dancers have finished a combination or playing too quickly for a dance step. It will be an important tool in the performance of all of his functions in the dance studio. It follows naturally that being able to focus visually on the dancers is enhanced and supported by some degree of music memorization and by improvisation.

Developing Rapport—The Esoteric Aspect. There is an esoteric, yet profoundly tangible and meaningful, aspect of working with dancers that—depending on the accompanist—may or may not evolve over time. It is the most rewarding and nourishing part of this otherwise demanding and often taxing work, but it is impossible to describe in a word or a phrase. Perhaps the most succinct way to capture its essence would be to call it *the ability to read dancers.*

Reading Dancers. The ability to read—and appreciate—dancers comes as a kind of "flowering out of the soil," created through the determined, persistent work that is necessary to master dance accompaniment and to be an artist in doing so. It is an awareness of the meaning to be discerned from every look, every facial expression, every stance of the body, every gesture and sigh that each dancer manifests. Perhaps it can best be called empathy.

From the Keyboard. From his vantage point at the keyboard, the accompanist watches the dancers—when they walk into class, during combinations, and between combinations. He sees when a dancer is pleased with what she had done, or when she is frustrated at not having satisfactorily completed a double pirouette, and he feels that emotion himself. He can see the kind of day a dancer is having, the type of temperament that makes her who she is, and whether she likes and respects the instructor. The dance studio is alive with visual messages, some subtle, some otherwise, and all of them communicate volumes to an empathetic accompanist, including—*very importantly*—the effect of his music on the dancers.

The Most Positive of Impulses. A really good accompanist loves dancers. He *must* love them. From this love comes a passion to please them. This profound and positive impulse drives him to lift them up in their dancing and to give them joy in their hard work. But this drive is not selfless. For the dance accompanist, there is no other reward that matches catching a subtle smile or a light in the eyes of a dancer who is uplifted by his music. When this unmistakable connection is made—even at the bar, and perhaps within the first few measures of plié—the dancers begin to *dance.* Bodies become more erect, the carriage of the arms more beautiful. And, in center work, when the music is, for whatever reason, just right, and when it communicates something special, the entire roomful of dancers becomes charged.

Dancers will smile at the accompanist who brings this kind of energy. They may come close to the piano. After class, they may offer a thank-you with special warmth. And the appreciation of the instructor will also be apparent—and everyone will look pleased the next time they walk into class and see this accompanist.

Accompanying at the Proper Dynamic Level

Monotony. For ballet technique classes, accompanists need to make an effort to play music at dynamic levels that are varied and also appropriate for the setting and any special circumstances, and for the character of each individual combination. Such an admonition may seem unnecessary and obvious to some accompanists, but to others it may come as a surprise. Therefore, the following observations and suggestions are directed primarily toward those accompanists who may seem not to have given much thought to the issue—which could be a contributing factor, if applicable, to why they sound like wallpaper. Let it be known here that there are, in fact, many ballet accompanists who play at pretty much the same dynamic level all of the time (generally, loud)—a practice that dulls the sensibilities of the dancers and, in fact, creates a monotonous, interest-killing droning sound from the beginning of class to the end.

Clarity. Music for ballet technique classes must always be clear and unambiguous in the logic of its phrasing and its rhythmic underpinnings. The music should help the dancers focus. It should never be vague or indistinctly articulated. Unclear, colorless music will compromise the dancers' concentration on the execution of their movements. If the accompaniment is weak and anemic, and the dancers cannot easily discern the phrasing and pulse of the music, the whole purpose of the music will be lost.

Appropriateness. Generally speaking, the dynamic level of the music will not need to be as intense during the barre exercises as it may be during the center work. There are exceptions—for instance, grand battement—although what is called for here, as much as the appropriate dynamic level, is an energetic, well-punctuated rhythm. The point is that an accompanist's playing can become obnoxious if he is incessantly hammering away without thought. This is especially applicable to smooth, slow, graceful combinations like pliés, fondus, and stretches, in which case boisterous music is out of character.

Balance. To reiterate, proper musical support is always a necessity, but pointless extremes offer nothing. The accompanist may render his playing as full and rich as he desires—even with a bit of judicious gushing, now and then—but overpowering sound can be just as distracting as weak sound.

Center Work. During some of the center work, and particularly in the case of various grand allegro combinations, the dancers will likely benefit from all the support and thrust that the accompanist can manufacture. This is especially true with the big waltzes. In this setting, the accompanist will want to approximate as much as possible a full symphony orchestra. This will, however, demand a lot of an accompanist. It can be taxing and, in order to endure, he will need to stay as physically relaxed as possible and not waste energy.

Other center combinations—like petit allegro—will generally call for light, bouncy music. Occasionally, a solid, heavy piece of music may work well, for instance, with the right adagio combination. Making these judgments is part of the accompanist's job. But speaking broadly, regardless of the step or the music used for it, a plodding, earthbound playing style works counter to the aims of ballet technique. This type of accompanying brings down the dancers in the worst way and, aesthetically, places weights on their ankles.

Temporarily Adjusting the Volume. During the performance of dance combinations, it is not unusual for the instructor to communicate verbally with the dancers, perhaps to count out beats, give corrections, or call out the next step. This is especially true when a combination is being marked. While exercising discretion as to when a volume adjustment may be appropriate, a discerning, courteous accompanist may wish to adjust his volume slightly downward on such occasions, so that the instructor will not have to shout over the music. All such decisions must be made judiciously, on a spontaneous, case-by-case basis, and never in such a way as to derail a combination.

Temporary adjustments in volume are generally more applicable to some combinations than to others. Such fine-tuning is more in keeping with slower barre exercises (pliés, certain tendus, stretches, etc.), whereas, during the performance of grand allegro steps, and certainly the big waltzes, attempting such accommodations is not recommended, since they could send confusing messages to the dancers—in effect, dropping the floor out from under them.

Pianos. Sometimes, the quality, size, and condition of the piano in the dance studio may influence how the accompanist plays—especially his volume. Each piano offers its own challenges. For example, new grand pianos—with softer felt hammers that have not been hardened by a lot of playing—can actually sound rather muffled and require more of the accompanist's muscle. On the other hand, an old spinet with hard felts can produce a lot of sound without requiring much effort. (Accompanists with a lot of experience in working under many conditions will just be grateful if the instrument, whatever it is, is reasonably in tune. This is one of the reasons why accompanying on a digital piano can be so enjoyable.)

Depending on the quality of the piano, the size of the studio and its acoustics, and the number of dancers (their bodies absorb sound), the accompanist may want to open the lid of the piano, as long as doing so is safe and is properly done. This can be appropriate for both the barre and the center, although the center portion of the class may especially benefit from a fuller sound. It is not necessary to fully open the lid of the piano; using the shorter of the two lid props is perfectly sufficient. Also, when the short lid prop is used, the lid itself is generally still usable as a place for setting music binders (unless the lid is too slippery). Generally, upright pianos also have lids. However, if these are opened, then it may not be suitable to place music there.

Dueling Pianos. Finally, when a location has multiple studios—especially with thin walls, and where doors are not kept closed—the accompanist may find that someone else's loud playing is interfering with his own—even to the point of almost drowning him out. Many professionally trained pianists will recall the tiresome, cacophonous racket generated by innumerable practice rooms, crowded together on a floor of the campus music building.

In a ballet school, this can be a problem. Perhaps a discreet request by management may be in order—or at least some door closings. But whatever the case, the recommendation is not to start a competition. Perhaps a small increase of volume will be in order, but not to the point of sacrificing musicality and good taste. This is management's problem to resolve.

Physical Considerations for the Accompanist

Ballet Accompanists as Athletes. Just as dancers are athletes, the ballet accompanist is an athlete in her own right, facing her own physical challenges, some of which are relatively unique to playing for ballet classes. An overview of this issue is provided here and is explored further in the three sections that immediately follow: "Frequent Stopping and Starting," "Long Combinations," and "Balancing Orchestral Textures with Lyricism and Avoiding Physical Strain." Each section addresses interrelated physical considerations that may arise in the particular contexts described. These physical issues are specific to the ballet technique accompanist's type of work and therefore will be problems only for her. Dancers have their own potential physical hazards to deal with and, in general, will not be aware of those with which the accompanist may have to contend. Still, these issues can be troublesome and potentially serious for the accompanist.

Tension. Some dance accompanists may be particularly susceptible to muscular problems. Accompanying in the context of ballet technique classes may either create problems or aggravate a preexisting condition. Tendonitis may become an issue, particular for those pianists who, by nature and habit, are physically tense or stiff in their overall approach to playing. Until a ballet accompanist feels comfortable and secure, at least relatively speaking, with her work (which can take a year or more), she will most likely—almost surely, in fact—find herself at times under some degree of mental tension—and therefore physical tension—as a result of the fact that, in plain terms, she is subject to scrutiny and criticism from the instructor and from the dancers. She is always on the spot, and therefore vulnerable. Even a condescending look from a student can be devastating.

Expectations and Anxiety. At each and every technique class, unrelenting expectations, even though often only implicit, are placed upon the accompanist. These expectations may be most keenly felt if the instructor is an experienced professional who is especially accustomed to a very high degree of accommodation and response from accompanists. Unfortunately for accompanists (especially unseasoned ones), some instructors (and some dancers) are uninhibited and even downright tactless when it comes to offering criticism to the pianist. This cannot fail to cause the accompanist emotional anxiety, which, in turn, may make her physically tense (see the section of this chapter entitled "Working with Dance Instructors").

Tension interferes with the proper working of the muscles and can negatively impact the accompanist's hands, wrists, arms, and shoulders. A professional dance pianist may accompany for twenty or even thirty hours per week, which is extremely demanding in and of itself. If the accompanist is in an environment that feels hostile, the tension can be significantly exacerbated. A pianist who works or practices significantly outside of the dance environment can carry over tension to these areas, which can aggravate physical issues.

Circumnavigation. Generally, the accompanist can avoid physically damaging herself by taking proper measures—in a very conscious, deliberate, systematic, and preemptive fashion. It is hoped that the ballet accompanist will have acquired, in advance of playing in this field, a solid, correct piano technique. Regardless, a focus on relaxation and on playing properly must be maintained; the natural weight of the arms can be used to produce large, full sounds while avoiding tight, aggressive playing.

Pianos and Chairs. If the piano in the dance studio has an especially stiff touch, the accompanist should take special care not to overwork her fingers and wrists in an attempt to compensate for this stiffness—particularly if she is unaccustomed to it. Keeping the piano lid open may help maximize the tone production. Benches or chairs can also be an issue. Sitting in a low chair that has a seat like a bucket or sitting on a bench that perches the pianist too high can cause physical discomfort and strain. Accompanists are encouraged to raise these issues and get them corrected.

Frequent Stopping and Starting

Downtime. During both the barre and the center portions of a ballet technique class, the accompanist may sit at the piano for several minutes between combinations, or between each side of a combination, without playing. The instructor may be explaining the previous, current, or upcoming combination or giving detailed corrections to the dancers. The more the class is oriented to actual teaching, the more downtime there will be; if the class is primarily a workout session—perhaps for a ballet company, a very advanced class, or an open class (see "Open Classes" in chap. 1)—the less downtime there will be. It bears stating—if it is not obvious—that it is impolite and completely unacceptable, for any reason, for the accompanist to be practicing when the instructor is talking to the class.

Taking Care. For the accompanist, the chief point to be made about sitting idle for a period of time is that he should take care that he does not strain or otherwise injure his hands or wrists when resuming his accompanying. This advice is especially applicable when the upcoming combination is going to be big, demanding, fast, or long. Even pianists who have never had any physical issues are urged to heed this guidance. There is *almost never* an occasion during a ballet technique class when the dancers will sit or lie on the floor idly, allowing their muscles to get cold and become more susceptible to strain. The exceptions are floorwork involving personal or group warm-ups, before or at the beginning of a class, or between the barre and center, when floor stretches are being done to maintain warmth and suppleness. The operating word here is *stretches*—since the dancers are not just sitting around, getting cold.

Cold Studios. A cold studio is hazardous to dancers. The studio should be comfortably warm, so as not to encourage tight or cramped muscles. However, occasionally studios are poorly heated or drafty—a problem more common in colder climates and during the cooler seasons. To help protect themselves, many dancers wear all sorts of warm-up gear, including sweaters, ankle warmers, and leggings either of wool, acrylic, or plastic. For the accompanist, keeping hands and wrists warm is of comparable importance.

Gloves. If the accompanist has a problem keeping his hands and wrists warm—this is worthy of attention—a good solution is to take of pair of knit gloves and cut off the ends of the fingers about an inch or an inch and a half, or buy such a pair, so that when he wears them in class, about a half to a third of each finger protrudes unencumbered. It is not recommended that they be warn unnecessarily throughout the duration of class, unless the accompanist really feels that he needs them, since he will not want to become unduly dependent on them. Analogously, the accompanist may observe that some dancers seem to develop a dependence on leg and ankle warmers that sometimes appears to have a psychological basis. Unless there are temperature issues indicating otherwise, most dance instructors will not allow dancers to continue to wear ankle and leg warmers after the barre and will often insist that the warmers be removed after the first few combinations at the barre. In addition, the dancers' wearing of leg and ankle warmers makes it more problematic for an instructor to detect issues that require giving corrections.

Long Combinations

Grand Allegro Combinations. The issue of playing for long combinations for ballet technique has been touched upon in other sections of this book, as it applies in particular contexts. It is briefly addressed here as a general issue with which the ballet accompanist will deal in many classes, especially advanced ones. Playing for long periods of time—sometimes ten minutes or more—without pause or rest is not uncommon. This is particularly the case for grand allegro combinations during the latter portion of center work, when the dancers proceed either in single file or in groups, one after the other, across the entire dance studio, either diagonally or from one side to the other.

If the accompanist is playing a huge waltz in symphonic style or a fast, intense gallop under these *unrelenting* conditions, she can become seriously taxed, both physically and mentally. Classical pianists know that, even in large-scale, virtuoso piano pieces, the composer generally builds in some periods of physical and emotional repose—if not to give the performer a brief rest, then certainly for contrast and dramatic effect. This will not be the case in much of the ballet grand allegro work.

A Marathon. The dancers can rest after each time they or their particular group completes a grand allegro combination, but the accompanist generally continues to play until each dancer or group has finished—perhaps on both sides, and even multiple times. For the accompanist, this can be a physical and mental marathon. The accompanist is fortunate if she works with an instructor who is sensitive to this—many of them are not—and manages to give her an occasional rest. The instructor can almost always use this time to give corrections to the dancers. But to keep an accompanist playing furiously without rest for wave after wave of dancers, although not unusual, is, one could even say, abusive. No accompanist ever wants to be in the position of *having to ask* for a moment or two of rest, out of fear of being seen somehow as weak. But sometimes, she might just have to ask for what should be obvious. Again, the dancers get this rest. The accompanist should get it too, when she needs it.

Balancing Orchestral Textures with Lyricism and Avoiding Physical Strain

Physical Strain and Its Causes. As discussed elsewhere in this book, muscle or tendon strain, particularly in the forearms, elbows, or wrists, or the aggravation of such issues previously incurred, may occur in the course of accompanying for ballet technique. This strain can be caused by various factors, one of which is the requirement—sometimes—to produce very full, massive sounds and textures for an extended period of time for certain big (grand allegro) combinations toward the end of center work. Another factor, often related to the one above, is many accompanists' tendency to think and play predominantly in a chordal fashion—as opposed to being, in general, more melodically or lyrically oriented at the appropriate times.

Circumventing Strain. The desirability of producing large (orchestral) sounds for the musical support of certain combinations has been touched on in "Accompanying at the Proper Dynamic Level" in this chapter and elsewhere in this book, and is again acknowledged here—and endorsed. Let the point here be that, when this type of playing is more or less compulsory for certain big combinations, the accompanist's approach should be the correct one. To maximize the chances of circumventing strain or injury, the accompanist should endeavor (first through mental calm and focus) to maintain physical relaxation throughout her arms and wrists and should employ the natural weight of the arms to produce large sounds—avoiding all tension and stiffness, but particularly in the wrists, so that they remain flexible and *give* upon the impact of the fingers on the keyboard.

Two Reasons for Taking Care. The principals of relaxation expressed above are extremely important, principally for two reasons. The first is that the kind of repetitious playing sometimes demanded in ballet technique class is *unnatural*, and therefore stressful. It occurs only very rarely, for example, in the normal course of performing classical music. The second reason is that, once the physical strain of excessively repetitive playing manifests, it is difficult to eliminate or mitigate. The only real cure—if altering playing habits is not enough—is rest. The kind of rest required likely means not playing again, at least for ballet, for a substantial period of time. To continue accompanying for ballet after the strain has occurred will almost certainly prevent healing, and likely will exacerbate the problem.

The Instructor. It bears repeating that an instructor who has awareness and a degree of sensitivity will not overwork the accompanist on the big combinations, and will take care that a little respite is provided. If the accompanist is doing his job, he will need a bit of a break. Accompanists will probably endure anything rather than complain about the strain and request a pause. Unfortunately, some instructors will not think to provide this, so the accompanist will likely suffer in silence and pay for it later. Dancers need to remember that accompanists are, in their own way, also athletes—playing for ballet is demanding—and need protection from injuries just like dancers do.

Becoming an Orchestra. It is expected that an accompanist who aspires to be the best she can be will work to develop her skills at improvisation and at embellishing existing musical scores (see chap. 7, Improvisation, for an in-depth discussion) to thicken and enrich them so that her music offers full support for dance combinations, especially the big ones—while at the same time practicing healthy playing habits. Some knowledge of music theory and harmony, whether objective or intuitive, helps. An ability to discern quickly the essential harmonic structure of a piece of music—to grasp it in its essential triadic, chordal contest—will provide the platform for the accompanist to improvise her own embellished chords, textures, and melodies. Thereby, she can render a fuller, symphonic sound when desired, while still focusing on the lyricism and phrasing necessary to give the music shape and movement.

Lyricism. Most articulate dancers will say that, in general, beautiful musical phrasing and the quality of melody are important to them, and that music which delivers a beat and little else is, if not downright deadening, not conducive to expressive dance movements. Exceptions abound, of course, and are acknowledged, since driving, primal music can, in the right context, generate enormous excitement and energy, and may work very well for frappés, fast tendus, or grand battement. Nevertheless, in the typical ballet technique class, the lyrical aspect of music is very important to almost any combination, and particularly to pliés, port de bras, ronds de jambe, adagios, waltzes, and other flowing choreography.

Balance. To summarize all of the above, and to speak generally about accompanying for ballet technique, thinking and playing in a predominantly or inordinately chordal fashion tends to work the wrists and arms and not the fingers. Therefore, for physiological as well as aesthetic reasons, it is very important that the accompanist maintain balance in his playing by emphasizing the melodic aspect of his improvisation. Over a period of time, not to do so may mean a compromise in basic piano technique and facility, overworked wrists and weakened finger action—and tendonitis.

Maintaining a Good Piano Technique. One good way to maintain a solid piano technique is to practice properly—outside the dance studio. This will help to avoid wrong habits that can be physically harmful to the accompanist and can erode the musicality that is so important both to the accompanist and to the dancer. The fact is that accompanying for ballet technique classes can have both general and specific downsides for pianism, or it can serve as an opportunity for significant musical growth. Accompanists have the power to make this choice.

Free Online Music Scores

The internet is a vast and often convenient resource for locating and downloading free music scores, and it is therefore an invaluable tool for ballet accompanists. Internet resources

- Facilitate quick location of specifically sought-after scores;
- Offer a portal for the exploration for music that the accompanist was not previously aware of;
- Often enable free downloading, so that the accompanist can gather an extensive collection of music, in hard copy, suitable for ballet technique class, the cost of which would otherwise be a handicap or prohibitive;
- Enable printout of music in an 8½" × 11" portrait format that can easily be stored in standard binders (Although printing out music on standard letter-size paper generally makes the score smaller than it would be in a published hard copy, the resulting copy is generally quite readable, as long as the printer being used is of high quality.);
- Make it convenient to print a critically important backup hard copy to be stored in a safe place;
- Prevent heavy wear and tear—and markups—on hard copies of published scores, which in some cases comprise a substantial collection of pieces, perhaps only one or two of which the accompanist wants to use; and
- Eliminate the need to make copies of published scores that, in many cases, are awkward and difficult to reduce and center for reproduction on letter-size paper.

In downloading online scores, the accompanist should always consider any applicable copyright issues.

Below is a brief discussion of the online Petrucci Music Library and other online sources and search techniques for finding free, downloadable music scores.

The Petrucci Music Library—International Music Score Library Project. Launched in 2006, the website for the International Music Score Library Project (IMSLP)—also known as the Petrucci Music Library, or "Petrucci"—offers hundreds of thousands of scores (the site also has recordings). It is, as far as this author can determine, the richest, most extensive, and best-organized online source for easily accessible, free, downloadable music on the internet. Any musician—a ballet accompanist, for instance—could spend a lifetime mining this resource. Although IMSLP offers standard, very economical monthly and annual subscriptions with specific advantages, there is no fee for downloading musical scores. Petrucci is recommended as the first place to look online to research music scores.

IMSLP content can easily be explored via numerous types of searches:

- Composer
- Genre or type of work
- Title
- Instrumentation
- Featured instruments
- Language (vocal or written works)
- Period or style

A search by composer yields an alphabetical list of musical works. For "Bach, Johann Sebastian," for example, there are nearly a thousand listings. A search of the term "waltz" yields thousands of entries by title, with the composer's name included. The same is comparably true, for example, for "bourée," "bransle," "concerto," "partita," "passacaglia," "pavane," "polka," "prelude," "rag" "tango," and just about any other musical genre or type of work that comes to mind.

One extremely advantageous attribute of the Petrucci site is that, in addition to finding almost anything sought for, users can discover, through browsing, composers and compositions not previously known to them.

Of enormous use to the ballet accompanist: very often, with works originally written for orchestra or other instrumental combinations (displayed as "full scores" and "parts"), the "Arrangements and Transcriptions" tab will usually include reductions and arrangements for, among other mediums, solo piano. Along the same lines, works for piano and orchestra (concertos, etc.) will also be offered under the "Arrangements and Transcriptions" tab in the common format of "two pianos, four hands."

As further discussed elsewhere in this book, the option of downloading orchestral reductions for piano and two-piano arrangements of piano concertos, etc., allows the ballet accompanist great flexibility and comparative ease in making musical arrangements for ballet technique classes.

The Petrucci site advises visitors about potential copyright issues specific to composers and musical scores. The ballet accompanist should read and understand any notifications regarding copyrights, and proceed accordingly, using good judgment.

Other Online Sources. In addition to the Petrucci Music Library, a number of other online sites offer free, downloadable music. Ballet accompanists are encouraged to explore all options. Accompanists who search often for free online music will learn, over time, which sites best suit their needs. In addition to Petrucci, two other mentionable sites are ScorSer (http://en.scorser.com/D/Sheet+music.html) and MuseScore (https://musescore.org/en).

For music scores online—especially free scores and, in particular, a specific score—virtually unlimited potential combinations of search words and phrases will yield pages of results. It is sometimes possible to locate an especially difficult-to-find piece of music by experimenting with many different search combinations. Persistence often pays off.

Working with Dance Instructors

Overview

Need for Detailed Discussion. The ballet technique class accompanist, especially one who plans on playing for a significant number of classes, and at various levels, will encounter many types of instructors. There are those who are difficult to work with and those who encourage positive working relationships. The instructor–accompanist relationship is a fundamental component of the dynamics of a dance class. The subsections of this "Overview" introduce the various issues that will be discussed in greater depth in the following pages.

Room for Interpretation. Generally speaking, even a well-intentioned instructor may occasionally confuse the accompanist or leave room for interpretation. The instructor may ask for music with a certain feeling or a specific tempo. For example, he may ask for a "lively three" (3/4), but the accompanist may have a piece of music that is in 6/8 time and that he believes would be perfectly appropriate. It all depends on the specific feeling and quality of the music in question. When the instructor asks for a piece in 2/4 time, he probably wants something bright and well-accented rhythmically; a 4/4 or 6/8 meter might be just as suitable—depending on how the accompanist plays it.

In other words, the dance accompanist will sometimes find that a dance teacher, in articulating his feelings about the music, does so in a manner that perhaps lacks the accuracy or precision in terminology that a formally trained musician might expect. This can lead to confusion or misunderstanding, although this need not be serious; plus, the more the accompanist works with a specific instructor, the more he will be able to interpret accurately what is needed and what degree of leeway he can exercise while meeting the requirements.

Precise Tastes. On other occasions, the instructor asks the accompanist for something very specific and is being quite precise and accurate—for example, a "bright mazurka" or a "stately polonaise." (When an instructor mixes up these two dance forms, however, which happens occasionally, the situation can be awkward for the accompanist.) Whereas some dance instructors are reasonably knowledgeable and musically articulate about what they want—some are downright picky and will reject music almost on a whim—others are willing to accept just about anything.

Trust in the Accompanist. At any rate, the accompanist should not allow himself to be ruffled too much by instructors with picky tastes in music. It goes with the profession. On the other hand—and especially when an instructor trusts the accompanist—the accompanist is able to exercise enormous freedom in his music choices, as long as they come across clearly and support the combination. For example, if the instructor asks for a "slow adagio," the skilled accompanist may select a slow, flowing 3/4, 4/4, or 12/8, or whatever else—even sometimes a lyrical tango—with equal success, as long as it compliments and supports the movements of the dancers.

A detailed exploration of the instructor–accompanist relationship follows.

Difficult—and Confusing—Dance Instructors

General Observations and Guidelines. In the course of their pursuit of success in this line of work, ballet accompanists will likely have some challenging experiences with dance instructors. They should be prepared for this, because it has happened to virtually every dance accompanist at one time or another.

Ironically, on the one hand an accompanist has the power to make or break a dance class. On the other hand, because of the dynamics in the dance studio, particularly between the instructor and the accompanist, the accompanist can be quite vulnerable, because he functions as an entire orchestra, the sole source of musical support for the dance class. Therefore, there can exist almost a love-hate relationship, although perhaps generally an unconscious one, between the instructor and the accompanist, because they are yoked together in their mutual dependency and the power they have to make each other's lives in the dance studio difficult.

This irony is implicit in a ballet accompanist's job description. But in addition to the everyday—although subtle—tensions inherent to the ballet studio, there may be, occasionally, that dance instructor who, for whatever reason, appears to the accompanist to make life unnecessarily and unreasonably difficult. This phenomenon, which usually manifests as discourteous treatment of the accompanist, or apparent blaming, is unacceptable and always unprofessional. It can occur in any dance studio, irrespective of whether the class is at a professional, university, or private school level.

An instructor may be hard on an accompanist or challenging to work with for a variety of reasons. At the root of the behavior may be insecurity, possibly due to lack of experience or competence, and in particular an indication of ignorance about how to communicate with a musician.

An insecure instructor can be an accompanist's worst nightmare and can cause him to question his own competence. However, if the instructor merely lacks experience but is basically well intentioned, a good accompanist can, with a little time, gain the instructor's trust and help him to realize that, if the instructor will let him, he can be their best friend and provide security and support in the music that he provides.

To survive difficult or impolite instructors relatively unscathed, the ballet accompanist should strive to develop a thick skin and never to appear unnerved when unpleasant things happen. The fact is that, whether the instructor is unnecessarily difficult or not, he and the dancers will often be aware of the inevitable slips, miscalculations, and errors in judgment that the accompanist is bound to make from time to time. In spite of this, or perhaps especially because of this, the accompanist should always appear to play with conviction and confidence, even when he feels shaky. As the expression goes, "Never let them see you sweat."

The accompanist is advised to respond to an instructor's criticism or negative behavior politely and professionally and, without hesitation, to seek clarification from a dissatisfied instructor. (The dissatisfaction will usually be about either the tempo or the character of the music; this will be discussed in detail elsewhere.)

Can You Play Something Else? One of the most unsettling comments an instructor can make to an accompanist is, "Can you play something else?" Or, "No, I don't like that. Can you play something else?" If this question is not followed by some kind of guidance, the accompanist can address it in one of two ways: first, by playing something else without saying anything, or second, by seeking clarification. Either way is alright, but if the accompanist simply picks another piece of music and the instructor is still dissatisfied, the parties need to have a brief conversation in order to get the situation resolved, because tension will now be building; that is, both the accompanist and the instructor will be feeling frustrated.

The Dancers Are Confused. An instructor may occasionally halt a combination and assert to the accompanist that the music is "confusing" the dancers. It may be true, and the accompanist should consider this possibility and either strive to play the music more clearly—likely with a stronger beat—or select another piece of music. The accompanist is advised, however, that an instructor is saying the dancers are confused when in fact the instructor himself is confused, probably because of inexperience or insecurity. If the accompanist is doing his job, the dancers will very rarely be confused. Nevertheless, regardless of who is confused, if one or two adjustments on the part of the accompanist are not successful, he will have to press the instructor for clearer feedback, just as in the "Can you play something else?" scenario presented above.

Often, the accompanist's first remedy for correcting confusion is to ensure that the introduction he is providing is crystal clear, steady, and appropriate in length. Usually, this is helpful. Also, although the introduction is clear to the accompanist, it may not be clear to the instructor or the dancers. Therefore, the accompanist should listen critically and open-mindedly to what he is playing.

Faster, Faster! Slower, Slower! Sometimes, instructors inadvertently send the accompanist mixed signals about tempos; they may or may not assume that they have been clear. Instructors who lack experience or sophistication often fail to note this, at least initially. A good instructor will likely be aware of a possible need for clarification before beginning a combination.

An instructor may first address a combination to dancers at the desired tempo—or not, then speed up significantly in their presentation in order to save time. By the time the instructor has completed his presentation and explanation of a dance combination, it may not be at all clear to the accompanist what tempo is actually desired.

If the instructor does not clarify to the accompanist precisely what the tempo of a combination is, prior to indicating to the accompanist to proceed with the music, the more experienced accompanist may choose to draw upon his own experience and instincts and select the tempo himself. He may guess correctly, especially if he has prior experience with the instructor. On the other hand, if the tempo he chooses does not please the instructor, the instructor may either quickly indicate to the accompanist during the combination—by a signal or with a word or two—that an adjustment is needed; or, if the combination has been significantly disrupted, the instructor may stop the dancers, clearly indicate the desired tempo to the accompanist, and then begin again.

Without proper input from the instructor, any accompanist, no matter how good, can sometimes misjudge the tempo of a combination. Generally, the instructor should forgive the error, quickly and clearly correct it, and move on with the combination. A problem can occur, however, if the instructor tries to handle the situation in the following way.

The combination is underway, and at some point the instructor calls out to the accompanist, "Faster!" After a few bars at an increased tempo, the instructor, by now possibly exhibiting some frustration, may again call out, "Faster!" The same may happen with "Slower! Slower!" If not rectified, this type of situation will ultimately end in a breakdown of the combination—a kind of failed guessing game, with both the instructor and the accompanist feeling frustrated.

This calls for calmness on the part of the accompanist. He should simply ask the instructor to provide the desired tempo and do his best to accommodate it. The accompanist's attention should be fixed, as much as possible, on the instructor during the first few bars of the new attempt in order to confirm that he is compliant—or to make a quick adjustment. Generally, the instructor will appreciate this.

One pitfall for the accompanist when the instructor suddenly asks for an unanticipated speedup or slowdown—especially a significant one—is that the music the accompanist has selected will no longer work, either because it does not sound right or support the combination, or because a faster tempo has rendered it unplayable. Although this situation is potentially frustrating, with experience the accompanist can overcome it, by simplifying or embellishing the music on the spot, as the situation requires, or by abandoning the music at hand immediately and switching over to an appropriate improvisation. Dealing with this type of challenge should be considered one of the accompanist's many essential survival skills.

It should be noted that, in relatively rare instances, the instructor may plan for a combination to be performed in part at a certain tempo and then, perhaps halfway through the combination, at a different tempo. Generally, the instructor will alert the dancers—and of course the accompanist—ahead of time.

Dealing with the Difficult Instructor. When an instructor behaves inappropriately toward an accompanist, the dancers may respond in various ways. They may appear not to notice unprofessional comments, or they may disregard them, although they generally do notice; or they may mirror the instructor's attitude, which, fortunately, is rare—especially if the dancers regard the accompanist as competent and as working in good faith. An accompanist will likely pick up on expressions or body language indicating that the dancers are aware of or are uncomfortable with an instructor's attitude toward the accompanist. The accompanist may catch an understanding look from a dancer; or sometimes dancers will be especially gracious to the accompanist at the end of class, during reverence, or upon leaving the studio, indicating that they are with the accompanist in spirit.

An instructor with a hostile attitude may also target the dancers. When this happens, dancers may be even more inclined to sympathize with the accompanist. It should be noted, however, that an instructor may be highly respectful to the accompanist while being hard on the dancers—especially in high-pressure, professional environments, in which the instructor may give dancers a hard time for their own good, to drive them to higher levels of performance. This is sometimes necessary and appropriate, but it should always occur with the goal of improvement.

As the ballet accompanist is exposed to many different dance instructors, the likelihood increases that, at some point in time, he will encounter an instructor who is, to put it simply, a pill. In such cases, the accompanist develops an expectation that, in every class with this instructor, some barb will be thrown, some subtle or not-so-subtle comment that can grind away at the accompanist's confidence and self-esteem. When this occurs, the accompanist has a number of choices, which include remaining silent and tolerating the poor treatment, discussing it with the instructor, or involving an appropriate third party, possibly as a mediator. Any of these choices may be daunting.

Delightful Dance Instructors

Appreciative, Knowledgeable. Many dance instructors are a delight to work with. They are deeply appreciative of good accompanists, they are flexible (as opposed to fussy and controlling), and they are knowledgeable about and interested in music—especially music that is new and fresh, and they are experienced in techniques of clear communication with accompanists. In addition to being appreciated by accompanists and inspiring their enthusiasm and loyalty, this type of instructor is respected and loved by the dancers. Dancers want to see a professional, affirming, relaxed relationship between an instructor and accompanist.

A Cherished Position. A cherished position for a talented, experienced dance accompanist is to play for an instructor of high caliber who has had to endure mediocre or bad accompanists. Such an instructor may regard the newly arrived accompanist almost as a messiah.

Communication Between Instructor and Accompanist

Different Approaches. Instructors come to dance classes with widely different temperaments, philosophies, and approaches—including the way they relate to and communicate with accompanists. The way an instructor conducts a dance class—which affects the accompanist—depends significantly on the level of the class and the degree of familiarity the instructor has with the students. A class for professionals in a dance company conducted by the ballet master will be very different from a class for beginning or intermediate dancers in a private school. Subject to this stipulation, some general statements are made below.

Depending on the experience and competence of both the instructor and the accompanist, it is quite possible for them to work together very successfully, at any level of dance, from the first time they meet—and with almost no direct verbal communication. Such collaborations can be highly positive. However, the accompanist must be very accomplished.

An accompanist may receive all direction imaginable—directly or indirectly—from an instructor prior to the students' execution of a combination. After announcing the combination, the instructor may demonstrate it in its entirety, slowly and thoroughly. The students may "mark" (refer to the following paragraph) the combination while watching the instructor's demonstration; or, after indicating the combination, the instructor may—or may not—ask the dancers to mark the combination prior to performing it "full out" (refer to the following paragraph).

Marking a Combination. When dancers "mark" a dance combination—either in learning it for the first time or in the process of reviewing it—they run through it mentally and physically, but with significantly reduced movement that may only suggest the full character and course of the combination when it is fully danced. To state this another way, marking constitutes a run-through of the combination, with the focus on remembering the routine itself, rather than on dancing the movements "full out"—that is, performing the combination with fully defined movements.

Conveying Information to the Accompanist. At some point during the demonstration described above, the instructor will, ideally, convey to the accompanist the meter and the precise tempo of the music desired, and perhaps even convey that it should be, for example, a waltz, a tango, a polonaise, or, simply, an adagio. He may even suggest a desired aesthetic quality. On rare occasions, the accompanist may encounter an instructor who is so conscientious that during the execution of the combination they will alert the accompanist that, for example, there are eight counts, or sixteen counts, left in the combination. This gives the accompanist certainty about when to end the music, since, based on the way combinations are sometimes demonstrated to dancers, the accompanist may not always anticipate the end point of the combination correctly.

Many instructors have received good training—probably during some course of academic education at a university or college—about how to communicate with an accompanist. This academic training may have included courses in music theory or music appreciation.

Little or No Direction. On the other end of the extreme, the accompanist may receive little or no direction directly from the instructor about a combination. The instructor's explanation of a combination to the dancers may appear to the accompanist to be sketchy—or, at least, insufficient or hasty. From the accompanist's standpoint, all of this may be true, but it is likely that the dancers understand the combination, sometimes because the instructor uses that same one in every class. The combination may not be marked prior to full execution. Finally, the instructor may give the accompanist little or no indication about the music, including meter or tempo.

When an instructor provides little to no information directly to an accompanist prior to the dancers' execution of a combination, it may indicate so many different things or possible permutations thereof that this dynamic can only be interpreted on a case-by-case basis. Any of the following may apply:

- The instructor and the accompanist recognize each other as seasoned professionals.
- The instructor and the accompanist may work together often.
- The instructor's high regard for the accompanist may indicate or suggest that little communication is needed, which the accompanist can interpret as flattering.
- The instructor does not know how to communicate with the accompanist—a situation that, at least at times, requires the accompanist to seek clarification from the instructor.

On-the-Spot Readiness—Music Binders, Memorization, and Improvisation. Occasionally, an instructor will ask the accompanist to play some music while the instructor is working out a combination before explaining it to the dancers. Much more rarely, the accompanist may work with an instructor who employs this modus operandi to every single barre and center combination of every class. In both cases, but especially in the latter, there is a heavy onus on the accompanist to be prepared to respond almost instantaneously when the instructor makes various requests like "Can I have a plié?" or "I'd like a grand battement" or "Please play a petite allegro."

In this type of environment, or any environment, the accompanist can minimize or even completely avoid being unprepared by employing a combination of strategies that include music binders, some memorization, and improvisation, all of which are valuable tools for any ballet accompanist, regardless of how the instructor runs the class.

Music Binders. The following practices will greatly assist the accompanist.

- Have music binders close at hand and open.
- For easy access, binders can be arrayed open and flat on top of an upright piano or on the lid of a grand piano, as long as the lid is either down or just partially open.
- At least one binder, or perhaps two, can be set up directly in front of the accompanist, on the music rack of an upright, a grand piano, or, depending on the weight of the binders, an electronic keyboard.
- If the accompanist is using an electronic keyboard, having music binders lying flat on the area above the keyboard will likely be impractical. In such cases, it is recommended that the accompanist have a couple of benches or chairs around him where binders can be set out open and immediately accessible.
- Every binder should be open, ideally with one each of the following types of music at hand:
- A slow to moderate 2/4 or 4/4
- A moderate to bright 2/4 or 4/4
- A slow to moderate 3/4
- A moderate to bright 3/4

These musical types can be modified as needed, according to whether the class is at the barre or in the center, and which portion thereof.

- An experienced accompanist should be able comfortably to modify and improvise on any of his scores at hand, such that, in most cases, a duple meter can be modified to a triple meter, and vice versa, and a slower piece of music can be modified to serve as a brighter one, and vice versa.
- Once an available score has been put to use, the accompanist can select another music candidate for the immediate lineup.
- To plan ahead even further, it is strongly recommended that the accompanist keep at hand a number of pieces of colored, 8½" × 11" card stock that can be inserted into binders as placeholders during class, so that other musical candidates can be quickly accessed in response to anticipated combinations.

Memorization. Although this book does not place significant emphasis on extensive memorization of music scores, judicious memorization of a number of scores, especially those that are amenable to more frequent use, is a useful skill. Of course, the limits thereto may be circumscribed by the accompanist's ability, motivation, and time.

Improvisation. As discussed more fully elsewhere in this book, the accompanist is very strongly urged to develop and practice improvisational skills outside of the dance class, so that anytime the need or desire arises in class he can naturally, with confidence, and at very short notice both improvise "new" music and create "new" works out of the musical scores in front of him.

Although having well-organized binders with a rich variety of music available and being able to improvise at a second's notice are extremely valuable tools, the accompanist who uses the combination of the two, freely and easily, is in a superior state of readiness and is maximally able to deliver what is needed.

Tempos for Pliés, Adagios, Selected Tendus and Ronds de Jambe, and Other Foundational Steps

Pliés, which are foundational to ballet technique, are usually the first combination given at the barre, although sometimes they will be preceded by some kind of gentle warm-up or slow step. Professional instructors who recognize the importance of pliés for all levels of students will generally want them to be executed slowly, fully, and with strong intention. Some instructors will even give two plié combinations.

The accompanist will find, however, that many instructors will require faster tempos for pliés, thereby rushing through them and depriving dancers of the full benefit of the exercise. In more extreme cases, pliés are executed to tempos that amount to a moderate waltz. This may be because of a flawed or compromised teaching methodology—sometimes to get pliés and even the whole barre over with quickly, so that the class can move on to "real" dancing; or, perhaps due to scheduling constraints, the class is actually insufficient in length for full, careful instruction of steps. Either way, the dancers derive less benefit.

All of this is to say that, depending on where the accompanist works and for whom he plays, he may become accustomed to playing pliés at faster tempos. Then, when the accompanist encounters a more knowledgeable instructor, he may receive a gentle correction or reprimand about a rushed tempo. Under such circumstances, the accompanist is free, if he wishes, to verbally acknowledge and reinforce the instructor's insistence for a slower tempo and to explain, very briefly, that playing faster tempos for pliés has become more or less a habit as a result of working with less fastidious teachers. The instructor may appreciate such an affirmation.

Tempos—Steadiness and Flexibility. In addition to other issues having to do with tempos (discussed elsewhere in this book) and, in particular, how these issues are communicated between dance instructors and accompanists, it is worth mentioning that, especially with slower and more lyrical combinations like pliés and adagios, instructors do not appear to be troubled when the music breathes slightly—the operative word being *slightly*. This is never to suggest that the accompanist is free to take all kinds of liberties with tempos—to wander all over the place, so to speak—because to do so in a ballet technique class would be out of place and highly disruptive. However, virtually all performances of any kind of lyrical music suggest at least a slight fluidity or elasticity, however subtle or even unnoticeable, that gives the music life.

It may be said that, in many instances, the challenge for the accompanist is to balance a very judicious fluidity of tempo within beats or bar lines while maintaining an overall, reliable steadiness. This discipline is, in itself, an art—or part of art—that deserves cultivation and that should enhance the appeal of the accompanist's music to the instructor and dancers.

However, the accompanist will occasionally encounter an instructor who, in general, is especially vigilant with respect to the maintenance of rigid, even metronomic tempos, with a few predictable exceptions like the culmination of an adagio. Such instructors may snap their fingers, consciously or unconsciously, through the entirety of every barre combination and most center combinations, or they may count out the music or click their tongue. The accompanist may run across an instructor who, to use an apt phrase, watches him like a hawk, and immediately raises an issue if the tempo varies to a degree that would be virtually imperceptible to most people. When the accompanist does work with such an instructor, or a finger-snapper or counter, the best advice is just to embrace the challenge. The accompanist will become accustomed to it. In fact, if the accompanist becomes highly accustomed to working with a finger-snapper or a counter, it will feel strange to him if, for whatever reason, the snapping or counting suddenly stops.

3/4 Versus 4/4 Meter for Slow Combinations. The accompanist will, not infrequently, encounter instructors who have strong prejudices against music in duple meter (2/4 and 4/4), at least for certain slower combinations. This almost knee-jerk attitude is not limited to relatively inexperienced or unknowledgeable instructors; it characterizes the mind frame of some experienced professionals as well.

Pliés are the obvious case in point. The instructors referred to herein either greatly prefer music in 3/4 time for pliés or even insist on it, while resisting or even refusing to consider the use of plié music in 4/4 time. An accompanist's attempt to slip in music in 4/4 time for pliés for such instructors may result in the instructor's immediate displeasure and discomfort, and a request for something in a 3/4 meter.

For some instructors, this prejudice against duple meters may extend not only to other slow combinations, like adagios (it is likely easier to slip in a 4/4 meter for stretches), but also to certain other combinations, like tendus.

This book strongly encourages accompanists to resist the prejudice against 4/4 meter; from a musically objective standpoint, such a bias is indefensible. The most common excuse from instructors for avoiding 4/4 time for pliés, for example, is because it is not "smooth" like a 3/4. To the contrary, there are countless pieces in 4/4 time that are every bit as smooth as music in 3/4 time. It all depends on how the music is played. It can, in fact, be justifiably argued—and demonstrated—that a smooth piece of music in 4/4 time is superior to a selection in 3/4 time because the former provides, aesthetically, a firmer base for a plié exercise.

The 4/4 meter bias also excludes innumerable musical compositions that, in fact, not only are beautiful but also are perfect candidates for plié exercises. Consider these compositions:

- *Pavane for a Dead Princess*, by Maurice Ravel (allowing for some alterations to square up the phrasing)
- Prelude no. 2 for Piano, by George Gershwin (allowing for some alterations to square up the phrasing)
- "Elegie," *Morceaux de fantaisie*, op. 3, no. 1 for Piano, by Sergei Rachmaninoff
- "Stranger in Paradise," from the musical *Kismet*, by Robert Wright and George Forrest—taken from music of Alexander Borodin's "Polovtsian Dances."

Regarding "Stranger in Paradise," for example, if the instructor is resistant to 4/4 time, the accompanist can modify it on the spot to a 3/4 time version, which is as beautiful as the original.

A final argument for the accompanist to incorporate 4/4 music for pliés and other combinations into his ballet class repertory is that it permits a virtually limitless expansion of musical possibilities, which will also enrich the dancers immeasurably and open them to new musical forms and styles.

Mixing Up Meters. In explaining and demonstrating a combination to dancers, instructors almost always call out the steps in the rhythm that, in the instructor's mind, matches the steps. This vocal articulation of the rhythm will generally be in the context of 2/4 or 4/4 time, 3/4 time, or 6/8 time, and is usually done in an automatic, almost unconscious way. In most cases, this will help the accompanist select appropriate music.

From time to time, however, the instructor—without realizing it—will count part of the combination in, for example, 2/4 time, and then switch, perhaps, to 6/8. This may occur more than once while the instructor is demonstrating a specific combination, and doing so is certainly unconscious. Although this can happen in many combinations, both at the barre (grand battement is a good example, although, when the instructor clearly adds "en cloche," a 6/8 may actually be preferred) and in the center, it seems to occur most frequently during the first part of the center work. It never seems to bother the dancers. However, it can leave the accompanist wondering what to play. This can be especially confusing to an accompanist when the instructor clearly and consistently counts an entire combination in one meter when, in the accompanist's view, a different meter seems to be called for.

If the desired meter has not been made clear to the accompanist, he has the option of making an educated guess, in which case the assumed or established tempo of the combination can be a very significant determining factor. Often, but not always, a combination that appears to bog down under a 2/4 meter will work much better with a 6/8. Conversely, when a 6/8 or 3/4 seems too rushed or compressed, a 2/4 meter may be the answer. Deciding on and committing to a particular meter under these circumstances is an accompanist's gamble. If the instructor does not like the musical choice, the accompanist can always change it. It is also perfectly acceptable for the accompanist to ask the instructor for clarification prior to the start of the combination.

Playing for Children and Young People. "Playing down" to children and young people out of concerns about confusing them is not recommended as standard procedure. This is not to imply that highly challenging, complex, or esoteric scores—which in fact may be confusing or disorienting to children and may undermine their efforts to focus on what they are learning—should be used. However, music of some sophistication, whether it be classical or popular, can generally be used, as long as the accompanist offers it with clarity and with sensitivity to what the children are doing and what they are striving to learn. If the accompanist is offering music properly, he may be pleasantly surprised at how readily children take to it. Children will generally respond to clear musical preparations and strong rhythm. They will feel these instinctively, and will take to them like a duck to water. After all, outside the ballet class, they are likely exposed to a great of deal of music from many sources. They do not need a diet of "Mary Had a Little Lamb" or "I'm a Little Teapot."

Maestro. Occasionally, dance instructors address dance accompanists as "maestro" (feminine "maestra"), a term of respect for a distinguished musician, especially a conductor of classical music, or an eminent composer or teacher of music. Instructors may use this term consistently or otherwise, or in certain contexts. The accompanist is advised not to be surprised if this convention manifests, and not to be disappointed if it does not. Not all accompanists are fond of being called "maestro," but it is advisable just to go with the inclination of the instructor.

Pay Scales for Ballet Accompanists

During the Dutch Baroque period—that Golden Age of seventeenth-century Dutch art—the lives of great painters like Johannes Vermeer (1632–1675) were powerfully affected by the Guild of Saint Luke of Delft. The Guild, a professional trade organization for artists and artisans, regulated the commerce and production not only of painters, but also of sculptors, potters, faïenciers (those who made glazed earthenware and pottery), engravers, glass makers, painting sellers; tapestry weavers, embroiderers, architects, engineers, surveyors, mapmakers, map coloring specialists, calligraphers, typeface makers, printers, book binders and sellers, and even chair painters and furniture joiners.

An analogy—perhaps *comparison* is a better term—between the Guild and pay rates for ballet accompanists today might seem tenuous to some, or even irrelevant. Yet something may be gained from looking at the two in a similar light. Therefore, the following observations are offered to ballet accompanists—and in particular, to aspiring ones—for consideration.

In the Los Angeles area, where the author has resided since 1985, pay rates for ballet accompanists often seem surprisingly low, and certainly so in comparison with the rates paid in other trades that require far less skill and specialization. Pay rates for ballet accompanists in the Los Angeles area vary markedly from school to school, with no clear inferences to be drawn based on the type of school, whether at a major university with a heavily endowed dance program, a charter high school for the arts, a conservatory, or a private business.

Although it is not the intent of this book to document pay scales for ballet accompanists in specific dollar amounts, limited investigation via the internet regarding pay rates in various parts of the United States indicates that the rates are far from impressive. This is not to say that rates in every locale, ballet school, and dance company are low or mediocre. It is reasonable to infer that some accompanists at the top of their profession and ensconced in the more prestigious institutions are better paid than accompanists at lower levels. Suffice it to say that aspiring, qualified accompanists will generally not be impressed with the pay. To make a viable living doing nothing but playing for ballet classes is not realistic. Many who play for ballet will certainly find it necessary to supplement their income by other means, whether in the music field or elsewhere.

Some disillusionment over unimpressive pay scales for ballet accompanists (generally in the context of no vacation or no health benefits) can be further exacerbated if the accompanist must piece together a "career" by picking up a limited number of classes at multiple schools. Especially in a sprawling geographical area (Los Angeles, for instance), driving times, car expenses, traffic congestion, or the challenges of using public transportation to get from class to class can be daunting.

Because of budgetary constraints, some ballet schools have only one accompanist. Other, larger institutions may employ many accompanists. In the latter case, it generally appears that, regardless of experience or competence or artistic level, accompanists within a given institution (as opposed to discrepancies between schools) are all paid the same rate—or, in rare exceptions, so nearly the same rate as to amount to an inconsequential difference.

In the recent past, the author was in communication with an individual who had entered a doctoral program in dance accompaniment (the first such program in the United States, as far as can be determined). Her expectations regarding potential salary appeared to be significantly at odds with demonstrable reality. Some skepticism about high pay as a result of possessing a doctorate in the field of dance accompaniment seems generally warranted, given the context presented above. A possible exception would be in the context of a major university with a large program, demanding an individual with a broad range of responsibilities and skills—a context in which most accompanists will never find themselves.

To put it another way, a ballet accompanist comparable in quality and sophistication to a "Vermeer" rather than to a "glass maker" or a "chair painter" may, with rare exceptions, nevertheless end up being paid a chair painter rate.

Balancing Traditional Piano Work and Ballet Accompaniment

Common Ground, with Restrictions. The level of standard for craftsmanship and artistry for playing as an accompanist for ballet technique classes should be on a par with that of a professional piano soloist or chamber player in the classical, pop, or jazz fields. The only distinction to be made is that, in work for ballet technique accompaniment, certain restrictions apply—primarily, that the music must be in uniform phrases (of four, eight, and sixteen measures, and multiples thereof) and that the tempo—subject, as appropriate, to very judiciously limited shaping—must be steady.

To Survive and Flourish. Although the demands peculiar to ballet class accompaniment can be very taxing and tend to erode musicality, the pianist should endeavor never to give ground. On the other hand, clinging to a certain attitude that might aptly be called "musical puritanism" will likely guarantee her demise as a studio pianist. The way to survive and *flourish* as a ballet accompanist is to regard all music as fertile ground to be explored and adapted, as needed, for dance technique, while maintaining—or reinventing, as necessary—its coherence and integrity. The aim of most of the technical material in this book is to enable her to do this.

Enjoying the Challenge. Some of the later sections of this book—specifically, chapter 4, Suggested Piano Repertory for Barre and Center Work; chapter 5, Preparing and Arranging Piano Repertory for Ballet Class; and chapter 7, Improvisation—provide detailed discussions on arranging traditional piano pieces to make them more suitable for ballet technique accompaniment—with numerous examples, techniques, and suggestions for adapting music for dance combinations. A piece of music may undergo a considerable metamorphosis before it can be used successfully in the studio. A really good ballet accompanist must do a great deal of this kind of work, something which, hopefully, the pianist will find to be an inviting challenge. If she discovers that this kind of work offends her tastes, she might want to rethink the whole matter of playing for ballet.

A Legitimate Form of Arranging. The modification of both traditional and unconventional piano music for dance work should, with full justification, be regarded in the same light as other types of music arranging and adaptation, and improvisation. This work falls in the same creative category as reshaping musical material for various scenarios in film scores, or large-scale classical instrumental works, or opera; or employing the traditional theme-and-variations approach; or jazz improvisation. Each of these avenues is an opportunity for new and original musical expression. Each challenges the imagination.

Balancing Structure and Freedom. Unless the creative imagination is allowed to flower in dance accompaniment, a significant opportunity for expression and growth is lost. Playing the piano in a freer (but disciplined), more spontaneous fashion does not mean abandoning traditional musical forms or compositions, but rather to enjoy the balance between the established and the experimental. Exploring this juxtaposition is an antidote to the musical stiffness that comes from sitting alone in a practice room day after day, merely practicing and memorizing traditional repertory like a machine. Playing for dance can open up a receptive pianist to new areas of artistic discipline and expression.

3 Barre and Center Combinations

Overview of Barre and Center

Order of Steps and Focus. While studying the discussions and charts for barre and center steps and combinations that follow, the accompanist should bear in mind that the order in which the steps and exercises are presented here reflects a *somewhat typical*—or even *theoretical*—format that is *generally* or *broadly* followed in the ballet technique class. This format is relatively flexible, however, particularly with respect to center work. A considerable amount of variation will be evident to the accompanist, in terms of what steps are focused on in a given class and how they are choreographed—depending largely on the dancers' experience level and the instructor's teaching plan. Further, given that the repertory of ballet steps is very large, only a limited number will be addressed in any given technique class. Therefore, this part should be viewed as a broad, flexible road map regarding the direction and focus that a class may take.

The Purpose of Barre Work. The ballet technique class is comprised of two portions, the barre and the center, in that order, each of which generally takes up about half of the time allotted for the class. The amount of time devoted to barre work and center work, respectively, may vary somewhat, depending on the instructor, his teaching plan, and the level of advancement of the dance students. Work at the barre is made up of a series of exercises that prepare and train the dancers for the dance steps and combinations that will be addressed during the center portion of the class. Barre work is extremely important, since it is foundational to ballet work and is intended to develop strength and coordination, to emphasize the correct carriage of the body, to perfect the execution of dance steps, and to enhance artistry, including consciousness of musicality.

An Indispensable Foundation. Besides preparing the dancers for the combinations that are choreographed in the center, the work at the barre warms up the dancers' muscles systematically and safely, while training and toning them and promoting flexibility. The feet, ankles, calves, thighs, hips, stomach, back, arms, hands, and neck all receive appropriate attention. Safe, proper work in the center is not feasible unless dancers first work properly at the barre and eliminate bad habits. Any deficiencies or weaknesses not fully addressed during the barre will be visible and exacerbated during center work—resulting in compromised technique and possible injury. Again, correct barre work is intended to provide a solid foundation for all ballet work.

The Physical Apparatus of the Barre. The physical barre itself, discussed in "The Ballet Studio" in chapter 1, provides dancers with the support and balance needed to learn steps and to develop and maintain technique. In ballet classes at the beginning levels, a significant portion of class time—perhaps the majority of class time—will be occupied with barre work. Barre work is never dispensed with in ballet technique classes—even at advanced professional levels. However, as training progresses, instructors take care that the barre does not become a *crutch* for dancers that compensates improperly—and very apparently—for technical deficiencies and poor balance.

General Order of Barre Work. The following discussion of barre work does not, by any means, include all of the exercises that could be performed at the barre. It does, however, include the major ones. The order of barre exercises is relatively routine, at least for the major steps. Stretching or other kinds of warm-ups may be done at the beginning of class, either on the floor or at the barre; or, if stretching or other warm-ups are not done, then pliés almost always begin the class. More than one plié combination may be given. The instructor will likely give at least two tendu combinations, which are usually followed by ronds de jambe or perhaps fondus. The steps that come after this will vary from class to class—perhaps frappés, développés, or other combinations. The last exercise at the barre will probably—or often, at least—be grands battements of one kind or another. At the end of barre work, the dancers may perform a series of stretches together, or they may limber up individually before commencing their center work.

Grouping of Center Steps for Discussion. In studying the chart and discussions of center steps presented later in this section, the accompanist should bear in mind the following. The dance steps listed are subdivided into various categories according to the type of step: adagios, linking steps, petit allegro steps, pirouettes, and grand allegro steps. Although this list is not exhaustive, it does include most of the major dance steps. Many of the steps in the respective categories are not performed exclusively by themselves or only with other steps in the same category. The essence of choreography is the combination of many different kinds of dance steps. Therefore, the accompanist will find, for instance, petit allegro steps in grand allegro combinations, and vice versa. Of course, there are some steps that may not work well together in a particular combination.

Dance Steps Discussed Individually. For the purposes of this book, and to simplify matters somewhat for the accompanist, dance steps are presented and discussed below as if they were being executed individually—that is, by themselves, and not in conjunction with other steps. This method of discussion will help give the accompanist a capsule idea of each step, along with some indication of what kind of tempo and meter will generally be suitable for it. The individual steps can be choreographed into many workable combinations. By studying the text, the accompanist can develop for herself a concept of what kind of music is required for combinations that involve various predominant categories of dance steps.

General Order of Center Work. In most ballet technique classes, the center work will include an adagio piece; several petit allegro combinations; possibly some work on different kinds of pirouettes, both slow and fast; and some grand allegro combinations. The order in which the adagio, petit allegro, and slow pirouette work is done is flexible. Slow pirouettes are used in many adagios, in context with other steps. Fast pirouettes, petit allegro steps, and grand allegro steps can be combined in innumerable ways. Grand allegro work will generally be reserved for the last part of class, and fast pirouettes will usually come at the very end. Again, the order of steps in the charts and discussions below is to be regarded as flexible.

Note Regarding Piano Repertory. The following descriptions of the various exercises at the barre and in the center are accompanied by appropriate general suggestions for musical accompaniment. In chapter 4, Suggested Piano Repertory for Barre and Center Work, the subject of suitable repertory for specific steps and combinations will be dealt with extensively.

Online Photos and Videos. Accompanists are encouraged to look online for photos and videos of the dance steps discussed in this part on barre and center combinations.

The Barre
Barre Exercises Chart

Warm-up and Stretching

Plié
Port de Bras

Battement Tendu
Battement Tendu Jeté
Battement Piqué

Fondu (Battement Fondu)

Rond de Jambe à Terre
Rond de Jambe en l'Air

Battement Frappé
Battement sur le Cou-de-Pied
Pas de Cheval

Développé

Grand Battement
Battement on Cloche

Stretching

The Barre: Discussion of Exercises and General Music Requirements

Note Regarding the Descriptions of the Barre Exercises. Any of the barre exercises discussed below can be described in various ways and from a number of perspectives that, depending on their intent, can vary in terms of their level of detail and anatomical precision. The descriptions of the exercises are brief and general in nature, and they are primarily intended to convey to the ballet technique accompanist a visual sense of the movements so that she can relate to them when she sees them in the studio.

Warm-up and Stretches (Optional). Often as a group and as prescribed by the instructor, the dancers may do a series of slow and gradual stretches. Generally, their purpose is to remove tightness from the dancer's body and to encourage suppleness. These stretches warm up the muscles and stimulate the circulation.

Appropriate Music. The music for stretches should generally be slow, smooth, and flowing.

Tempo and Meter. Slow. 3/4 or 4/4.

Plié. Bent, bending. A bending of the knees. Proper execution involves gradually bending and straightening the knees, while maintaining an erect, straight back. The plié promotes flexibility of the muscles and tendons of the legs and hips. It also helps the dancer develop a refined sense of balance, as well as establishing turnout at the beginning of class. Pliés are generally coordinated with a movement (or carriage) of the arms, known as port de bras. There are two kinds of plié: grand plié, a full bend of the knees until the thighs are parallel with the floor; and demi plié, a half bend, during which the heels do not come off the floor.

Appropriate Music. The music for pliés should be broad, slow, smooth, and flowing. The phrasing should connote spaciousness and grace; it should be flowing in character, and never clipped or choppy. Some instructors, however, stipulate a tempo that tends to rush this exercise, depriving dancers of the plié's full benefit.

Tempo and Meter. Slow. 3/4 or 4/4. (A slow, smooth 6/8 may also be used, if in character with the movements.) A 4/4 sometimes makes instructors uncomfortable—something it would benefit them to overcome, since really this is not a logical bias.

Port de Bras. Carriage of the arms. The port de bras is a movement of the arms from one position to another. The rest of the body may complement the movement of the arms by bending from the waist in any direction desired or stipulated. The arms should be graceful in their execution of this movement, and the bending of the body should be done in a smooth, controlled manner. Note: Port de bras also fits very appropriately, and is often executed, in the context of Adagio exercises, in the center portion of class.

Appropriate Music. The music that is appropriate for pliés should be suitable for port de bras as well.

Tempo and Meter. Slow. 3/4 or 4/4.

Battement Tendu (Tendu). *Battement* means "beating." *Tendu* means "stretched." The working leg (moving leg) is stretched away from the supporting leg (stationary leg) and is then brought back to its original position, thereby creating the beat. The dancer glides the working foot along the floor without lifting the toes off the floor. She learns to move the working leg in any direction without moving the hips, which remain stationary, while maintaining turnout. Tendus warm up and strengthen the ankles and feet.

Appropriate Music. The instructor may give more than one tendu exercise. If this is the case, the first tendu combination will probably be comparatively slow, while the second tendu combination will be quicker in tempo.

Tempo and Meter. For slower tendu combinations, a broad 3/4 or 4/4; for more brisk tendu combinations, a moderate to quick 3/4, 4/4, or 2/4. In any case, the beats should be clear and defined.

Battement Tendu Jeté (Battement Tendu Dégagé). *Jeté* means "thrown." This exercise is very similar to battements tendus, with the very important distinction that, in battement tendu jeté (dégagé), the toes of the working foot are allowed to come slightly off the floor. The working foot is "thrown" away from the supporting leg.

Appropriate Music. The music for battement tendu jeté (dégagé) is generally moderate to quick in tempo. The rhythm should be sharp and clear, and well accented.

Tempo and Meter. A sharp 2/4, 4/4, or 6/8.

Battement Piqué. *Piqué* means "pricking," designating the position in which the working leg is stretched away from the supporting leg. Only the toes of the working leg are touching the floor; then they are lifted from the floor in quick, light movements. The toes tap the floor lightly. The exercise teaches the muscles of the leg to move in a quick, controlled fashion.

Appropriate Music. Since battement piqué is generally a rather fast exercise, the music should be correspondingly fast and light.

Tempo and Meter. A quick 2/4, 4/4, or 6/8.

Fondu (Battement Fondu). A melting or sinking down. This is a plié on one (the supporting) leg, causing the body to be lowered. A fondu is much like a plié in terms of its general character and grace, but perhaps a little quicker.

Appropriate Music. The music for fondus is similar to that used for pliés, although it may be a little bit brighter. A tango in moderate tempo can be excellent.

Tempo and Meter. A slow to moderate 3/4 of 4.4, including a tango.

Rond de Jambe à Terre. A circle of the leg on the ground. The working leg traces a circular movement on the floor. The toes of the working foot stay in contact with the floor, and both legs (supporting and working) are kept straight. The focus of this exercise is to stabilize the hips, while promoting hip flexibility and strengthening the ankles.

Appropriate Music. This exercise generally calls for a smooth, even waltz feeling, although the accompanist need not feel compelled to play a waltz. Many pieces in triple meter would be suitable. Some instructors like to use a 4/4, especially at the more fundamental levels, when establishing the proper coordination for this exercise. The tempo may vary considerably, depending on the instructor's preference.

Tempo and Meter. A smooth 3/4 or a rather broad 6/8. Also, per the above, a smooth 4/4.

Rond de Jambe en l'Air. A circle of the leg in the air. The working leg is opened to second position in the air. The working calf, foot, and toes make an oval in the air, moving in toward the supporting leg and then away from it. The upper part of the working leg must remain stationary, while the lower part of the leg executes the movements. This exercise teaches the dancer to isolate the parts of the working leg and to control the moving parts.

Appropriate Music. The music for this combination may vary as appropriate, given the possible range in tempos, depending on the instructor's preference. This rond de jambe exercise will most likely be somewhat quicker than the (generally preceding) rond de jambe à terre exercise.

Tempo and Meter. Possibly an energetic 3/4, or a moderate 2/4 or 4/4. Often, a well-articulated mazurka is excellent.

Battement Frappé. Striking or struck battement. The heel of the working foot touches—"beats"—the ankle of the supporting leg, and the ball of the working foot strikes the floor, finishing several inches off the floor. The upper portion of the working leg remains stationary. Frappés strengthen the ankles and feet, and they teach the dancer to execute and control quick, sharp movements.

Appropriate Music. The tempo for this combination will vary, although the music should be very marked and distinct, with a well-punctuated rhythm.

Tempo and Meter. A duple meter is generally the most suitable. A sharp 2/4 or 4.4.

Battement sur le Cou-de-Pied. Beating at the "neck" of the foot (ankle). The working foot is wrapped around the ankle of the supporting leg. The heel of the working foot rapidly beats alternately in front of and then in back of the supporting ankle. This exercise prepares the dancer for batterie—or jumps with beats.

Appropriate Music. The music for this combination will generally be very fast and correspondingly light, even nervous.

Tempo and Meter. A very fast 2/4, 4/4, or 6/8.

Pas de Cheval. Horse's step. With respect to the working leg, this exercise is reminiscent of the movement of a horse's hoof as the horse paws the ground with one leg. The chief purpose of pas de cheval is to increase the dexterity and flexibility of the dancer's feet.

Appropriate Music. The most suitable music for this step is usually something in a moderate, duple meter.

Tempo and Meter. A moderate 2/4 or 4/4.

Développé. Developed. The working leg is drawn up along the supporting leg and is opened—that is, extended—into the air. The hips remain straight and square. This exercise is performed slowly and smoothly, without making jerking movements and without disturbing the carriage of the rest of the body.

Appropriate Music. The music for développés should be slow and graceful, and similar in style to music used for pliés and fondus.

Tempo and Meter. A slow, smooth 3/4 or 4/4.

Grand Battement. Large battement. The purpose of this exercise is to strengthen the working thigh and associated muscles, increase flexibility in the hip joints, and turn out the legs from the hips. The working leg is raised energetically upward and away from its original position to a maximum height as determined by the instructor, and then brought back down again in a controlled manner. The working leg may be raised in any number of directions, according to the particular exercise. The movement of the working leg should not throw the hips, the back, or the rest of the body out of proper placement.

Appropriate Music. Grand battement requires strong, energetic music, generally with relatively heavy downbeats and upbeats. A march, or a marchlike selection, is excellent in most cases. Some tangos, if sufficiently powerful, work well.

Tempo and Meter. A moderate, marchlike 2/4 or 4/4.

Battement en Cloche. Battement like a bell. A type of grand battement in which the working leg swings from front to back—freely, but always under the dancer's control—resembling the pendulum of a clock. The rest of the body is kept still, unless choreographed otherwise by the instructor. This exercise loosens the hips but should not interfere with the general placement of the body.

Appropriate Music. Music for battement en cloche should be in a strong, swinging, triple meter, with a heavy or very pronounced downbeat.

Tempo and Meter. A moderate, swinging 3/4 of 6/8.

Stretching(Optional). After the barre work has been completed and before center work begins, the dancers may do a series of stretches, often as a group and as prescribed by the instructor, or otherwise at their own discretion. Like all stretches in ballet technique class, these will be slow and gradual. Music may or may not be asked for, but generally it is used.

Appropriate Music. The music for these stretches should, as for any stretches, generally be slow, smooth, and flowing, comparable to that used for stretches at the beginning of the class or for pliés.

Tempo and Meter. Slow. 3/4 or 4/4.

The Center

Note. The ballet accompanist is advised that many of the barre exercises and steps discussed above under barre work can be—and are often—revisited in the center portion of the class. These specifically include, but are by no means limited to, battement tendu, grand battement, and, potentially, rond de jambe.

Center Dance Steps Chart

Adagio
Temps Lié
Port de Bras

Linking Steps
Glissade
Pas de Bourrée
Chassé

Petit Allegro
Assemblé
Ballonné
Ballotté
Brisé
Brisé Volé
Changement
Coupé
Échappé Changé Sauté
Emboité
Entrechat
Jeté
Jeté Passé
Pas de Chat
Sauté
Saut de Basque
Sissone (Ouverte or Fermée)
Soubresaut
Temps Levé

Pirouettes
Slow, in Place
- Attitude
- Arabesque
- Other Posés
- From Fourth Position—Preparation from Two Feet
- From Fifth Position—Preparation from Two Feet
- From Second Position—Preparation from Two Feet
- En Promenade

Quick, in Place
- From Fifth Position
- Flic-Flac (en Tournant)
- Fouetté

Quick, Moving
- Assemblé Soutenu en Tournant
- Chainné (Déboulé)
- Piqué Posé

Tour en l'Air (Men's Step)

Rising Steps
Relevé
Sous-Sus

Grand Allegro
Cabriole
Grand Echappé
Grand Jeté en Avant
Jeté en Tournant (par Terre)
Grand Jeté Entrelacé
Grand Jeté en Tournant
Pas Balancé
Pas de Basque (Grand)
Pas de Ciseaux
Pas de Poisson
Pas Failli
Renversé Sauté
Sauté Fouetté
Sissonne Tombée
(Quick pirouettes; tour en l'air)

Reverence

The Center: Discussion of Steps and General Music Requirements

Note Regarding the Descriptions of the Center Steps. Like the steps in "The Barre" (above), any of the center steps discussed below can be described in various ways and from a number of perspectives. Depending on their intent, these steps can vary in terms of their level of detail and their anatomical precision. The descriptions of the exercises that follow are brief and general in nature and are primarily intended to convey to the ballet technique accompanist a visual sense of the movements that she can relate to when she sees them in the studio.

***Adagio*.** At ease, at leisure. An adagio is a combination comprised of various steps and movements. Generally, it is slow, graceful, and drawn out. It teaches the dancer stamina and control. Its principal difficulty and challenge lie in the great demands that it makes on the dancer's ability to execute beautiful, slow, continuous movements without showing strain or fatigue, and while projecting an image of perfect control. The step called temps lié is frequently used in adagios. It teaches control in the transference of weight from one foot to the other.

Appropriate Music. Depending on the character of the adagio, appropriate music will vary somewhat in its general mood and feeling. However, adagios are typically comprised of one or more of the following qualities: gracefulness, stateliness, continuity of movement, sustained poses, smoothness, elegance, and sweeping, expressive gestures.

Tempo and Meter. The music should be appropriately slow, full, broad, etc. A 3/4 or 4/4 of expressive quality.

Linking Steps—Glissade, Pas de Bourrée, and Chassé. These three dance steps may be used in virtually any dance combination. They are linking steps, meaning that they are used to link, or connect, other steps together. That is to say, they get the dancer from one step to another. They may be practiced as separate, individual steps in beginning dance classes. Since these steps are generally used in combination with other steps, they are included here chiefly for the accompanist's general information and reference.

Appropriate Music. Appropriate music may be selected as the occasion demands. Usually, a moderate, smooth waltz or waltzlike piece will work, or an appropriate tango.

Tempo and Meter. When these steps are practiced as separate, individual steps in beginning dance classes, the tempo will vary, depending on the instructor's approach. A moderate 3/4 or a nonaggressive tango rhythm is generally good.

***Petit Allegro*.** Appropriate music for petit allegro will be discussed as a whole, after the following individual presentations of the various petit allegro steps.

Assemblé. Assembled, joined together. As the foot of the working leg is brushed out along the floor, the supporting leg pushes off the floor, into the air. The legs are joined together (assembled) in the air before the dancer returns to the floor.

Ballonné. Bounced, like a ball. As the supporting leg pushes the dancer off the floor, the working leg executes a battement. As the supporting leg returns to the floor, the working leg finishes its movement in such a manner that the working foot touches the ankle of the supporting leg.

Ballotté. Tossed. The body performs a backward and forward swaying movement in the air, as the weight changes from one leg to the other. The legs open sharply in the air.

Brisé. Broken or beating. A brisé is like an assemblé with beats, which travels. It covers space.

Brisé Volé. Flying brisé. This brisé is finished on one foot, with the other leg crossed in front or in back, allowing the dancer to perform another brisé in the opposite direction, finishing on the opposite foot.

Changement. Changing. A jump that begins with both feet and finishes on both feet, but the feet change positions in the air, so that the one that was originally in front ends in back.

Coupé. Cut or cutting. A small jump or step from one foot to the other, used as a preparation for other steps. This term also designates the position of the working foot at the ankle of the supporting leg.

Échappé Changé Sauté. Escaping with a jump. This step is comprised of two jumps in succession. It is begun from two feet, the legs opening before landing. The second jump, which immediately follows, brings the feet back together.

Emboité. Fitted together, or boxed. This is a small, traveling jump from one leg to the other, in which the working leg always finishes at coupé in front of the ankle of the supporting leg.

Entrechat, Even-Numbered and Odd-Numbered. Interweaving, braiding; a beating step. The dancer jumps off the floor and quickly crosses the legs before and behind each other. Entrechats are numbered from two through ten, depending on the number of crossings; if deux, quatre, six, huit, dix (two, four, six, eight, ten), the dancer lands on two feet; if trois, cinq, sept, neuf (three, five, seven, nine), she lands on one foot.

Jeté. Thrown. There are many kinds of jetés. This is a jump from one leg to the other. The working leg is "thrown" out, as the supporting leg pushes off into the air.

Jeté Passé. A jeté passed forward (en avant) or backward (en arrière). In this step, the legs cross, resembling the action of a pair of scissors.

Pas de Chat. Cat's step. Pas de chat is a traveling jump, which, in its movement, resembles the leap of a cat. The legs are drawn up quickly, one after the other, while the dancer is in the air.

Sauté. Jumped or jumping. A sauté is a simple jump. It can be executed in many positions and may stay in place or travel.

Saut de basque. A Basque jump. The dancer turns in the air, with one foot drawn up to the knee of the other leg. The landing is on one foot. One or two turns may be executed during the jump. In the latter case, the jump is designated as a double saut de basque.

Sissonne (Ouverte or Fermée). A traveling jump, named after François César de Roussy, Count of Sissonne, a seventeenth-century French nobleman credited with the invention of the step. In sissonne ouverte, the dancer jumps off of two legs and finishes on one leg. In sissonne fermée, the dancer begins and finishes the jump on two legs. Both sissonnes travel in the air.

Soubresau. A sudden spring. The jump begins from both feet. As the feet push off the floor, they are held tightly together, well pointed. The knees are straight. This jump may travel in any direction.

Temps Levé. A raising motion. Temps levé is a hop that is done from one foot and lands on the same foot. It can be executed in any position.

Appropriate Music, Tempos, and Meters for Petit Allegro Steps—Discussed as a Single Category. These steps may be practiced individually or in many different combinations. However, any one step or combination of steps in the petit allegro category will fall into a general range of requirements for musical characteristics, tempos, and meters, as explained below. Thus, it is appropriate to treat petit allegro steps as a single category.

Bright, Uplifting, Energetic. Generally, petit allegro requires music that is moderate to bright, often a 2/4 or 4/4, or sometimes a lively 3/4 or 6/8. Occasionally, a bright, uplifting 3/4 or 6/8 may be appropriate for providing a bit of extra time or lift for some petit allegro combinations. Regardless of the choreography or the innumerable possible variations for petit allegro, the music should always be lively, bright, light, dancelike, and well-articulated rhythmically. The quality of this music should never pull the dancers down or make them feel sluggish, heavy, or earthbound. The purpose of the music is to support the dancers getting up into the air. It should convey a sense of buoyancy, or bounce.

Flexibility of Duple and Triple Meters. A light polka or one of the livelier Chopin waltzes—or a 3/4 similar in feeling and style (something easier to play readily)—is often ideal. If the accompanist chooses a waltz for a petit allegro combination and the tempo seems too rushed of stiff, it is a good indication that a 2/4 meter should be used instead. On the other hand, if the accompanist decides to play something in a 2/4 or 4/4 meter and the music turns out to be sluggish, given the combination or the tempo at which the instructor wants it executed, then a bright 3/4 or possibly a 6/8 will very likely be a better fit. Again, depending on the combination and the tempo, one meter will tend to fill out the spacing of the steps better than the other. Experience will help the accompanist make the best judgment the first time around; also, it is ideal if the instructor provides a precise tempo prior to the execution of the combination.

Pirouettes.

Stated simply, pirouettes are turns. They can be executed on one or two feet, and they can be in place or traveling. From the accompanist's point of view, it will be convenient to divide pirouettes into three basic, somewhat arbitrary but recognizable categories: (1) pirouettes executed slowly, in place; (2) pirouettes executed quickly, in place; and (3) pirouettes executed quickly, while traveling. Many pirouettes are practiced at the barre, but here it will be most practical to discuss them in relation to center work. Any discussion of appropriate music may be applied to pirouettes at the barre as well as to combinations in the center, when applicable.

Pirouettes—Slow, In Place

Attitude, Arabesque, and Other Posés. These pirouettes are executed on one spot, on one foot, and in a slow and controlled manner. They are used frequently in adagio combinations, in conjunction with other steps.

APPROPRIATE MUSIC, TEMPO, AND METER. In general, these movements will warrant music with an adagiolike quality, smooth and sustained. Particularly in the case of attitudes, a slow to moderate waltz tempo may be appropriate.

Preparation from Two Feet. Turns from the fourth, fifth, and second positions are executed on one foot, but they are prepared from two feet. They are executed in place, at a moderate tempo, and each pirouette may be comprised of one, two, three, or more turns, depending on the choreography or the ability of the dancers. They may be practiced by themselves, or performed in conjunction with other steps.

APPROPRIATE MUSIC, TEMPO, AND METER. Music for the above turns should, in most cases, be moderate in tempo and relatively smooth in quality. A moderate waltz, somewhat rich and full, will likely work well in many instances. Occasionally, a very broad 4/4 meter will work more successfully that a 3/4. The choice of whether to use a 3/4 meter or 4/4 meter will depend on various factors and considerations analogous to those discussed in the section above on petit allegro.

En Promenade. In a walk. This is a very slow turn that is executed on one flat foot. The supporting leg performs a series of small movements in which the supporting heel changes position by slight shifts. The rest of the body is held in a posé. En promenade is executed in context with movements that have an adagio quality.

APPROPRIATE MUSIC, TEMPO, AND METER. Music used for any combination that employs promenades and comparable movements should have adagio qualities. The accompanist is referred to the preceding discussion on adagio.

Pirouettes—Quick, In Place

From Fifth Position. These pirouettes are executed in place, rapidly, and in succession. They are prepared from two feet and executed on one foot.

APPROPRIATE MUSIC, TEMPO, AND METER. Music for this step should be bright and fast—a 2/4 or 4/4 only. A polka or something similar would be suitable. A cancan is ideal.

Flic-Flac (En Tournant). A flicking movement, used in adagio, turning. The working foot executes the flicking movement in front of or behind the supporting leg, as the dancer executes a full turn. Flic-flac may be practiced at the barre, because of its difficulty.

APPROPRIATE MUSIC, TEMPO, AND METER. Music for flic-flacs should be a 2/4 or 4/4 meter, similar in quality to the music for pirouettes from fifth position, except that the tempo will be somewhat more moderate.

Fouetté. Whipped. For a fouetté, the dancer executes a full turn on one leg, while the other leg whips the body around. These fast turns are executed in place, in succession, on one foot.

APPROPRIATE MUSIC, TEMPO, AND METER. The music should be in the same style as that used for pirouettes from fifth position. Dancers may perform sixteen fouettés in succession, or even thirty-two or sixty-four, depending on the level of virtuosity of the dancer.

Pirouettes—Quick, Moving

Assemblé Soutenu en Tournant, Chainné (Déboulé), Piqué Posé. All of these turns are fast. Any number of them may be done rapidly in succession. In the ballet technique class, they may be done straight across the floor or in a diagonal from corner to corner. A number of dancers may form a large, moving circle and perform them in that manner.

APPROPRIATE MUSIC, TEMPO, AND METER. The music for these steps should be similar to that used for quick pirouettes in place—bright, fast 2/4s or 4/4s. The tempo may be extremely fast, in which case the accompanist will have to play very lightly and with all possible speed.

Tour en l'Air. A turn in the air. This is almost exclusively a male dancer's step. It is executed in place. The dancer leaps into the air, turning once, twice, or perhaps several times (called single tour, double tour, etc.). These turns may be practiced on one spot, in succession, and frequently they are used in grand allegro combinations.

APPROPRIATE MUSIC, TEMPO, AND METER. The music for successive tours in place should be either a very large and powerful 3/4 (waltz or waltzlike) tempo with a strong downbeat or, on occasion, an equally assertive, powerful, broad 4/4.

Rising Steps—Relevé and Sous-Sus. Raised and over-under, respectively. Both the relevé and the sous-sus are rising steps. In performing these steps, the dancer goes up quickly onto toe (on pointe) or half-toe. These steps are basic to dancing and are employed everywhere. They can be practiced at the barre or in the center, and they are often practiced by themselves in pointe class (for further discussion, see "Pointe Class," chap. 8). Relevés can be executed on one foot or two feet; a sous-sus is done on two feet, with one foot placed in front of the other, the legs and feet drawn tightly together, and the heels forward.

Appropriate Music, Tempo, and Meter. Music that is suitable for relevé and sous-sus, whether practiced at the barre or in the center, may be in a 2/4 or 4/4 meter and moderate in tempo. The character of the music should be sharp, clear, and well accented, although not too fast. These exercises may put considerable strain on the dancers' legs, and a tempo that pushes too much will not be good for the dancers' muscles.

Grand Allegro. Grand allegro combinations are generally reserved for the latter portion of center work, when the dancers are fully warmed up. Grand allegro steps are bigger than petit allegro steps, and they are characterized by big jumps that cover a considerable distance and height. These steps may be combined with various fast pirouettes and petit allegro work. During grand allegro, the accompanist will need her biggest, most powerful waltzes, and fast, brilliant galops, codas, and polkas.

Note Regarding Men's Grand Allegro Work. In general, men's jumps and associated men's combinations in grand allegro work—and specifically, traditional men's variations in the ballet repertory—call for big, powerful music, performed at appropriately restrained (slower) tempos that permit full execution of the choreography. Pursuant to this, and as suggested elsewhere in this book, when it comes time for men to perform grand allegro work in class separately from women, keep this in mind: Tempos may need to be adjusted downward for men.

Cabriole. A caper. The legs beat against each other while they are extended in the air during this big jump. The dancer lands on one leg.

APPROPRIATE MUSIC, TEMPO, AND METER. The most suitable music for this step is a big, powerful waltz, as is the case with many of the grand allegro steps.

Grand Échappé. A large escaping or slipping movement. This is a very big jump, usually executed in place. It is a larger version of the échappé, which is also done straight up and down.

APPROPRIATE MUSIC, TEMPO, AND METER. For grand échappé, a 4/4 is generally more appropriate than a waltz. A large, powerful 4/4 or 2/4, with a strong lift, is recommended.

Grand Jeté en Avant. A large jeté forward. In this big forward leap, one leg pushes off the floor and is thrown up and back, while the other leg is thrown forward, into the air. While the dancer is in the air, his legs form a split, and he holds this position for as long as possible. As he descends, he lands on the forward leg.

APPROPRIATE MUSIC, TEMPO, AND METER. Grand jeté en avant may be included in a typical big waltz combination. However, when the dancers are leaping across the floor in a straight line or in a circle, a strong 2/4 or 4/4 galop or a coda is very good.

Jeté en Tournant (par Terre). A jeté, turning across the floor. This is a large leap, with the dancer traveling forward while staying close to the floor, followed by a complete turn in the air that ends with a landing on one foot.

APPROPRIATE MUSIC, TEMPO, AND METER. A fast, strong 2/4 or 4/4 meter is best for this step, which may be done successively in a straight line or in a circle. A galop or a coda is very good.

Grand Jeté Entrelacé. *Entrelacé* refers to the "interlacing" of the legs. This is a large jump in which one foot is thrust forward, the body does a half turn to face the direction from which the jump originated, and the other leg is thrust toward the back, thus creating the interlacing effect.

APPROPRIATE MUSIC, TEMPO, AND METER. This step is usually performed to a big waltz, as for cabrioles or grand jeté en tournant.

Grand Jeté en Tournant. A large jeté, turning. In this large jump, the dancer springs from one foot, throwing the other leg upward and around to the outside, while turning in the air.

APPROPRIATE MUSIC, TEMPO, AND METER. The most appropriate music for this step is, again, a big, powerful waltz.

Pas Balancé (Balancé). A rocking step. This is a smooth, graceful, sweeping waltz step. It is comprised of three steps, in which the weight of the body is shifted from one foot to the other.

APPROPRIATE MUSIC, TEMPO, AND METER. A gracious, smooth, but dancy waltz is good for balances. This step is not as big as many other grand allegro steps, and the music need not be as imposing.

Pas de basque (Grand). A large Basque step. This step is comprised of three basic movements and is somewhat slower than most grand allegro steps. Both of the dancer's legs make large, sweeping movements in the air.

APPROPRIATE MUSIC, TEMPO, AND METER. Pas de basque is best danced to a very slow, stately mazurka, or perhaps to a polonaise, depending on the tempo of the combination and the character of the music. A waltz is too fast and does not place enough emphasis on the individual beats within the measure.

Pas de Ciseaux. Scissors step. One leg is thrown forward into the air as the dancer jumps off the floor. The dancer then swings the leg back, past the other leg—thereby resembling scissors—as the dancer lands.

APPROPRIATE MUSIC, TEMPO, AND METER. The accompanist should use a large, strong waltz for pas de ciseaux.

Pas de Poisson. Fish's step. The dancer jumps into the air, forming an arch with his back—resembling a fish leaping out of the water. The dancer's legs are held straight and close together. The crossed feet resemble the tail of a fish.

APPROPRIATE MUSIC, TEMPO, AND METER. This step best fits into a 2/4 or 4/4 galop or coda tempo.

Pas Failli. Giving way. This step is similar to sissonne. The body does a slight turn in the air, so that the head begins to look over one shoulder. As the dancer lands, the back leg immediately slides forward, and the head finishes looking over the opposite shoulder.

APPROPRIATE MUSIC, TEMPO, AND METER. A strong 3/4 or 4/4 meter would be appropriate for this step, depending on the tempo desired. The quality of the music should be comparable to that which would be used for other grand allegro steps.

Renversé Sauté. A jump, upset or reversed. The dancer's body bends so that the balance is angled but controlled. The supporting leg pushes off from the floor in a jump, as the other leg executes a battement front and circles to the back.

APPROPRIATE MUSIC, TEMPO, AND METER. The standard, strong grand allegro waltz should be used for this step.

Sauté Fouetté. A sauté whipped. As the working leg executes a battement from back to front, the supporting leg executes a jump. When the working leg is lifted high to the front, the body does half a turn away from it, and the dancer finishes facing the opposite direction, with the working leg to the back.

APPROPRIATE MUSIC, TEMPO, AND METER. Generally, the standard, strong grand allegro waltz should be used. A strong 4/4 meter with a lift may also work.

Sissonne Tombée. A sissonne falling. The dancer jumps off two feet and lands on one foot, immediately falling forward onto the other leg. This step is usually not practiced by itself, but is done with various other steps.

APPROPRIATE MUSIC, TEMPO, AND METER. The standard, strong grand allegro waltz should be used.

Reverence. A curtsey. Many ballet classes end with a reverence (not all instructors include it), which, in essence, is an elaborate series of bows. It may be combined with other elements. Its main purpose is to practice bowing. In bowing, the dancers generally acknowledge the instructor, the accompanist, and the real or imaginary audience.

APPROPRIATE MUSIC, TEMPO, AND METER. The music for the reverence will probably have a slow, adagiolike quality. It may be strong, assertive, and triumphant—a slow or moderate 3/4or 4/4 meter with a rich, full texture. Occasionally, a piece with a subdued, poetic quality lends a striking mood for the reverence.

4 Suggested Piano Repertory for Barre and Center Work

General Guidelines on Repertory and Its Use

Compatible Music for Each Step

Wide Variety of Composers and Styles. This chapter is devoted to a discussion of both general categories and specific examples of piano literature that can be used, either in its original form or in appropriately edited versions, for the ballet technique class. In this chapter, each barre exercise and center step is either treated individually or discussed in conjunction with other combinations that warrant similar musical accompaniment. For each dance step, there is a list of compatible compositions that musically reinforce the characteristics and quality of that particular step. A wide variety of composers and styles has been suggested for most steps. This will enable the ballet accompanist to acquire a broad sense of what is musically appropriate for each step while becoming aware of specific pieces that are individually suited for the purpose.

Essential Information Provided

Time Signatures, Metronome Markings, Cadences. For the accompanist's reference, several items of essential information are included with each listing. The time signature of the piece is provided. A metronome marking (MM) is offered, which is intended to be a general indication of the appropriate tempo for each step when performed in that particular composition. The metronome suggestion indicates an average, comfortable tempo that may vary considerably in an actual situation, depending on the preference of the instructor, her approach to teaching, and the dancers' skill level. Following the metronome markings, the accompanist will find instructions regarding which measures of the music to use; how to arrange them into square, even musical phrases that will accommodate the dance combination; and where to cadence. The accompanist will rarely use all of any given piece of music; sometimes, she will need only a small section—for instance, sixteen measures. She may, in fact, take a handful measures from different sections of the piece and knit them together into a logical, continuous musical fabric .

Avoid Excessive Repetitiousness

Short Musical Excerpts. The accompanist is strongly advised against excessive repetitiousness when using very short pieces or very short sections of larger pieces. For example, if the accompanist is using only sixteen measures of music to accompany a comparatively long combination, or one that is fast-moving and that uses up the music rapidly, or one that repeats itself many times for successive dancers or groups of dancers, the repetition of those same sixteen measures over and over to fill out the exercise will likely have a noticeable effect on the dancers and become a bit deadening. There are one or two tactics that the accompanist can and should use to ameliorate this circumstance.

Improvisation. First, if the accompanist has any skill at improvisation, she can embellish, enrich, and otherwise vary the music each time, or every couple of times, that she repeats it. She should drive herself, within reason, to improvise until she becomes relatively comfortable and proficient in doing so. (See chap. 7, Improvisation)

Ample Music. The accompanist's second alternative to excessive repetition of limited phrases is simply to make sure that she has enough music immediately available (or memorized) so that she can shift around from one selection to another. If done skillfully, these transitions can be seamless and provide energizing variety. Key changes are fine.

Listen to the Instructor. By listening to the dance instructor while she demonstrates a combination, the accompanist should be able to ascertain generally how long the combination will take and how much music will be required to avoid excessive repetition. (See chap. 2, "Long Combinations.")

Notebooks. The subject of music notebooks is especially relevant here. The accompanist is referred to chapter 2, "Organizing Music for Ballet Class," for a complete discussion of music binders and how to organize them.

It is very strongly recommended that the ballet accompanist compile and arrange for herself notebooks of musical repertory for use in the ballet technique class. This is practical—if not indispensable—for a number of reasons. Individual piece of music are much easier to locate quickly when they are organized into notebooks. Although such notebooks can be arranged by category—either by dance step or by composer—the method highly endorsed here is by composer, alphabetically. If the notebooks are arranged in categories according to dance steps, the question will then arise—over and over again—as to the category of dance step to which a particular piece of music should be classified, since any given piece of music is often suitable or can be made suitable—for a very wide variety of dance steps and combinations (pursuant to this, it would be a poor idea to try to categorize and divide music according to *barre* and *center* work). A central point of this book is that the accompanist should become highly skilled at arranging and *manipulating* music so that the possibilities for the use of any given score become almost unlimited. Therefore, again, arranging ballet notebooks by composer is the most practical method.

Assembling music into logical collections of copies also avoids wear and tear on the accompanist's personal scores. In addition, she will not have to make ballet-related notations on her personal scores, that is, measure numbers, repeat signs, and various alterations. Furthermore, since she may use only one or two pieces for class out of a much larger collection, there is no point in hauling around excess music. Surplus and irrelevant music encumbers the accompanist and interferes with her ability to offer music efficiently. The longer the accompanist plays to ballet, the more repertory she should accumulate. Notebooks are the ideal alternative to the accumulation of irrelevant scores.

Coordinating Various Chapters of this Book

Four Closely Coordinated Technical Chapters. The accompanist is strongly encouraged to compare and coordinate the information in this chapter and chapter 3, Barre and Center Combinations. Doing so will help her acquire a sound, general knowledge of the structure of ballet technique classes, the approximate order and basic nature of the dance steps and their relationships to other steps, and a reliable idea about what kind of music is appropriate for any particular dance step or combination. The accompanist is urged to examine and analyze carefully this chapter's many musical recommendations and to research, confirm, and employ the music that she is attracted to while drawing from her own repertory and conducting her own musical research. The development of her repertory will find substantial fulfillment through her study of the following the next three chapters in this book.

Building One's Own Personal Repertory. The broad spectrum of music presented in this book encompasses many styles and varying degrees of technical skill. Some can be played readily, or at least with minimal practice and preparation, while other pieces may require more work. Many technically challenging pieces can and, for practical reasons, should be simplified for ballet technique accompaniment purposes (see "When Music is Too Difficult or Too Complex," chap. 5), while retaining the essential features that make them good candidates for use in the studio. The accompanist is strongly encouraged to build up her own individual ballet repertory, rather than purchasing collections of ballet pieces, which is limiting and does comparatively little to develop the latent talents of an accompanist. Her musicality and powers of musical analysis will be much more stimulated to grow and develop if she does most of her own work. Therefore, while the repertory suggestions provided in this section of the book are extensive and absolutely suitable for use as a ballet technique musical syllabus, they comprise foundational knowledge and guidance that will enable the accompanist to independently research, develop, and implement her *personal* collection of ballet repertory.

Avoidance of Standard Ballet Repertory. It has been recommended that the accompanist avoid playing most of the standard repertory from famous ballets for the technique class. However, given the text immediately above about building a personal repertory for ballet class, a bit of judicious reiteration is included here.

Among the repertory suggestions in this section, there are relatively few examples from the standard ballets. In general, it is recommended to avoid as much of the standard ballet music as practicable. If the accompanist is working with professional ballet dancers, they will likely be overly (perhaps nauseatingly) familiar with the ballet standards. For them, hearing this music in class all the time and during rehearsals and on stage as well may be, to say the least, trying.

There are occasions, however, when it is challenging for the accompanist to find good pieces that are as appropriate in feeling for certain dance combinations as ballet literature. For instance, traditional piano repertory offers little when it comes to finding appropriate (and technically accessible) music for fast pirouettes and 2/4 grand allegro steps. At such times, the codas, galops, and fast 2/4's from the ballet scores, as well as polkas, cancans, and other galops from outside the traditional ballet settings, are ideal. In the upcoming section on music for grand allegro steps, appropriate suggestions are provided.

The Special Challenge of Grand Allegro Waltzes

A Special Issue. A general discussion of waltz music for grand allegro combinations is offered here, since it is somewhat of a special issue.

Lining Up Several Pieces. The accompanist is reminded once again that many of the 2/4 and 3/4 combinations for grand allegro work toward the end of the center portion of technique class may go on for some time—perhaps a long time—without a pause in the music. In these circumstances, her musical selections should not be so technically ambitious as to exhaust her. To avoid or at least ease this strain, the potential for which is very real, the accompanist might want to string together several different pieces, both for aesthetic and technical relief. If the accompanist has not memorized a good deal of music or does not improvise readily, she may wish to remove several compatible grand allegro pieces from her notebooks temporarily and line them up across the music rack of the piano.

Lifting the Dancers. It can be challenging to find waltzes in the traditional piano repertory that ideally convey the sense of lift and energy that the dancers need in grand allegro waltzes. Most waltzes in the traditional piano repertory are, as written, too stylized; they do not possess that simple, ungarnished, elemental power that drives the dancers up into the air and inspires them to become, for a moment at least, unbound from the force of gravity. It bears mention here that some of the big waltz melodies from Broadway can serve nicely, if played appropriately.

Downbeats. With grand allegro waltzes in general, the first beat of each odd-numbered measure will be the beat on which the dancers push off from the floor. This beat should be correspondingly strong and powerful, and should convey a sense of intense, upward drive, or lift. Since the dancers will generally land on the first beat of the even-numbered measures, this beat should be comparatively lighter, so as not to encourage a sense of weight and heaviness upon landing. In other words, as a general principle in grand allegro waltzes, the heaviness of the downbeat of each successive measure will alternate as follows:

Measure 1: Heavy downbeat
Measure 2: Light downbeat
Measure 3: Heavy downbeat
Measure 4: Light downbeat
Etc.

Powerful Left Hand, Uplifting Rhythmic Motifs in Right Hand. Grand allegro waltzes should, overall, have a strong, powerful bass— especially downbeats. Octaves should be used on most left-hand downbeats, rather that single notes. In conjunction with this, rhythmic motifs with uplift should generally be employed in the right hand. One right-hand rhythmic motif, two measures in length, that conveys very well a sense of lift to the dancers may be illustrated as follows:

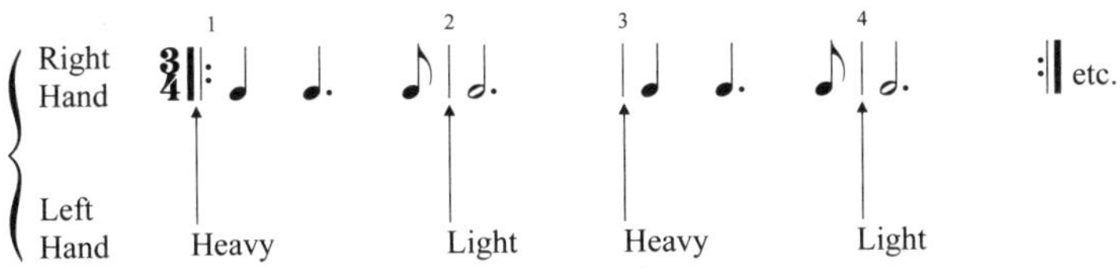

This motif should be put to excellent use—frequently, as appropriate, but not overdone—in grand allegro waltzes, in conjunction with a strong left hand with an emphasis on the odd-numbered downbeats.

Note on Duple Meters. Relevant to the present discussion on grand allegro waltzes, it is appropriate to make a point here about playing accents in 2/4 or 4/4 grand allegro combinations. Generally, the principal outlined above for alternating heavy and light downbeats will have an analogy for grand allegro (and some other) music in duple time. That is to say, the odd beats are more heavily accented; the even beats are lighter. This alteration of heavy and light beats gives the music rhythmic life and prevents it from sounding stodgy and earthbound.

To illustrate the same point with a very different example, this approach to accenting music would apply very well in a march-like (2/4 or 4/4) grand battement combination (end of the barre portion of class). The dancer's leg swings up quickly and energetically on the odd counts, as the accompanist plays a heavier, more accented beat, and comes down lightly on the even counts, as the accompanist plays a lighter, less accented beat.

There are, naturally, instances when the above principle does not apply, for example, in a barre combination that calls for beats with consistent, regular, even accents—a feature which the observant, experienced accompanist would, ideally, reflect in her playing.

The Transformative Grand Allegro Waltz Motif. Regarding grand allegro waltzes, accents, and rhythmic motifs, it is pointed out here that the two-measure, right-hand rhythmic motif highlighted above can be used—with relative ease—to help transform almost any waltz that is otherwise a good candidate into a better grand allegro waltz—simply by modifying the melody to accommodate the motif. In addition, and not uncommonly, many ¾ pieces of music that are not, at first glance, amenable to transformation into a grand allegro waltz can be converted into just such a showpiece by following the practices discussed in this section. This is also true of many 4/4 pieces that can be converted!

The Score is Only the Starting Point. Grasping the essence of grand allegro combinations—both 3/4 and duple—will likely be one of the most challenging issues for the inexperienced ballet technique accompanist. Whatever combination the accompanist is playing for, she should always strive to convey musically, and support, the essential qualities of the dance movements, whether they reflect the smoothness and grace of an adagio or the sharp, accented brilliance of a petit allegro jumping step. Of foremost importance is the manner in which a grand allegro waltz is played—not what is written on the score. Following this, in the hands of a skilled accompanist, the same 3/4 piece could be arranged, on the spot, in any number of ways so as to be quite suitable for many combinations—pliés, ronds de jambe, battement en cloche, or a powerful grand allegro. This is, in fact, nothing more than practicing the principle of variation. Except for some outstanding thematic familiarity (which can also be skillfully modified), dancers might not ever suspect that the same material was being used, perhaps over and over again, for different combinations. The methods for making such arrangements are discussed in the chapter 5, Preparing and Arranging Piano Repertory for Ballet Class.

Suggested Piano Repertory for the Barre

Applicability of Suggestions. The accompanist should note that many suggestions put forth throughout this book apply, as appropriate, to all repertory suggestions. The accompanist is encouraged to experiment and to refine any suggestion to make it especially appropriate for the combination.

Metronome Markings. All metronome markings (MM) provided are approximate and should be adjusted as appropriate.

Viewing and Downloading. Most of the suggested repertory can be viewed online, and downloaded at no charge. Observe copyright notices. (See "Free Online Music Scores," chapter 2.)

Music for Pliés, Port de Bras (Suitable for Stretches)

BACH: SARABANDE, ENGLISH SUITE IN F MAJOR

3/4, MM quarter note equals 80

Play and repeat the first eight measures, then play the remaining sixteen measures. This totals thirty-two measures. Repeat as necessary.

Bach: Menuet II, Partita in B-Flat Major

3/4, MM quarter note equals 88

Play the entire movement straight through, taking the repeats. This totals thirty-two measures. Repeat as necessary.

Brahms: Intermezzo, op. 119, no. 2

3/4, MM quarter note equals 88

Begin with the middle section, marked *Andantino Grazioso.* Play the first thirty-two measures as written. Repeat at necessary.

Brahms: Romance in F Major, op. 118, no. 5

6/4, MM quarter note equals 80

Use the first sixteen measures. Since this piece is a 6/4, sixteen measures will be the equivalent to thirty-measures of 3/4. Repeat as necessary. In measure 16, cadence in F major, rather than in D minor.

Chopin: Nocturne in B Major, op. 32, no. 1

4/4, MM quarter note equals 66

Use the first sixteen measures. Repeat as necessary. Cadence in B major in measure sixteen.

Chopin: Nocturne in E Major, op. 62, no. 2

4/4, MM quarter note equals 66

Use the first sixteen measures. Measures 17–24 may be repeated to form another sixteen-measure phrase. Cadence in B major in measure 24, after the repeat. This totals thirty-two measures. Repeat as necessary.

Fauré: Nocturne in E-Flat major, op. 36

4/4, MM quarter note equals 50

Play the first eight measures. Omit measures nine through eleven, and play measures twelve through nineteen, Cadencing in B-flat in measure nineteen. This totals sixteen measures of 4/4. Repeat as necessary.

Gershwin: Prelude no. 2 in C-Sharp Minor

4/4, MM quarter note equals 88

Play measures 5–12 for the first phrase, including the pickup to measure five. Play measures 13–18 for a second phrase, repeating measures 15 and 16 before playing measures 17 and 18. The accompanist now has an even, sixteen-measure phrase.

Play measures 19–26 to complete the third eight-measure phrase. For the final eight-measure phrase, play measures 27–30, repeating measures 29 and 30, rounding out the phrase with two measures of F-sharp major. This totals thirty-two measures. Although these alterations sound rather elaborate, the accompanist will find that he can make the music sound quite smooth and convincing.

Rachmaninoff: Prelude in G-Flat Major, op. 23, no. 10
3/4, MM quarter note equals 60

Play measures 3–34, including the pickup to measure 3. This will make an even, thirty-two measure phrase. Cadence in G-flat major in measure 34. Repeat as necessary.

Ravel: Waltz no. 2 in G Minor, Valses Nobles et Sentimentales
3/4. MM quarter note equals 88

This piece falls into four equal sections of sixteen measures each, so no alterations in the measures are necessary.

Satie: Three Gymnopedies, no. 1
3/4. MM quarter note equals 84

Measures 5–12 comprise the first eight-measure phrase. Measures 13–21 (omitting measure twenty) comprise the second eight-measure phrase. Measures 22–30 (omitting measure twenty-six) comprise the third eight-measure phrase. Omit measure thirty-one. The last eight-measure phrase is made up of measures 32–39. This totals thirty-two measures of four even phrases. Repeat as necessary.

Wright and Forest: "Stranger in Paradise," from Kismet
4/4. MM quarter note equals 88

Consider where the words start as measure 1. Play measures 1–16 as written and repeat as necessary. Cadence in F major in measure 16. (Note: This selection is very easy to convert to 3/4.)

Music for Fondus, Développés, Battements Tendus (Slow)

Brahms: Intermezzo, op. 117, no. 1
6/8, MM eighth note equals 92

Play measures 1–16, and cadence in E-flat major in measure 16. Repeat as necessary.

Brahms: Variations on a Theme by Paganini, op. 35, Book I, Var. XI
2/4, MM eighth note equals 50

This piece can be played straight through as written. It has sixteen measures. Repeat as necessary.

Brahms: Variations on a Theme by Paganini, op. 35, Book II, Var. IV
3/8, MM eighth note equals 96

This piece can be played straight through as written. It is sixteen measures. Repeat as necessary.

Brahms: Waltz in E Major, op. 39, no. 2
3/4, MM quarter note equals 96

Play this waltz straight through without any alterations, taking the repeat after the first eight measures. This will total thirty-two measures. Repeat as necessary.

Brahms: Waltz in D Minor, op. 39, no. 9

3/4, MM quarter note equals 108

Play measures 1–8 twice, then the remainder of the waltz, taking the second ending. This will total thirty-two measures. Repeat as necessary.

Brahms: Waltz in C-Sharp Minor, op. 39, no. 16

3/4, MM quarter note equals 96

Play the entire waltz as written, taking the repeat. This totals thirty-two measures. Repeat as necessary.

Chopin: Nocturne in F Minor, op. 55, no. 1

4/4, MM quarter note equals 80

Play measures 1–16, cadencing in F minor in measure 16. Repeat as necessary.

Chopin: Nocturne in C Minor, op. 48, no. 1

4/4, MM quarter note equals 60

Play measures 1–16, repeating them if necessary. The last time through, cadence in measure sixteen in C minor.

Gluck: Ballet des Ombres Heureuses from Orpheo et Euridice

3/4, MM quarter note equals 88

Play measures 1–8 twice. Then play measures 9–16 and measures 17–28, omitting measures 21–24. This will yield four smooth phrases of eight measures each. Repeat as necessary.

Granados: Valses Poeticos, no. 3

3/4, MM quarter note equals 104

Play measures 1–8 as written. For the second eight measures, play measures 1–4 again and then skip to measures 9–12. Play measures 13–20 for the third phrase. For the last eight measures, play measures 13–16 again and then measures 21–24. This process totals thirty-two measures. Repeat as necessary. Notice that this waltz was originally in twelve-measure phrases, through measure 24.

Rachmaninoff: Variations on a Theme of Corelli, op. 42, Var. IV

3/4, MM quarter note equals 88

Play this piece straight through. It is sixteen measures long. Repeat as necessary.

Ravel: Mouvement de Menuet (II), from Sonatine

3/8, MM quarter note equals 88

For the first phrase, play measures 1–4 twice. Then play measures 5–12 for the second phrase. The third phrase will consist of measures 13–20. Measures 21 and 22 are omitted. The final phrase is formed as follows: play measures 23–26, then repeat measures 23 and 24, and round out the phrase with one measure of improvised A-flat major tonality and a cadence in the final measure on D-flat major. This will total four phrases of eight measures each. With a little bit of care, the accompanist can make the above procedure sound quite natural and convincing. Repeat as necessary.

Saint-Saëns: Menuet in F Major, op. 90

3/4. MM quarter note equals 96

Play measures one through eight for the first phrase. The second phrase will be measures 9–12, played twice. Measures 13–24 are identical to measures 1–12, so the entire process may be repeated for these measures, yielding a total of thirty-two measures of four even eight-measure phrases.

Schubert: Impromptu in A-Flat Major, op. 142, no. 2

3/4, MM quarter note equals 96

Play measures 1–24 to complete the first three phrases of eight measures each. The last eight-measure phrase may be done as follows: play measures 25–30 as written and add two measures of suitable A-flat major tonality in which to cadence. Repeat at necessary.

Schumann: "Erinnerung" (Remembrance), from Album for the Young, op. 68

2/4, MM quarter note equals 52

Play measures 1–10, omitting measures seven and eight, for the first phrase. Repeat to make a second phrase of eight measures. For the last two phrases of eight measures each, play measures 11–18 twice. The second time through, change the last chord in measure 17 to E major (V^7 of A), and cadence in measure 18 in A major. Repeat the piece as necessary.

Schumann: Drei Stücklein (Three Little Pieces), op. 99, no. 1

4/4, MM quarter note equals 60

Use measures 1–8. In measure eight, improvise chords of appropriate E major tonality to go with the B major dominant chord at the end of measure 7. If the accompanist wishes to use the entire piece, he may play it straight through as written, which is sixteen measures. The suggestion for cadencing in measure eight will be handy if the accompanist has played the entire piece and is going through it for a second time, only to discover that the combination is twenty-four measure long (as occasionally happens), instead of thirty-two.

Smetana: "Charming Landscape," from The Sketches, op. 5, Book II, no. 3

2/2, MM eighth note equals 69

Play the first sixteen measures as written. The last two phrases of eight measures each will be measures 17–24 and measures 31–38. Measures 25–30 are omitted. Repeat as necessary.

Music for Ronds de Jambe à Terre

Bach: Menuet II, English Suite in F Major

3/4, MM quarter note equals 104

This piece, without repeats, totals thirty-two measures. It would be unwise to play it in this fashion, however. Measure sixteen would be halfway through the piece and is not clear and distinct harmonically, as it should be in order to sound convincing to the dancer's ear. Therefore, it would be better to play this piece in the following manner. Play measures 1–8 twice, to total sixteen measures (at measure eight, the second repeat should be taken). Then play measures 9–16 and skip directly to measures 25–32. Measures 17–24 are omitted. The accompanist still has four phrases of eight measures each, and the music is more harmonically convincing. Repeat as necessary.

Bach: Passepied II, Partita in B Minor (Overture in the French Manner)

3/8, MM eighth note equals 104

Play measures 1–8 twice. Play measures 9–24. This makes four phrases of eight measures each. Repeat as necessary.

Beethoven: Theme, and Variations I, IV, and VI, from Six Variations on "Nel cor più non mi *sento,*" *La Molinara*

6/8, MM eighth note equals 112

The number of measures and the straightforward harmonic structures of the theme, and variations I, IV, and VI are identical, and therefore the alteration that follows may be applied to the theme and each variation. Play measures 1–12 as written. Omit measures 13–16 and proceed directly to measures 17–20. This makes sixteen full measures. Repeat as necessary, or change from one variation to another.

Brahms: Waltz in E Major, op. 39, no. 5

3/4, MM quarter note equals 112

Play the opening eight measures twice. Then play from measure 9 through to the end of the piece. The accompanist will be two measures short of completing four even eight-measure phrases. In other words, the last eight-measure phrase begins in measure 17 and ends with measure 22. The fill in the last two absent measures, simply repeat the last two measures (21 and 22), including the pickup note to measure 21. This will sound natural and will square off the phrase. Repeat the piece as necessary.

Brahms: Waltz in B-Flat Major, op. 39, no. 8

3/4, MM quarter note equals 112

Play measures 1–4 twice, then play measures 5–12. This makes sixteen measures. For the second sixteen measures, play measures 13–20 and complete the last eight-measure phrase in the following way: play measures 21–29, omitting measure 26 and ending on measure 29. In examining the final phrase of the waltz, the accompanist will see that omitting measure 26 is the best choice, since it interferes minimally—the least—with the melody and the phrase structure.

Chopin: Nocturne in B-Flat Minor, op. 9, no. 1
6/4, MM quarter note equals 116
Begin in measure 19, the D-flat major section. The next thirty-two measures will fall naturally into four phrases of sixteen measures each. Repeat the thirty-two measures as necessary.

Chopin: Prelude in A-Flat Major, op. 28, no. 17
6/8, MM eighth note equals 116
Begin with measure 3 and play through measure 18. This sixteen measures of 6/8 equals thirty-two measures of 3/4. Repeat as necessary.

Granados: Valses Poeticos, no. 1
3/4, MM quarter note equals 116
Play the first thirty-two measures as written. If needed, play measures 33–48 (the remainder of the piece) twice, for another thirty-two measures.

Mozart: Sonata in A Major, K . 331, First Movement, Variations III and IV
6/8, MM quarter note equals 116
For both variations, play measures 1–16 as written. In measure 16, cadence on the last beat (A minor in Var. III and A major in Var. IV). Repeat as necessary.

Poldini: Poupeé Valsante (Dancing Doll)
3/8, MM eighth note equals 116
After the five-measure introduction, the following thirty-two measures fall into four equal eight-measure phrases. Repeat as necessary.

Ravel: Menuet on the Name of Haydn
3/4, MM quarter note equals 116
Play measures 1–16 as written. In the interests of harmonic clarity, play the last two phrases of eight measures each in this way: play measures 17–24 twice, substituting a suitable B-flat major configuration in measure 24 each time. Repeat the piece as necessary.

Saint-Saëns: Valse Nonchalante, op. 110
3/4, MM quarter note equals 116
Play the first thirty-two measures as written. In measure 32, cadence in D-flat major. Repeat as necessary.

Scriabin: Prelude in A Major, op. 11, no. 7
6/8, MM eighth note equals 116.
Play the first sixteen measures and cadence on A major on the second beat of measure 16. Sixteen measures of 6/8 equals thirty-two measures of 3/4. Repeat as necessary.

Smetana: Chanson, from Six Feuilles d'Album, Op 2, no. 2

2/4, MM quarter note equals 40

In this piece, each quarter note is subdivided into two groups of sixteenth-note triplets. In his case, it is very useful to change the rhythm so that a quarter note sound as if it is subdivided into three groups of sixteenth-note duplets. Thus, each quarter note will have three pulses, which resembles as 6/8 or a 3/4. This is more suitable for ronds de jambe à terre. This piece is divided into two equal sections of sixteen measures each. Each section will now seem to the dancer to be thirty-two measures of ¾ or sixteen measures of 6/8. If the combinations ends at the first sixteen measures, cadence in E minor on the second beat of measure 16. Repeat as necessary.

Tchaikovsky: Schneeglöckchen (Snow-Drops), op. 37, no. 4

6/8, MM eighth note equals 116

Play the first sixteen measures as written. Cadence in G minor in measure 16. For the second sixteen measures, play measures 25–40. Cadence in D minor in measure 40. Repeat as necessary.

Vogt: Twenty-Four Octave Exercises, op. 145, no. 23

3/8, MM eighth note equals 108

This piece may be played as written. It is comprised of four even eight-measure phrases. Repeat as necessary.

Music for Ronds de Jambe en l'Air

Bach: Menuet I, Partita in B-Flat Major

3/4, MM dotted half note equals 60

Use the first thirty-two measures of this movement. In measures 31 and 32, play two measures of a B-flat cadence, instead of playing what is written. This will sound rounded out and natural. Repeat the movement as necessary. The first sixteen measures may be repeated rather than continuing.

Bach: Passepied I, Partita in B Minor (Overture in the French Manner)

3/8, MM dotted eighth note equals 56

Play this movement straight through without repeats. This equals thirty-two measures. Repeat the movement as necessary.

Bach: Prelude in C Major, Well-Tempered Clavier, Book I

4/4, MM half note equals 50

There will be one rond de jambe for each half note. The first phrase will be measures 1–7, with measure 7 repeated to make eight measures. On the repeat of measure 7, play a G for the root of the arpeggio instead of B. The second phrase is measures 8–15. For the third phrase, play measures 16–21 as written, which totals six measures, and finish the last two measures as follows. In measure 22, use the first half-note arpeggio and skip immediately to measure 24, playing only the first half-note arpeggio of that measure—in other words, measure 7 of the third phrase consists of the first halves of measure 22 and measure 24, combined. Use measure 25 to finish the third phrase. For the last phrase of eight measures, use measures 26–32. Insert one measure of improvised C major arpeggios between measures 28 and 29, and play a tonic C major arpeggio in measure 32 instead of the G^7 arpeggio that is written.

The accompanist now has four phrases of eight measures each, in which the harmonic rhythm and motion will be clear the ear, that is to say, unambiguous to the dancers. Ironically, there are exactly thirty-two measures of music up to the point at which this discussion ended. However, as written, the music does not sound like even phrases of eight measures each and is not, therefore, immediately usable for the ballet technique class. The arranged version sounds quite musically acceptable if played intelligently, and is a good example of the kind of thing that, with patience, the accompanist can work out. (This prelude, as well as two others from *The Well-Tempered Clavier*, are discussed in chap. 6.)

BEETHOVEN: BAGETELLES, OP. 119, NO. 9

3/4, MM dotted half note equals 56

Play measures 1–8 and repeat. Measures 9–12 repeated make up the third phrase of eight measures. Measures 13–20 make up the fourth phrase. Repeat as necessary.

BRAHMS: WALTZ IN G-SHARP MINOR, OP. 39, NO. 3

3/4, MM quarter note equals 138

Play the piece as written. It will be either sixteen or thirty-two measures, depending on whether the repeats are taken. Repeat as necessary.

CHOPIN: ETUDE IN F MINOR, OP. 10, NO. 9

6/8, MM dotted quarter note equals 56

The tempo indicated above is much slower that the correct performance tempo. However, for the purposes intended, it is quite acceptable musically. Use the first thirty-two measures as written. In the last half of measure thirty-two, cadence in F minor. Repeat as necessary.

CZERNY: THE ART OF FINGER DEXTERITY, OP. 740, NO. 4

6/8, MM dotted quarter note equals 56.

The tempo indicated above, although much slower than the original, is very suitable in this context. Use the first sixteen measures and repeat as necessary. Cadence in B-flat major in measure sixteen.

FAURÉ: BERCEUSE, OP. 56, NO. 1

2/4, MM quarter note equals 52

Begin in measure 3. Measures 3–10 are the first phrase. Play measures 11–14 twice for the second phrase of eight measures. The second time through, cadence on B major in measure 14. Repeat as necessary.

Schumann: "Bittendes Kind" (Entreating Child), from Kinderszenen, op. 15, no. 4

2/4, MM quarter note equals 50

Play measures 1–16 as written. Cadence on A major on the second beat of measure 16. Repeat as necessary.

Schumann: "Wiegenliedchen" (A Little Cradle Song), op. 124, no. 6

2/4, MM quarter note equals 56

Play the first thirty-two measures as written, if needed. In measure 32, cadence on D major. Repeat as necessary.

Scriabin: Etude in E Major, op. 8, no. 5

4/4, MM half note equals 50

The first phrase is measures 1–8. The second phrase of eight measures may be played in this way: play measures 9–12 and then return to measure 1–4. In measure 4, cadence strongly on E major. Repeat as necessary.

Tchaikovsky: Chanson Triste, op. 40, no. 2

4/4, MM half note equals 50

Play measures 1–8 as written. For the second phrase of eight measures, proceed as follows: play measures 9–12, and then skip directly to measures 17–20. Repeat as necessary.

Vogt: Twenty-Four Octave Studies, op. 145, no. 7

3/8. MM, dotted quarter note equals 50

Play the first sixteen measures as written. Repeat this section or continue. The piece consists of three phrases of sixteen measures each. Arrange and repeat as necessary.

Music for Battement Tendu (Quick), Pas de Cheval

Bach: Aria, Partita in D Major

2/4. MM quarter note equals 60

Play the first sixteen measures as written, and repeat as necessary.

Bach: Gavotte I, Partita in B Minor (Overture in the French Manner)

2/2, MM quarter note equals 120 (half note equals 60)

Play the entire piece as written, taking the first repeat. This is thirty-two measures of two equal sixteen-measure phrases. In listening to this movement, one would think that the first full measure of music begins with the pickup, and not where the bar line actually is. If the accompanist plays this movement as written, it will confuse the dancers. Therefore, imagine all the bar lines to be one half note in front of where they actually are. This will sound more "correct" to the dancer's ear. In playing through Gavotte, will be readily aware of the issue pointed out above.

Bach: Rondeau, Partita in C Minor

3/8, MM dotted quarter note equals 60

The first sixty-four measures of this movement fall into even sixteen-measure sections, so the accompanist may play the music as written and cadence where appropriate, for instance, in C major in measure thirty-two. Repeat as necessary.

Bartók: First Movement (Bagpipe) and Second Movement (Bear Dance) from Sonatine

2/4, MM quarter note equals 60

In the first movement, after the introduction of four measures, use the next sixteen measures, which are square. Repeat as necessary. In the second movement, play measures 1–8 and repeat. For the second sixteen measures, play measures 9–12 and repeat, and then play measures 13–20. Repeat the piece as necessary.

Brahms: Variations on a Theme by Handel, op. 24, Var. 1

4/4, MM quarter note equals 60

Play this variation as written (sixteen measures with repeats). The rapid thirty-second note figures may be omitted if desired. Repeat as necessary.

Dvořák: Humoresque, op. 101, no. 7

2/4, MM quarter note equals 60

Play the first eight measures as written. For the second phrase, play measures 9–12 and repeat. Repeat the entire section (sixteen measures) as necessary.

Satie: Les Pantins Dansent

2/4, MM half note equals 56

Play the first sixty-four measures as needed, and repeat if necessary. This piece falls into even sixteen-measure sections, and an improvised cadence at any phrase ending is no problem.

Scharwenka: March, op. 62, no. 1

4/4, MM half note equals 60

This entire piece falls into distinct eight-measure phrases. Play as necessary.

Schubert: Impromptu, op. 142, no. 3

4/4, MM quarter note equals 60

Play the first sixteen measures as written, and repeat as necessary.

Schumann: "Armes Waisenkind" (Poor Orphan), from Album for the Young, op. 68

2/4, MM quarter note equals 56

This piece is thirty-measures of even phrases. Play and repeat as necessary.

Vogt: Twenty-Four Octave Studies, op. 145, no. 6
2/4, MM quarter note equals 54
This exercise consists of two even sections of sixteen measures each. Play and repeat as necessary.

Music for Battement Tendu Dégagé, Battement Frappé

Bach: Bourée I, Partita in B Minor (Overture in the French Manner)
2/2, MM half note equals 88
Measures 1–4, repeated, are the first phrase. Measures 5–12 are the second phrase. Measures 13–16, repeated, are the third phrase. The first time measure 16 is played, two A-minor chords are sufficient; this sounds smoother and clearer, harmonically. The second time through measure 16, play as written, and proceed to the fourth phrase. Phrase four is measures 17–24. Repeat the piece as necessary.

Bach: Bourée II, Partita in B Minor (Overture in the French Manner)
2/2, MM half note equals 88
The first phrase of eight measures consists of measures 1–4, repeated. Phrase two is measures 5–12. The third and fourth phrases are measures 13–28 as written. Repeat as necessary.

Bach: Echo, Partita in B Minor (Overture in the French Manner)
2/4, MM quarter note equals 96.
Use only the first sixteen measures of this piece, since the measures that follow may lead to confusion. Repeat the first sixteen measures as necessary, cadencing in F-sharp minor in measure sixteen.

Bartók: Peasant Dance, from Mikrokosmos, Vol. V, no. 128
2/4, MM quarter note equals 100
The first four measures are introductory. Play measures 5–22 for the first two phrases of eight measures each. If stopping in measure 20, cadence on a strong E-flat. Repeat as necessary. This piece would not be useful after measure 20.

Brahms: Variations on a Theme by Paganini, op. 35, Book II, Var. III
2/4, MM quarter note equals 92
Play this variation straight through without repeats, a total of sixteen measures. Then repeat as necessary.

Liszt: Hungarian Rhapsody no. 6
2/4. MM quarter note equals 96
Begin in measure 96, which is the opening of the B-flat major section. Play the first sixteen measures of the theme as written. For the second sixteen measures, play the next eight measures and repeat them, ending in the last measure (119) on D major. Repeat the entire section as necessary.

Satie: La Diva De L'Empire

2/4, MM quarter note equals 88

Begin in measure 9. The following sixty-four measures fall into even phrases, so the accompanist may use and repeat whatever amount of music is necessary.

Schubert: Acht Ecossiasen, D. 529

2/4, MM half note equals 92

Numbers 1 through 4 and 6 through 8 are sixteen measures long. Play and repeat as necessary. Number 5 is twenty-four measures long, so the last eight measures may be repeated.

Schubert: Moment Musical, op. 94, no. 3

2/4, MM quarter note equals 92

After two introductory measures, the next thirty-two measures are square. The last eight measures of the piece may also be used. Except for measures thirty-five through forty-four, which is a phrase of ten measures, the other sections may be played as written and combined in any fashion desired.

Schumann: Nachstücke, op. 23, no. 1

4/4, MM quarter note equals 96

The first sixteen measures of this piece are sufficient. In measure sixteen, cadence on a strong E-minor chord on beat three. If repeating and going back to the beginning, play measure sixteen as written.

Schumann: Scherzino from Faschingsschwank aus Wien, op. 26

2/4, MM quarter note equals 100

Use the first sixteen or thirty-two measures. In measure thirty-two, cadence on a strong A-flat major chord. Repeat as necessary.

Tchaikovsky: Humoresque, op. 10, no. 2

2/4, MM quarter note equals 96

The first phrase begins in measure 10. The following thirty-two measures are comprised of four even phrases of eight measures each. Beginning in measure forty-two (the E-flat section), the next sixteen measures may be used and repeated as necessary. The opening G major section and the second E-flat major section may be used separately for different combinations.

Vogt: Twenty-Four Octave Studies, op. 145, no. 2

2/4, MM quarter note equals 100

The first sixteen measures may be played as written. For a second sixteen-measure section, play measures 17–24 twice. The second time through these measures, cadence on A minor on the second beat of measure 24. Repeat the entire section as necessary.

Music for Battement Sur le Cou-de-Pied, Battement Piqué

Bartók: Third Movement (Finale) from Sonatine

2/4, MM quarter note equals 120

Begin in measure 5, and include the pickup from measure 4. Use measures 5–20, and repeat as necessary. Repeated once, this equals thirty-two measures. When ending in measure 20, cadence on a strong G-major chord.

Beethoven: Rondo a Capriccio, op. 129

2/4, MM quarter note equals 144

Play the first sixteen measures as written. Measures 17–24 played twice may be used for a second sixteen measures. Measures 25–40 may be used for another sixteen-measure phrase, if needed, and then repeated, if necessary, to make a full sixty-four measures of music.

Brahms: Variations on a Theme by Handel, op. 24, Var. VII

4/4, MM quarter note equals 112

Play this variation as written (sixteen measures with repeats). Repeat as necessary, and cadence on B-flat major on the third beat of measure 8 the last time through. If the dance combination happens to be an uneven one and ends on measure 4 the second time through, then cadence on F major on the third beat.

Burgmuller: L'Hirondelle (The Swallow)

4/4, MM quarter note equals 132

Use measures 1–16, and repeat if necessary. Cadence on D major in measure 16.

Chopin: Etude in A Minor, op. 25, no. 4

4/4, MM quarter note equals 132

Use the first sixteen measures of this etude, and repeat if necessary. In measure 16, cadence on E minor on the third beat.

Czerny: The Art of Finger Dexterity, op. 740, no. 7

4/4, MM quarter note equals 132

Use the first sixteen measures of this exercise as written, and repeat as necessary.

Czerny: The Art of Finger Dexterity, op. 740, no. 9

2/4, MM quarter note equals 132

Use the first sixteen or thirty-two measures as written, repeating as necessary. In measure 32, end on B major (as a tonic); or, if repeating and going back to the beginning, play as written (B major V^7 of E major.

Czerny: The Art of Finger Dexterity, op. 740, no. 11

4/4, MM quarter note equals 126

Use measures 1–16 as written, and repeat as necessary.

Czerny: The Art of Finger Dexterity, op. 740, no. 30
2/4, MM quarter note equals 126
Use the first sixteen or thirty-two measures, repeating as necessary. If ending with measure 32, cadence on C major.

Mozart: Third Movement (Rondo), Sonata in A Major, K. 331
2/4, MM quarter note equals 126
Play measures 1–8 twice. Measure 9–24 are the second sixteen-measure phrase. If more music is needed, play measures 25–32 twice for a third phrase, and then go back to the beginning and play measure 1–8 twice to make the fourth phrase.

Rodgers (Richard): "The Sweetest Sounds," from No Strings
2/4, MM quarter note equals 120
Use the first thirty-two measures of this refrain. Cadence on a strong B-flat major in measure 32. Repeat as necessary.

Schumann: "Wilder Reiter" (Wild Rider), from Album for the Young, op. 68
6/8, MM dotted quarter note equals 126
Play measures 1–8 twice. Then play the remainder of the piece, which is sixteen additional measures. Repeat as necessary.

Music for Battement en Cloche

Beethoven: Theme, from Variations on a Waltz by Diabelli, op. 120
3/4, MM dotted half note equals 69
The theme is divided into two phrases of sixteen measures each. Play and repeat as necessary.

Brahms: Waltz in B Major, op. 39, no. 1
3/4, MM dotted half note equals 63
Play the first eight measures and repeat, then play the last sixteen measures of the waltz. Play and repeat as necessary.

Brahms: Variations on a Theme by Paganini, op. 35, Book I, Var. VIII
6/8, MM dotted quarter note equals 66
Play this variation straight through (sixteen measures) and repeat as necessary. When ending in measure 16, cadence on a strong A-minor chord on the second beat.

Schubert: Twelve Valses Nobles, op. 77, D. 969, Nos. 1, 2, and 3
3/4, MM dotted half note equals 66
Play the first or thirty-two measures of any of these waltzes. They are all square, and clear-cut harmonically. Repeat as necessary.

Schumann: Marche des Davidsbündler Contre les Philistines, from Carnaval, op. 9

3/4, MM dotted half note equals 54

Play the first eight measures and repeat. Then play the last sixteen measures. This totals thirty-two measures. Use only the first ending (measures 22–24), cadencing on a clear F minor.

Schumann: Arlequin, from Carnaval, op. 9

3/4, MM dotted half note equals 66

Play measures 1–16 as written. Then play measures 17–24 twice. This totals thirty-two measures. Whether in measure sixteen or in measure twenty-four, finish with a strong B-flat major cadence.

Vogt: Twenty-Four Octave Studies, op. 145, no. 12

6/8, MM dotted eighth note equals 66

Play the first sixteen or thirty-two measures as needed, and repeat as necessary.

Music for Grand Battement

Beethoven: Variations on a Waltz by Diabelli, op. 120, Var. I

4/4, MM whole note equals 63

Play this piece straight through to sixteen or thirty-two measures. Repeat as necessary. If ending in measure sixteen, cadence on a strong G major.

Bizet: "Toreador Song," from Carmen

2/4, MM half note equals 60

The main theme from the "Toreador Song" (the first sixteen measures) is often useful for grand battement. Repeat as necessary.

Brahms: Variations on a Theme by Handel, op. 24, Var. XXV

4/4, MM quarter note equals 69

Play this variation straight through and repeat as necessary. The accompanist may provide a stronger beat by playing the first sixteenth note of each bass figure *on* the beat, rather than one sixteenth note *off* the beat, as written. The second sixteenth note of each bass figure may remain as written, on the "and" of each beat.

Brahms: Variations on a Theme by Paganini, op. 35, Book I, Var. XIII

2/4, MM quarter note equals 69

Play this variation with the first repeat. This will total sixteen measures. Repeat the variation as necessary.

Fauré: Theme (Quasi Adagio), from Theme and Variations, op. 73

4/4, MM quarter note equals 60

Omit measures 5–8. The first phrase of eight measures is 1–4 and 9–12. The second phrase is measures 13–20. Repeat as necessary.

Grieg: Wedding Day at Troldhaugen, op. 65, no. 6
4/4, MM half note equals 60
There is an introduction of two measures. The first phrase of eight measures is measures 3–10. Omit measures 11 and 12–twelve. The second phrase is measures 13–20. Repeat these two phrases as necessary. Cadence on a full, strong D-major chord.

Liszt: Etude no. 6, Var. III, from Six Paganini Etudes
2/4, MM quarter note equals 69
Play this variation as written (sixteen measures) and repeat if necessary.

Liszt: Opening Theme from Hungarian Rhapsody no. 6
2/4, MM quarter note equals 60
Measures 1–4 are introductory. Use measures 5–20 (sixteen measures). Measures 21–36 may also be used for another sixteen-measure phrase. If ending at measure 36, play a strong cadence on D-flat major, rather than as written. Repeat as necessary.

Prokofiev: March, from Love of Three Oranges
4/4, MM half note equals 60
The first phrase begins in measure 3 and ends with 10. The second phrase is measures 11–18. Repeat as necessary, or cadence in measure 18 on C minor, the third beat.

Vogt: Twenty-Four Octave Studies, op. 145, no. 15
2/4, MM quarter note equals 60
Play the first eight measures and repeat. For the second phrase of sixteen measures, play measures 9–12 and repeat, then play measures 13–20. Repeat the exercise as necessary.

Suggested Piano Repertory for the Center

Applicability of Suggestions. The accompanist should note that many suggestions put forth throughout this book apply, as appropriate, to all repertory suggestions. The accompanist is encouraged to experiment and to refine any suggestion to make it especially appropriate for the combination. All metronome markings (MM) provided are approximate and should be adjusted as appropriate.

Viewing and Downloading. Much of the suggested repertory can be viewed online, and downloaded at no charge. Observe copyright notices. (See "Free Online Music Scores," chap. 2.)

Classical Ballet Pieces. Although this book generally recommends avoidance of standard classical ballet music, the accompanist will note that, in fact, a number of classical ballet pieces are included in the suggestions for center repertory. This is because these recommendations are particularly illustrative of the desired style and feeling for the steps under discussion and should be in the ballet technique accompanist's awareness and repertory for judicious use.

Music for Adagio (Attitudes, Arabesques, Other Posés; Promenade; Temps Lié)

Bach: Sarabande, French Suite no. 1
3/4, MM quarter note equals 72
Play the first eight measures and repeat. Then play measures 9–24. This totals thirty-two measures. Repeat as necessary.

Beethoven: Second Movement from Sonata no. 8 in C Minor, op. 13 (Pathétique)
2/4, MM eighth note equals 60
Play the first sixteen measures as written. For an additional sixteen measures to complete the combination, the recommended choice is measures 51–66. Cadence on A-flat major in measure 66. Repeat as necessary.

Brahms: Intermezzo, op. 119, no. 2
3/4, MM quarter note equals 104
Begin in measure 36, the opening of the E-major section. Use the first thirty-two measures of this section. Repeat as necessary.

Brahms: Variations on a Theme by Paganini, op. 35, Book II, Var. XII
6/8, MM eight note equals 104
Play this entire variation, taking only the first repeat. This totals sixteen measures, Repeat as necessary.

Chopin: Etude, op. 25, no. 5
3/4, MM quarter note equals 138
Begin in the E-major section (piu lento). Play the first sixteen measures as written. The next phrase of sixteen measures may be arranged as follows: play measures 17–28 and then skip directly to measures 33–36. The accompanist may cadence at the end of measure 36 or, if more than thirty-two measures of music are required, she may repeat the entire section. Or, instead of repeating, she may elect to play measures 37–52 for an additional sixteen measures, and repeat this much music for another sixteen measures (thirty-two additional measures total).

Chopin: Prelude, op. 28, no. 15
4/4, MM quarter note equals 66
Measures one through eight are the first phrase. The second phrase is measures 9–12, played twice. The third phrase is measures 13–19, with measure 19 played twice. The last phrase is measures 20–27. Repeat the entire section as necessary.

Chopin: Third Movement (Funeral March), from Sonata in B-Flat Minor, op. 35

4/4, MM quarter note equals 60

Use the middle section of the funeral march, which begins in D-flat major. (This section will not be as readily recognized, by any means, as the opening of the movement.) Use this entire section, taking only the first repeat. This totals thirty-two measures. Repeat as necessary.

Glazunov: Barcarolle, from The Seasons

6/8, MM eighth note equals 116

The opening eight measure are introductory. Begin with measure 9, and use the following thirty-two measures as written. In the last measure (forty), cadence on E-flat major on the second beat.

Liszt: Consolations, no. 2

4/4, MM quarter note equals 116

Play the first sixteen measures as written. For the second phrase, play measures 17–24 twice. Repeat as necessary.

Mozart: Second Movement, from Sonata in F Major, K. 332

4/4, MM eighth note equals 76

If the combination is not too heavy, this material is refreshing in its simplicity and purity. Measures 1–8 will be sufficient. Cadence on F major in measure 8 or, if repeating, make the last beat in measure 8 an F^7, in preparation for the opening in B-flat major.

Puccini: "Oh! Mio Babbino Caro" (Oh! My Beloved Daddy), from Gianni Schicchi

6/8, MM eighth note equals 112

Play measures 1–16 as written. For the second sixteen measures, play measures 17–24, repeat measures 17–22, and then skip directly to measures 25 and 26. The above procedure will result in a logical sequence of thirty-two measures. Repeat as necessary.

Rachmaninoff: Piano Concerto no. 1, op. 1

4/4, MM quarter note equals 63

Begin with measure 172, using the pickup from the preceding measure. Use measures 172–179 (eight measures). This little section may be easily repeated, as necessary. When ending in measure 179, resolve the C-sharp^7 chord (fourth beat) to a strong F-sharp minor chord on the following, final beat.

Rachmaninoff: Prelude, op. 23, no. 4

3/4, MM quarter note equals 66

The first two measures are introductory. Begin in measure 3. Use the following thirty-two measures as written, repeating as necessary. At the end of the thirty-two measure section, cadence on D major.

Rachmaninoff: Prelude, op. 23, no. 5

4/4, MM quarter note equals 66

Begin in measure 35, the middle section of this prelude. The first phrase is measures 1–7, playing measure 7 twice. For the second phrase, play measures 8–15, and cadence on D major—or repeat if necessary.

Rachmaninoff: Prelude, op. 23, no. 6

4/4, MM quarter note equals 72

The phrase begins with measure 2, ending on measure 9. The accompanist may incorporate the pickup from measure 1 into the introduction. For the second phrase, skip directly (and smoothly, to make it sound natural) to measures 16–23. The accompanist may cadence in measure 23 on E-flat major. This entire section may be repeated, or measures 24–39 may be played as written to fill out another sixteen measures. The accompanist may play a strong E-flat major cadence in measure 39, if ending at that point.

Ravel: Waltz no. 2 in G Minor, Valses Nobles et Sentimentales

3/4, MM quarter note equals 88

This piece falls into four equal sections of sixteen measures each, so no alterations are necessary.

Rimsky-Korsakov: "A Flight of Passing Clouds," op. 24, no. 3

12/8, MM dotted quarter note equals 48

This is a song, so the score is piano-vocal. The accompanist should be able to arrange the accompaniment and melody in order to use it for ballet technique class. Besides playing the melody, the right hand may fill in the harmonic texture, in order to ease the burden of the left hand. The first measure is introductory. Measures 2–9 are the first phrase. Omit measure 10. For the second phrase of eight measures, use measures 11–18. In measure 18, improvise a C-sharp^7 (V^7 of F-sharp minor) arpeggio for the first two beats, and fill out the last two beats of the measure with a strong F-sharp minor tonality. Repeat the entire piece as needed.

Scriabin: Prelude, op. 11, no. 11

6/8, MM eighth note equals 126

The first sixteen or thirty-two measures of this prelude may be used. If ending in measure sixteen, the accompanist may cadence on D-sharp minor on the second beat. If ending in measure 32, she may cadence on a full B-major chord on the second beat.

Music for Slow Pirouettes from 4th 5th, 2nd

Brahms: Waltz in B Major, op. 39, no. 13

3/4, MM quarter note equals 138

Play this waltz as written—sixteen measures without repeats. Repeat as necessary.

Brahms: Waltz in A-Flat Major, op. 39, no. 15

3/4, MM quarter note equals 126

Play measures 1–8 and repeat. For the next sixteen measures, play measures 9–22; measures 13 and 14 must be repeated to round out the first eight-measure phrase of this second section. The above process makes a total of thirty-two measures. Repeat as necessary, or play a full A-flat cadence in measure 22.

Chopin: Waltz, op. 69, no. 1

3/4, MM quarter note equals 126

The first sixty-four measure will be adequate, being comprised of even phrases of eight and sixteen measures. Repeat as necessary.

Chopin: Waltz, op. 70, no. 2

3/4, MM quarter note equals 132

Play the first sixteen measures as written. Omit measures 17–20. The second sixteen measures are 21–36. Cadence in E-flat major in measure 36. Repeat as necessary.

Delibes: Valse, from Act I of Coppelia

3/4, MM quarter note equals 126

Begin with measure 5. Use the following thirty-two measures as written, and repeat as necessary.

Granados: Valses Poeticos, no. 2

3/4, MM quarter note equals 138

Use the first thirty-two measures of this waltz and repeat as necessary.

Liszt: Opening Theme, from Hungarian Rhapsody no. 6

2/4, MM quarter note equals 42

Measures 1–4 are introductory. Use measures 5–20 (sixteen measures). Measures 21–36 may also be used for another sixteen-measure phrase. If ending at measure 36, play a strong cadence on D-flat major, rather than as written. Repeat as necessary. Although generally a slow to moderate 3/4 is used for this exercise, a 2/4 like the one under discussion here can sometimes work quite well. Some judicious experimentation is not inappropriate.

Schubert: Twenty Waltzes, op. 117, D. 146, Nos. 17 and 18

3/4, MM quarter note equals 126

Each waltz is comprised of sixteen measures. Play and repeat as necessary.

Schumann: Promenade, from Carnaval, op. 9

3/4, MM quarter note equals 138

Use the first thirty-two measures as written, and repeat as necessary.

Schumann: Valse Noble, from Carnaval, op. 9
3/4, MM quarter note equals 138
Play measures 1–16 (taking no repeats). Omit measures 17–24. For the second phrase of sixteen measures, play measures 25–40. Repeat as necessary.

Music for Petit Allegro (2/4)

Since a 6/8 meter is often as good as a 2/4 or 4/4 meter (providing that it is appropriately sharp and bright), a tarantella (which is a bright 6/8, MM dotted quarter note equals 104) is often good for petit allegro steps. The accompanist is encouraged to locate several of these Italian character pieces to have on hand—and to learn to improvise in a corresponding style.

Chopin: Etude, op. 10, no. 5
2/4, MM quarter note equals 100
Use the first sixteen measures of this etude. In measure 16, cadence on G-flat major on the second beat. Repeat as necessary.

Chopin: Etude, op. 25, no. 9
2/4, MM quarter note equals 104
Use the first sixteen measures as written, and repeat as necessary. In measure 16, cadence on a strong D-flat major chord on the second beat.

Czerny: The Art of Finger Dexterity, op. 740, no. 29
2/4, MM quarter note equals 100
Begin in measure 56. Use the following sixteen measures (56–71). Measure 71 should be on a strong D-major cadence. Repeat as necessary.

Czerny: The Art of Finger Dexterity, op. 740, no. 33
6/8, MM dotted quarter note equals 96
Use the first thirty-two measures of this exercise. Measure 32 should be replaced with a strong E-flat major cadence. Prepare this by playing a strong B-flat^7 chord in measure 32, the first beat. Repeat the exercise as necessary.

Czerny: The Art of Finger Dexterity, op. 740, no. 35
2/4, MM quarter note equals 84
Use the first thirty-two measures as written. Cadence in measure 16 or measure 32, repeating as necessary.

Czerny: The Art of Finger Dexterity, op. 740, no. 44
2/4, MM quarter note equals 88
Begin in measure 44 and use the following thirty-two measures, ending with measure 75. Cadence on a strong G-major chord in measure 75. Repeat as necessary.

Czerny: The Art of Finger Dexterity, op. 740, no. 47
2/4, MM quarter note equals 76
Use the first thirty-two measures as written. Cadence as the harmony indicates, and repeat as necessary.

Debussy: "Golliwogg's Cake Walk," from Children's Corner
2/4, MM quarter note equals 92
Begin in measure 10, and use the following thirty-two measures. Cadence on a strong E-flat major chord in measure 41. Repeat as necessary.

Dvořák: Slavonic Dance no. 2
2/4, MM quarter note equals 92
Play measure 1–16 as written. Then play measures 17–24 twice for the second sixteen measures. Repeat as necessary. Play this entire section in the same bright tempo, disregarding sudden tempo changes indicated in the score.

Gershwin: Prelude no. 3
2/4, MM quarter note equals 100
Begin with measure 5. Use measures 5–20, and repeat as necessary. In measure 20, cadence on a strong E-flat major chord.

Grieg: Album Leaf, op. 12, no. 7
2/4, MM quarter note equals 88
Use measures 1–16, repeating as necessary. Cadence in measure sixteen on B minor, with a strong F-sharp^7 major chord in measure 15. Play this music in a staccato, bright manner—not slurred.

Schubert: Nine Ecossaises, from op. 18, D. 145
2/4, MM quarter note equals 92
All of these pieces are in clear, eight-measure phrases. Play and repeat them as necessary.

Schubert: Galop and Eight Ecossaises, op. 49, D. 735
2/4, MM quarter note equals 88
All of these pieces, also, are in clear, eight-measure phrases. Play and repeat as necessary.

Schumann: Aveu, from Carnaval, op. 9
2/4, MM quarter note equals 104
Play the first four measures and repeat, then play measures 5–12. This totals sixteen measures. Repeat as necessary.

Schumann: Reconnaissance, from Carnaval, op. 9
2/4, MM quarter note equals 88
Use the first sixteen measures, repeating as necessary. In measure 16, cadence on a strong A-flat major chord.

SCHUMANN: DAVIDSBÜNDLERTÄNZE, NO. 12
2/4, MM quarter note equals 92
Use the first sixteen measures, cadencing on a solid E-major chord in measure 16. Repeat as necessary.

Music for Petit Allegro (3/4)

CHOPIN: WALTZ, OP. 64, NO. 3
3/4, MM dotted half note equals 80
Use the first thirty-two measures of this waltz, and repeat as necessary. Cadence on a strong E-flat major chord in measure 32.

CHOPIN: WALTZ, OP. 70, NO. 1
3/4, MM dotted half note equals 80
Used the first thirty-two measures, and repeat as necessary. Cadence as appropriate.

DELIBES: VALSE DE LA POUPÉE, FROM ACT II OF COPPELIA
3/4, MM dotted half note equals 66
Begin in measure 9 of the 3/4, using the pickup from measure 8. Use the following thirty-two measures and repeat as necessary.

GRANADOS: VALSES POETICOS, NOS. 4 AND 6
3/4, MM dotted half note equals 66
The fourth waltz is thirty-two measures. Play and repeat as necessary. Use the first thirty-two measures of the sixth waltz, and cadence as appropriate. Repeat as necessary.

PORTER (COLE): "TRUE LOVE," FROM *HIGH SOCIETY*
3/4, MM dotted half note equals 66
This refrain is thirty-two measures long. Play and repeat as necessary. The tempo is somewhat faster than in the original music, and this changes the mood, making a suitable light waltz.

RAVEL: WALTZ NO. 3 IN G MAJOR, VALSES NOBLES ET SENTIMENTALES
3/4, MM dotted half note equals 72
Play the first sixteen measures as written, Play measures 17–24 twice. This totals thirty two measures. When ending in measure 24, cadence on a strong D-major chord.

SCHUBERT—A General Note Regarding Petit Allegro Repertory. As stated elsewhere in this section of the book, there is a plethora of Schubert's music that can be used for ballet technique. And there are dozens of Schubert waltzes that could be used here, for 3/4 petit allegro exercises. Two specific examples that are applicable are given below. The accompanist may collect and use many more of Schubert's waltzes if he desires.

Schubert: Twelve Valses Nobles, op. 77, D. 969, no. 2
3/4, MM dotted half note equals 76
Play this piece straight through (thirty-two measures) and repeat as necessary.

Schubert: Twelve Valses Nobles, op. 77, D. 969, no. 3
3/4, MM dotted half note equals 76
Play the first thirty-two measures of this waltz as written. If more music is desired, repeat or do as follows: play measures 33–48 and measures 53–68 (omit measures 49–52).

Tchaikovsky: Tempo di Valse, from Weihnachten (December), op. 37, no. 12
3/4, MM dotted half note equals 80
Play measures1–16 as written. For a second phrase of sixteen measures, do as follows: play measure 17–30 as written, and improvise one bar of G^7, leading to a final C-major bar for the closing two measures. Repeat as necessary.

Vogt: Twenty-Four Octave Studies, op. 145, no. 8
3/4, MM dotted half note equals 80
Play the first thirty-two measures as written, and repeat as necessary.

Music for Grand Allegro (3/4)

Brahms: Waltz in B Major, op. 39, no. 1
3/4, MM dotted half note equals 63
Play this waltz as written, taking only the first repeat. This totals thirty-two measures. Repeat as necessary.

Brahms: Waltz in G Major, op. 39, no. 10
3/4, MM dotted half note equals 63
Play this waltz with all repeats (thirty-two measures). Repeat as necessary.

Brahms: Waltz in B Minor, op. 39, no. 11
3/4, MM dotted half note equals 63
Play the first sixteen measures and repeat. For another thirty-two measures of music, play measure 17–32 as written, then play measures 33–40 twice. Repeat this piece as necessary (sixty-four measures).

Chopin: Waltz, op. 18
3/4, MM dotted half note equals 69
Play the score energetically and strongly throughout. The first four measures are introductory. Use the next eighty measures, and repeat as necessary. (Eighty measures is five phrases of sixteen measures each.)

Chopin: Waltz, op. 34, no. 1
3/4, MM dotted half note equals 69
Begin with measure seventeen. Use the next sixty-four measures and repeat as necessary.

Chopin: Waltz, op. 42
3/4, MM dotted half note equals 69
Begin with measure nine. Use the following sixth-four measures and repeat as necessary.

Chopin: Waltz, op. 64, no. 2
3/4, MM dotted half note equals 63
Use the first thirty-two measures. The second section of this waltz, which has a smoother, more running character, will not be suitable for many combinations with big leaps. However, for fast waltzes which stay closer to the floor, this section may be suitable.

Glazunov: Entrée, from Raymonda
6/8, MM dotted quarter note equals 63
Begin with measure 35 (tempo di valse). Use the following sixteen measures (which equal thirty-two measures of 3/4), and repeat as necessary.

Glazunov: Valse des Bluets et des Pavots, from The Seasons
3/4, MM dotted half note equals sixty-three
Measure 1–4 are introductory. Use the following ninety-six measures, and repeat as necessary (six phrases of sixteen measure each).

Granados: Valses Poeticos, no. 5
3/4, MM dotted half note equals 66
Measures 1 and 2 are introductory. Use measures 3–26 (twenty-four measures), repeating the last eight measures. This totals thirty-two measures. Repeat as necessary.

Minkus: Pas de Deux, from Don Quixote
3/4, MM dotted half note equals 63
Begin with the tempo di valse in measure 17. Play the entire waltz (forty-eight measures) and repeat as necessary. This is an excellent example of a grand allegro waltz, and the accompanist should strive to achieve a similar feeling in other waltzes that she uses for grand allegro.

Rodgers (Richard): "Lover," from *Love Me Tonight*
3/4, MM dotted half note equals 66
Think of measure one as where the words begin. Use all sixty-four measures of this waltz as needed. It breaks down into four phrases of sixteen measures each. Repeat as necessary.

Rox (John): "It's a Big Wide Wonderful World"
3/4, MM dotted half note equals 66
Use all sixty-four measures of this waltz as needed, and repeat as necessary.

Schubert: Waltzes, op. 9, D. 365, Nos. 1, 12, and 13

3/4, MM dotted half note equals 63

Each waltz is sixteen measures long and has repeats. Play and repeat as necessary. These waltzes may easily be combined for long combinations. Play them strongly and energetically.

Schubert: Twelve Valses Nobles, op. 77, D. 969, no. 4

3/4, MM dotted half note equals 69

Play all forty-eight measures as written, repeating as necessary. Play strongly and energetically throughout, using octaves in the left hand on the first beat of each measure. A stronger lift will be implied if the rhythm in the right hand of measure one (and all or most other measures with the same rhythm) is changed:

From: Dotted Quarter + Eighth + Quarter
To: Quarter + Dotted Quarter + Eighth

This latter rhythmic pattern is characteristic of many grand allegro waltzes and should be generously—but judiciously—employed.

Schubert: Twelve Valses Nobles, op. 77, D. 969, no. 9

3/4, MM dotted half note equals 66

Play measures 1–16 as written. For another phrase of sixteen measures, play measures 17–28, and repeat measures 25–28. Repeat as necessary. The right-hand rhythm may again be changed:

From: Dotted Quarter + Eighth + Eighth + Eighth or
From: Quarter + Quarter + Quarter
To: Quarter + Dotted Quarter + Eighth

Schumann: Waltz, op. 124, no. 4

3/4, MM dotted half note equals 66

Play measures 1–16. For the second phrase of sixteen measures, play measures 17–20 and repeat, followed by measures 21–28. Octaves should be used for the first beat of the left hand in each measure. This waltz uses the rhythmic motif discussed in the preceding example, which is very effective in grand allegro waltzes—for example, measure four: *quarter rest + dotted quarter + eighth.*

It falls, however, on an even-numbered measure rather than on the more desirable odd-numbered ones.

Music for Pas de Basque

General Comments

3/4, MM quarter note equals 72—104

This step was previously described as a slower 3/4, with three distinct beats. Suitable music would be a slow, stately mazurka or a moderate polonaise. Generally, use a polonaise for slower tempos and a stately mazurka for the faster tempos. If the tempo is a slow one, a mazurka will likely sound too draggy. Although many mazurkas (for example, a large number of those by Chopin) will be too fast to be suitable, they will be very appropriate for faster combinations on many occasions (petit allegro 3/4), so the accompanist is therefore advised to have on hand a stock of mazurkas in vary styles (including some by Chopin).

Chopin: Mazurka in G Minor, op. 24, no. 1
3/4, MM quarter note equals 104
Play the first thirty-two measures as written, and repeat as necessary.

Chopin: Polonaise, op. 40, no. 1
3/4, MM quarter note equals 76
Play the first fifty-six measures as written, with measures 1–8 being played twice. Repeat as necessary.

Chopin: Polonaise, op. 40, no. 2
3/4, MM quarter note equals 72
Begin in measure 3. Use the following thirty-two measures and repeat as necessary.

Chopin: Polonaise, op. 44
3/4, MM quarter note equals 80
Begin with measure 9. Use measures 9–26 (omit measures 19 and 20 to make the phrase square). Repeat as necessary.

Delibes: Mazurka, from Act I of Coppelia
3/4, MM quarter note equals 104
Use measures 1–32 (do not count the opening measure with the tremolo and scale), and repeat as necessary.

Delibes: Bolero, from Act II of Coppelia
3/8, MM eighth note equals 104
Begin with measure ten. Use measures 10–25 (sixteen measures). Repeat as necessary. Measures 36–67 (thirty-two measures) may also be used. If ending in measure 67, cadence on a strong B-Major chord. Repeat as necessary.

Liszt: Polonaise in E Major, SA. 223, no. 2
3/4, MM quarter note equals 72
Begin with measure 6. Use measures 6–21 (sixteen measures). Measures 22–37 may also be used. When ending with measure 37, cadence on B major. Prepare for this by playing B major on beat two of measure 36, and F-sharp major V^7 on the third beat. This will steer the harmony clearly to the B-flat major cadence.

Scharwenka: Polish Dance, E-Flat Minor, op. 3, no. 1

3/4, MM quarter note equals 104 (considerably slower than the original tempo, but suitable for the purpose intended)

Use the first forty-eight measures as written, and repeat as necessary. Make the left sharp and accented, to increase the feeling of vitality.

Music for Relevés and Sous-Sus

General Comments

Sometimes during the grand allegro work, the female dancers will put on their point shoes (if they are not already wearing them). Since they may warm up their feet by doing relevés or sous-sus, music for these steps will be inserted at this point. In addition to the music suggest below, many of the 2/4 petit allegro pieces previously mentioned may be used here, with a somewhat slower tempo. In addition, much of the bright 2/4 and 4/4 music from the barre work would be suitable.

Delibes: Thème Slav Varié, from Act I of Coppelia

2/4, MM quarter note equals 76

Begin with measure 3 and use the following twenty-four measures. Repeat the last eight measures (19–26). This totals thirty-two measures. Repeat as necessary.

Delibes: Gigue, from Act II of Coppelia

2/4, MM quarter note equals 84

Begin with measure 9. This piece calls into consecutive eight-measure sections. Play and repeat as necessary.

Delibes: Marche des Guerrières, from Act III of Coppelia

2/4, MM quarter note equals 69

Begin with measure 3 and use the following thirty-two measures, repeating as necessary.

Delibes: Dance de Fête, from Act III of Coppelia

2/4, MM quarter note equals 62

Begin with measure 8 and use the following thirty-two measures. Repeat as necessary.

Gershwin (George): "Fascinating Rhythm," from *Lady Be Good*

4/4, MM half note equals 72

Consider measure 1 to be where the words begin. Use sixteen measures, or all thirty-two if needed. Repeat as necessary. If cadencing in measure 16, prepare the E-flat resolution with a strong B-flat major V^7 chord in measure 15.

Glazunov: Variation II, from Raymonda

2/4, MM quarter note equals 72

Begin with measure 3. Use the following thirty-two measures, and repeat as necessary.

Schubert: Military March, op. 51, no. 1

2/4, MM quarter note equals 82

Begin with measure 7. Use the following sixteen measures (7–22). Repeat as necessary.

Music for Grand Allegro (2/4), Fast Pirouettes in Place and Moving

General Comments

Besides the music listed below, the accompanist is encouraged to collect numerous pieces from the following categories: cancans, polkas, krakoviaks (Polish), galops, and codas from various ballet scores as *The Nutcracker* and *Swan Lake*. These kinds of pieces are ideal for grand allegro 2/4 steps and for fast pirouettes.

Brahms: Hungarian Dance no. 5

2/4, MM quarter note equals 138

Play the first forty-eight measures as written, and repeat as necessary.

Delibes: Czardas, from Act I of Coppelia

2/4, MM quarter note equals 144

Begin with measure 82 (plus animé). Use the first forty-eight measures of this section, plus the final section of the czardas (marked presto) for another sixteen measures. Play in a uniform tempo throughout, and repeat as necessary.

Delibes: Galop Final, from Act III of Coppelia

2/4, MM quarter note equals 138

Begin with measure 7. Play the following thirty-two measures as written. Play the next sixteen measures (40–55) twice, for another section of thirty-two measures. Repeat the piece as necessary.

Glazunov: Coda, from Raymonda

2/4, MM quarter note equals 132

Use as much of this coda as needed, and repeat as necessary. It falls into consecutive sixteen-measure sections.

Glazunov: Galop, from Raymonda

2/4, MM quarter note equals 132

Use as much as desired, and repeat as necessary. This galop falls into consecutive sixteen-measure sections.

Liszt: Hungarian Rhapsody no. 2

2/4, MM quarter note equals 126

Measure 1 begins at the F-sharp major section, marked *tempo giusto*. Play measures 1–16 as written, and then skip directly to measures 57–72 (second sixteen measures). Then skip directly to measures 129–144, for the third sixteen measures, and repeat this last section to total sixty-four measures. These sixty-four measures may then be repeated as necessary. Since these measures are rather spread out, the accompanist is advised to copy or rearrange her score for visual and page-turning practicality.

Loewe (Frederick): "With a Little Bit of Luck," from *My Fair Lady*
4/4, MM half note equals 138
Measure one is where the words begin (use the preceding pickup). Play measures 1–8 twice (sixteen measures). Then play measures 9–20, repeating measures 17–20 (include the pickup to measure 17), for another sixteen measures. Play measures 21–28 twice (include the pickup to measure 21) for a third sixteen-measure phrase. This totals forty-eight measures of music. Repeat and cadence as appropriate.

Minkus: Pas de Deux and Coda, from Don Quixote
2/4, MM quarter note equals 136
This is an excellent coda, which is very accessible technically. Use as much music as needed, and repeat as necessary. This music falls into consecutive sixteen-measure sections.

Rodgers (Richard): "Oklahoma," from the musical by the same name
2/4, MM quarter note equals 138
Begin measure 1 at the refrain. The refrain is fifty-six measures long. Repeat the last eight measures to total sixty-four measures. Repeat and cadence as appropriate.

Rodgers (Richard): "There is Nothin' Like a Dame," from *South Pacific*
2/4, MM quarter note equals 138
Measure 1 begins where the words start (include the pickup to measure 1). Play measures 1–16. Omit measures 17–19. For the second sixteen measures, use measures 20–35. This totals thirty-two measures, Repeat and cadence as necessary.

Schumann: "Traumes Wirren" (Restless Dreams), from Fantasiestücke, op. 12
2/4, MM quarter note equals 138
Play the first sixteen measure as written. Then play measures 17–24 twice. Repeat the entire section as necessary.

Tchaikovsky: Russian Dance, from The Nutcracker
2/4, MM quarter note equals 138
Play measure 1–32 as written. For another thirty-two measures, play measures 33–48, then play measures 49–56 twice. Repeat his entire section as necessary (sixty-four measures).

Tchaikovsky: Czardas, from Swan Lake

2/4, MM quarter note equals 126

Begin at the *vivace* section of the czardas. Measures 1–4 are introductory. Use the following sixty-four measures and repeat as necessary.

Tour en l'Air

General Comments

Tour en l'air is performed by male dancers (almost exclusively) in many grand allegro combinations. When this step is practiced alone, the accompanist may use a broad, powerful grand allegro waltz or perhaps another strong 3/4. He may also use as broad, powerful 4/4 with drive and energy. This music must help to thrust the dancer up into the air.

Glazunov: Var. III, from Raymonda

2/4, MM quarter note equals 69

Measures 1 and 2 are introductory. Use measures 3–34, as written, and cadence where appropriate.

Schubert: Twelve Valses Nobles, op. 77, D. 969, no. 1

3/4, MM dotted note equals 60

Use measures 1–32 as written. Cadence where appropriate.

Schumann: Marche des Davidsbündler Contre les Philistins, from Carnaval, op. 9

3/4, MM dotted half note equals 60

Use the first eight measures and repeat, for the first sixteen measures. For the second sixteen measures, play measures 9–24. Cadence where appropriate.

Composer Resources for Ballet Class Repertory

The following is a representative list of composers that the author has used for ballet classes. The list changes over time. It should not in any way be considered exhaustive, and may be expanded almost without limit. Composers included the list below who, in the author's opinion, are not or may not be well known to many pianists are marked with an asterisk, with nationality, birth and death dates, and a very short descriptor.

Many or most of these and other composers offer numerous works that can be employed for ballet class accompaniment and for a wide range of steps and combinations, subject to the accompanist's modification and imagination. The author has used one or two pieces of music for some of the composers and up to fifteen or more pieces for others.

It is restated here that this book is not intended to be an anthology, by composer, of music for ballet class. Such an anthology would constitute a book in itself. Rather, accompanists are encouraged to access online sites for exploring and downloading music, as discussed elsewhere in his book, especially the Petrucci Music Library site, which offers a virtually unlimited resource.

Albéniz, Isaac
Bach, Johann Sebastian
Bartok, Béla
Beethoven, Ludwig von
Brahms, Johannes
Chopin, Frédéric
Cobb, George Linus*
American, 1886–1942; ragtime, marches, waltzes
Confrey, Edward Elzear "Zez"*
American, 1895–1971; novelty piano and jazz music
Czerny, Carl
Debussy, Claude
Delibes, Léo
Dvořák, Antonín
Fauré, Gabriel
Finzi, Gerald Raphael*
British, 1901–1956; largely choral works, with smaller body of instrumental pieces (see especially Eclogue for Piano and String Orchestra, op.10)
Gershwin, George
Glazunov, Alexander
Gluck, Christoph Willibald
Granados, Enrique
Grieg, Edvard
Griselle, Thomas*
American, 1891–9155; large body of chamber music (see especially *Two American Sketches* for piano)
Horst, Louis*
American, 1884–1964; composer and choreographer, contemporary music for dance scores
Liszt, Franz
Lloyd, Norman*
American, 1909–1980; scores for modern dance, documentary films, classical chamber music
Milhaud, Darius*
French, 1892–1974; polytonality (see especially *Saudades do Brazil*)
Minkus, Ludwig*
Russian, 1826–1917; ballet music, author uses the pas de deux and coda from *Don Quixote*
Moreno-Buendía, Manuel*
Spanish, 1932–; conductor and composer for theater and instrumental music, and songs
Mompou, Federico*
Spanish, 1893–1987; solo piano music and songs (fresh, distinctive moods, tonalities, melodies, and rhythms)
Mozart, Wolfgang Amadeus

Poldini, Ede
Poulenc, Francis
Prokofiev, Sergei
Puccini, Giacomo
Rachmaninoff, Sergei
Ravel, Maurice
Rózsa, Miklós*
Hungarian-American, 1907–1995; numerous Hollywood and British film scores, concert works, piano music
Satie, Eric
Scarlatti, Domenico
Note: 500 keyboard sonatas
Scharwenka, Xaver
Schubert, Franz
Schulhoff, Erwin*
Czech, 1894–1942; piano and instrumental works, songs (rich variety of remarkably original and inventive works, often in traditional forms, with many for piano, linking
the late romanticism of Max Reger and Scriabin to the experimental music of John Cage)
Schumann, Robert
Scriabin, Alexander
Smetana, Bedřich
Tchaikovsky, Pyotr Ilyich
Tcherepnin, Alexander*
Russian-born pianist and composer, 1899–1977; numerous piano works, and orchestral and chamber music
Villa-Lobos, Heitor

Accompanists are reminded that, in addition to organizing ballet music by composer, it is strongly recommended that ballet class repertory be richly supplemented with bodies of works organized first by genera and then, if applicable, by composer, such as but not limited to the following:

Blues
Boleros
Broadway
Character music
Folk dances
Galops
Jazz styles
Krakowiaks (Polish)
Novelty pieces (example: "Kitten on the Keys," Confrey, Edward Elzear "Zez")
Polkas
Pop

RAD syllabus music (if desired)
Ragtime
Rock
Tangos
Tarantellas

Fertile Musical Territory for Exploration

A Solid Ground From Which to Start. This section has suggestions for fertile musical territory when the pianist wishes to expand her repertory for ballet technique class music. It is noted here that the numerous repertory ideas provided in this chapter were selected because they are, in general, relatively traditional and standard classical and popular pieces—but of very high quality—that, when offered in ballet class, will not distract the dancers or the instructor, or raise any eyebrows. Said another way, these repertory ideas offer solid ground for any ballet accompanist to embark on.

Exploring the Wide Terrain. In light of the very substantial—more than ample—specific music suggestions put forth in preceding sections, and rather than just running up more, this section is intended to provide motivated accompanists with some limited, although meaningful, direction about where they might wish to explore, in the vast terrain of keyboard literature available (and with immediate, generally cost-free online access), in their peregrinations to find interesting, challenging compositions for the dance class. Therefore, the following list offers a wide range of targeted music, some of which is definitely in the vein of the more standard fare, but also that which is more unique and very rarely, if ever, brought to light in the ballet technique class—or known at all by most pianists—and which will challenge and attract the attention of dancers and instructors—and capture the curiosity of more curious and intrepid keyboard players.

Ballet technique classes need this kind of musical stimulation.

Something for All Accompanists. From the accompanist's perspective, the literature referenced herein ranges, technically speaking, from immediately accessible to highly challenging (sometimes requiring significant practice and preparation). In parallel with this, while the phrasing structure of some the music requires no or little modification, other music would call for sophisticated editing in order to render it "square," while preserving an acceptable music logic. Thus, the offerings will likely have something for all needs, preferences, tastes, and levels of motivation.

Many of the composers are well known, at least to pianists, but others are not, and have music to offer that most pianists with standard training have not even been exposed to. If it is new material for pianists, it is almost certainly new material for dancers.

It is expressed here, once again, that, in addition to the need for having all music phrasing squared up, many other appropriate modifications and embellishments are appropriate—and absolutely necessary, in many cases, requiring the pianist's skill and imagination. If the accompanist studies all of the information in this book, she will be well equipped to embark upon such tasks.

Not an Anthology, but a Guide. Finally, it is not the purpose of this book to be an anthology of music for ballet class but rather a comprehensive body of reliable guidelines that will assist motivated accompanists in finding their way to beautiful, exciting music for dance.

List of Composers (A Relatively Small Sampling of the Unlimited Waters)

Bach, Johann Sebastian
English Suite no. 1, A Major, BWV 806
English Suite no. 2, A Minor, BWV 807
English Suite no. 3, G Minor, BWV 808
English Suite no. 4, F Major, BWV 809
English Suite no. 5, E Minor, BWV 810
English Suite no. 6, D Minor, BWV 811
French Suite no. 1, D Minor, BWV 812
French Suite no. 2, C Minor, BWV 813
French Suite no. 3, Minor, BWV 814
French Suite no. 4, E-Flat Major, BWV 815
French Suite no. 5, G Major, BWV 816
French Suite no. 6, E Major, BWV 817
Partita, B-Flat Major, BWV 825
Partita, C Minor, BWV 826
Partita, A Minor, BWV 827
Partita, D Major, BWV 828
Partita, G Major, BWV 829
Partita, E Minor, BWV 830
Well-Tempered Clavier, Books I and II
Each set contains twenty-four pairs of preludes and fugues in all major and minor keys. Research only the preludes.

Bartók, Béla
Romanian Folk Dances, Sz. 56

Brahms, Johannes
Variations on a Theme by Paganini, op. 35, Books I and II
These generally virtuosic variations include many levels of technical accessibility—some of which are formidable. Many are not suitable for ballet technique class; however, many are, and they can also be modified in many ways for the accompanist's own imaginative variations. Each book includes the theme and fourteen variations.

It is noted here to accompanists that the great modern dance choreographer, Twyla Tharp, did, in fact, choreograph Book I of this set for a solo dancer—a choreographic triumph and an astonishing tour de force for dance.
Waltzes, op. 39
Most of these lovely waltzes are usable, and can be modified as desired.

Chopin, Frédéric

Mazurkas, op. 6, 7, 17, 24, 30, 33, 41, 50, 56, 59, 63, 67, 68

Nocturnes, op. 9, 15, 27, 32, 37, 48, 55, 62

Waltzes, op. 34, 64, 69, 70

These waltzes, and other waltzes of Chopin, offer plentiful material, subject to editing for ballet technique. Some are not usable, and some are highly virtuosic. The accompanist must judge what is suitable and practical.

Cobb, George Linus (American, 1886–1942)

Ragtime, marches, waltzes. Very worthy of exploration for variety and stimulation. Samples listed below.

"A Happy Group (Barn Dance)"

"Alabama Jubilee"

"Rubber Plant Rag"

Confrey, Edward Elzear "Zez" (American, 1895–1971)

Novelty Piano and Jazz Music. Very worthy of exploration for variety and stimulation. Nearly 100 known piano works.

"Kitten on the Keys"

A famous example of Confrey's work, composed in 1921, great for ballet technique.

Dvořák, Antonín

Slavonic Dances, op. 46 and 72

Plentiful material for dance technique.

Waltzes, op. 54

Plentiful material for dance technique.

Gibbons, Orlando (1583–16 25)

Complete Keyboard Works

There are several volumes of these unique and fascinating works. They merit research by a motivated accompanist who understands ballet technique and who knows what kind of music can be used—or modified for use.

Ginastera, Alberto

Twelve American Preludes

These pieces vary in range from moody and poetic to dissonant and wild. Some of the material is definitely not usable for the ballet class. However, for an advanced and musically sophisticated accompanist who succumbs to the appeal of these compositions and can pluck the fruit of these exotic and intense scores, some really effective, head-turning material can be gleaned for judicious use with open-minded dance instructors.

Granados, Enrique

Twelve Spanish Dances

Exuberant music, rich with material. The accompanist can pick and choose based on accessibility.

Ochos Valses Poeticos (Eight Poetic Waltzes)

Includes a *Preludio.*

Milhaud, Darius (1892-1974)

Saudades do Brasil, op. 67 (1920)

Suite of twelve dances (each named after a Rio de Janeiro neighborhood) for piano, famous for its polytonality. Uses tango and samba rhythms.

"Sorocaba" (dedicated to Madame Regis de Oliveira)
"Botafogo" (dedicated to Oswald Guerra)
"Leme" (dedicated to Nininha Velloso-Guerra)
"Copacabana" (dedicated to Godofredo Leão Velloso)
"Ipanema" (dedicated to Arthur Rubinstein)
"Gávea" (dedicated to Madame Henrique Oswald)
"Corcovado" (dedicated to Madame Henri Hoppenot)
"Tijuca" (dedicated to Ricardo Viñes)
"Sumaré" (dedicated to Henri Hoppenot)
"Paineiras" (dedicated to La Baronne Frachon)
"Laranjeiras" (dedicated to Audrey Parr)
"Paysandu" (dedicated to Paul Claudel)

Mompou, Federico(Spanish, 1893–1987)

Solo piano music and songs, with fresh, distinctive moods, tonalities, melodies, and rhythms.

Cançons i Danses (Songs and dances) (1921–1979)

Very large body of work, rich for mining and arrangement for ballet technique.

Paisages (Paysages)

Three pieces, rich with ideas and unique, beautiful harmonies and textures for the adventurous accompanist.

Twelve Préludes

Published over many years. Rich with ideas.

Poulenc, Francis

15 Improvisations

Some of these yield usable music, with varying levels of technical challenges. Relatively advanced.

8 Nocturnes, FP 56

Some of these yield usable music, with varying levels of technical challenges. Relatively advanced.

3 Novelettes

The first and the third are good candidates and are technical accessible.

"Pastourelle," from the ballet L'Éventail de Jeanne (collaborative children's ballet by ten French composers)

"Songful," with lush harmonies.

Suite Française pour Piano (after Claude Gervaise—16th century)

Includes: 1. Bransle de Bourgogne, 2. Pavane, 3. Petite Marche Militaire 4. Complainte, 5. Bransle de Champagne, 6. Sicilienne,7. Carillon

Beautiful music, sometimes graceful, sometimes highly energetic. Requires doctoring of some phrases to square up, and other modifications as desired.

Scarlatti, Domenico

Keyboard Sonatas

There are 555 brilliant keyboard sonatas—all in one movement, and relatively short.

Schubert, Franz

Complete Dances

Generally collected into two volumes, or available in other formats. Hundreds of short pieces in duple and triple meter, with clear phrasing. Almost immediately technically accessible. A great resource (but not to be overworked). Includes minuets, waltzes, ländlers, ecossaises, and galops.

Schulhoff, Erwin (Czech, 1894–1942)

Many refreshingly inventive piano works.

Esquisses de Jazz (Six Easy Pieces for Piano)

Includes: Rag, Boston, Tango, Blues, Charleston, Black Bottom

Fünf Pittoresken (Five Picturesque Pieces)

Includes: Foxtrot, Ragtime, In Futurum (blank score, never done, ignore), One-Step,

Maxixe

Ostinato

Includes: Papa, Mama, Da....Da, Hopp....Hopp, A....A, Trara

Suite Dansante en Jazz

Includes: Stomp, Strait, Waltz, Tango, Slow, Fox Trot

Suite no. 2 for Piano

Includes 1. Preludio, 2. Melodia, 3. Toccatina, 4. Pastorale, 5. Gigue (a possibility, but challenging and work-intensive)

Tchaikovsky, Pyotr Ilyich

18 Pieces, op. 72

Best candidates, but presenting significant technical challenges: 2. Berceuse, 3. Tendres Reproches, 4. Danse Caractéristique, 6. Mazurque Pour Danser, 14. Chant Élégiaque, 17. Passé Lointain

Villa-Lobos, Heitor

Bachianas Brasileiras, no. 4, for Solo Piano

In several movements, parts of which can be worked into sequences of beautiful, unique, attention-getting material for ballet technique—but generally for *advanced* pianists and *experienced* accompanists who would embrace a challenge.

Ondulando (Estudo, op. 31)

A'Minba Afilhadinba Izaht—Petizada (Children)

Includes: 1. The Right Hand Has a Rose, 2. My Mother Used to Lullaby Me Like This, 3. The Poor Little Country Girl, 4. The Little White Dress, 5. Sacy, 6. The Story of Caipirinha

Sul America, for piano

Other Groupings

Broadway Music

Broadway music is an excellent source of potential repertory for ballet technique class. Many show tunes are perfect for all kinds of steps and combinations—including bright, dancy waltzes, energetic 2/4's, lovely adagios, etc. This music lends a very nice change of pace from the straight classics.

Blues and Boleros to Tangos and Tarantellas

Refer also to the previous section, "Composer Resources for Ballet Class Repertory," that recommends exploration, as well, of blues, boleros, character music, folk dances, galops, jazz styles, Krakowiaks), novelty pieces, polkas, pop, the RAD Syllabus, ragtime, rock, tangos, and tarantellas.

5 Preparing and Arranging Piano Repertory for Ballet Class

How to Play a Musical Preparation

The First Thing. Since a preparation is the first thing that an accompanist plays for any combination in the ballet technique class, preparations are the opening topic of discussion in this section. Before reading this section, read or review "Musical Preparations and Their Functions" in chapter 1 for foundational information on this topic.

Two Types. The preparation, or musical introduction, precedes—and sets up—the music to be used for the dance combination. Preparations can be divided into two basic types. The first is generally used with slower, smoother combinations. The second is chiefly appropriate for combinations that are quicker and sharper. On the following pages, several specific examples are given for each type of preparation.

Slower Preparations. In its simplest form, the type of musical preparation to be used for the slower, smoother combinations is two introductory chords. If this type of preparation is used, the two chords should be played in the same tempo as that to which the combination will be danced. However, while it is not uncommon for accompanists to use just two chords, it is not recommended. The two-chord preparation does not convey enough information, and generally it does not give the dancers enough time to prepare themselves. At a minimum, if two chords are used, they should at least be arpeggiated in a way that defines the tempo and the rhythmic pulse.

Instead, the accompanist is strongly encouraged to provide a fuller preparation that is four counts in length—in order to match, generally, the time that the dancers require to set up, and to convey a clear sense of what the coming music will be like.

Quicker Preparations. The preparations that are employed for sharper, brighter combinations must indicate very precisely the exact pulse (tempo) and feeling of the music that is to follow. Such preparations may consist, for example, of either four or eight counts for 2/4 or 4/4 steps. If the step is extremely fast, generally eight counts are desired, to give the dancers more time in which to prepare. These counts, or beats, may consist simply of an ostinato figure or, as an alternative, they may be the closing two or four bars of the musical selection to be played. In the case of bright waltzes or other 3/4s, two or four bars of introduction will be required. Generally, four bars are preferred—again, to give the dancers time to prepare. As with duple-meter music, the preparations for 3/4s may be four bars of improvised waltz rhythm or perhaps the final four bars of the music to be used. If a mazurka or a polonaise is specifically desired, identical principals apply: Two bars are appropriate, or the generally preferred four bars of a characteristic mazurka or polonaise rhythm, or perhaps the closing two or four bars of the piece itself.

Preparations Chart and Examples. The Preparations Chart below is divided into the two main types of preparation: (1) the slower, chordal, arpeggiated, or generally smoother type, and (2) the faster, ostinato-type preparation. The text sections of the chapter then divide the broad categories of dance exercises and steps by barre and center work. The examples of preparations that follow the chart explicitly convey what an appropriate preparation would be for any given exercise or step. All of the musical examples are taken from the repertory lists in chapter 4.

Clearly, there are many variations on or alternatives to the preparations shown that can be just as suitable. Introductory chords and arpeggios, if used, do not have to be on the tonic. Any chord progression or passage is acceptable if it clearly leads to the opening harmony of the music itself. The accompanist is encouraged to be imaginative in his use of musical preparations, in terms of both harmony and rhythm. Again, the chief requirement is that the preparation lead naturally and clearly to the music about to be played.

Preparations Chart

Slow Preparations

(slower, chordal, arpeggiated, or generally smoother type)

BARRE	CENTER
Stretches	Adagio
Pliés	Slow Pirouettes, in Place
Port de Bras	Reverence
Fondus	
Développés	
Slow Battements Tendus	
Ronds de Jambe à Terre	

Fast Preparations

(ostinato type or as otherwise appropriate; two or four bars of music)

BARRE	CENTER
Fast Battements Tendus	Petit Allegro steps (2/4, 4/4, and 3/4)
Battement Tendus Dégagés	Pirouettes: Quick, in Place, and Quick, Moving
Battement Piqués	Tours en l'Air
Ronds de Jambe en l'Air	Relevés and Sous-Sus
Battements Frappés	Grand Allegro steps (2/4, 4/4, 3/4)
Battement sur le Cou-de-Pied	
Pas de Cheval	
Battements en Cloche	
Grands Battements	

Slow Preparations at the Barre

Pliés: Ravel: Waltz no. 2 in G Minor, Valses Nobles et Sentimentales
MM quarter note equals 88

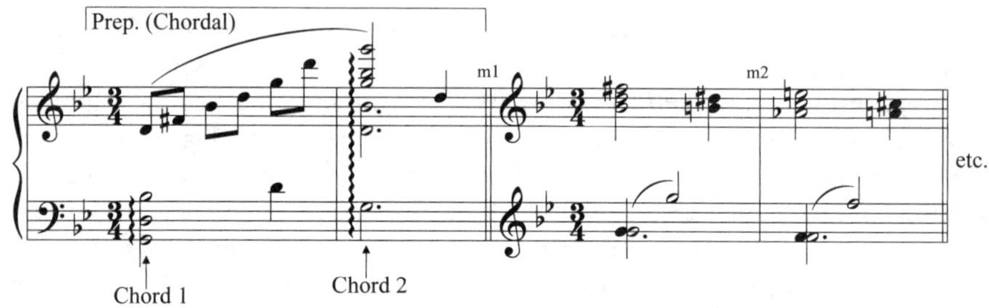

Fondus: Chopin: Nocturne in F Minor, op. 55, no. 1
MM quarter note equals 80

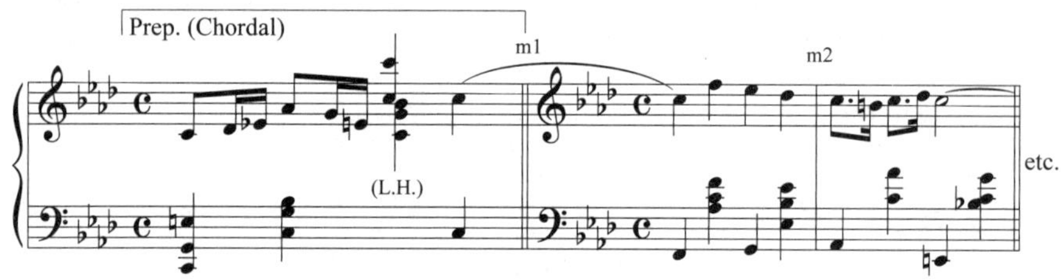

Ronds de Jambe à Terre: Bach: Passepied II, Partita in B Minor (Overture in the French Manner)
MM eighth note equals 104

Développés: Brahms: Intermezzo, op. 117, no. 1
MM eighth note equals 92

Fast Preparations at the Barre

Battement Tendu Dégagé: Liszt: Hungarian Rhapsody no. 6
MM quarter note equals 96

Battement Frappé: Bach: Bourée II, Partita in B Minor (Overture in the French Manner)

MM half note equals 88

In this example, the two-measure introduction consists of the last two measures of the first sixteen-measure section. (Remember that this original twelve-measure phrase has measures 1 through 4 repeated to make sixteen measures.)

Battement sur le Cou-de-Pied: Schumann: "Wild Rider," from Album for the Young, op. 68

MM dotted quarter note equals 126

In this example, the two-measure introduction consists of the final two measures of the piece.

Battement en Cloche: Beethoven: Theme, from Variations on a Waltz by Diabelli

MM dotted half note equals 69

Grand Battement: Brahms: Variations on a Theme by Paganini, op. 35, Book I, Var. XIII

MM quarter note equals 69

Adagio: Brahms: Variations on a Theme by Paganini, op. 35, Book II, Var. XII
MM eighth note equals 104
In this example, the preparation is the final measure of the variation (measure 12)

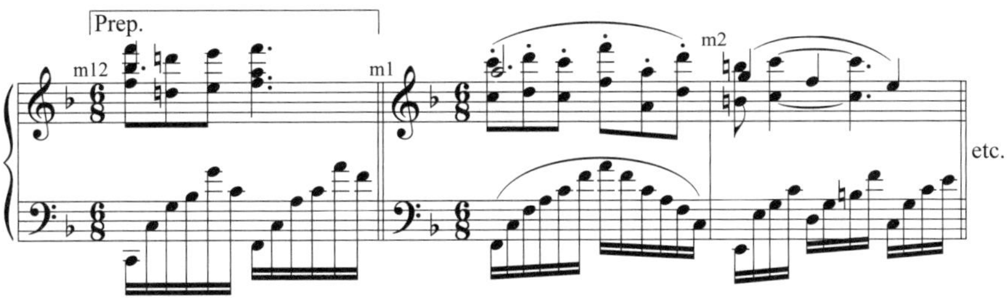

Adagio: Glazunov: Barcarolle, from The Seasons
MM eighth note equals 116
Use the imagination in playing preparations. Do not always just play dominant and tonic chords.

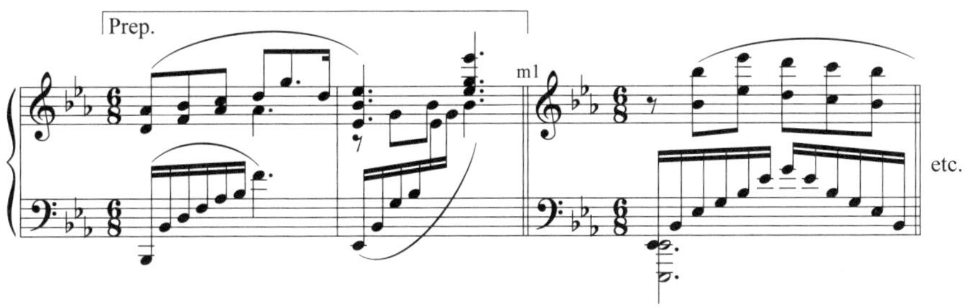

Adagio: Rachmaninoff: Prelude, op. 23, no. 5
MM quarter note equals 66

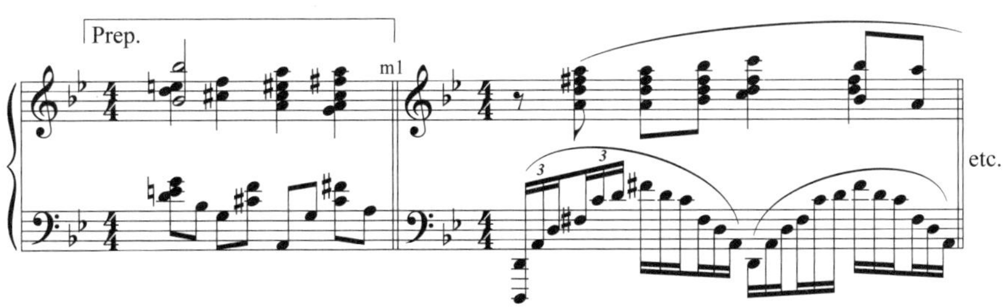

Slow Pirouette from Fourth, Fifth, Second: Brahms: Waltz in A-flat Major, op. **39, no. 15**

MM quarter note equals 126

Fast Preparations in the Center

Petit Allegro (2/4): Grieg: Album Leaf, op. 12, no. 7
MM quarter note equals 88

Grand Allegro Waltz: Shubert: Twelve Valses Nobles, op. 77, no. 9
MM dotted half note equals 66

or:

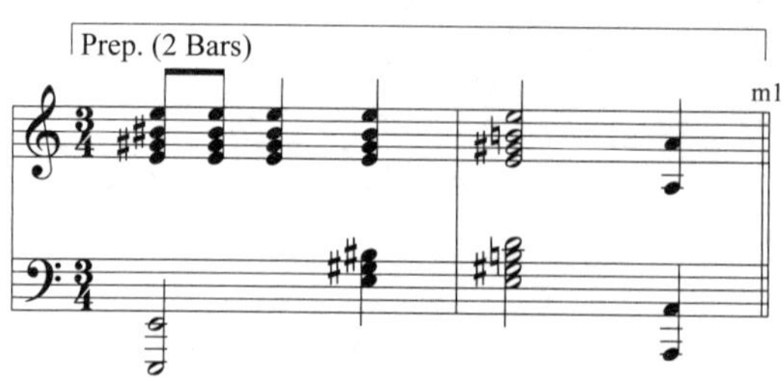

Grand Allegro Waltz: Schumann: Waltz, op. 124, no. 4
MM dotted half note equals 66
The following inventive preparation is suggested.

Fouetté: Minkus: Pas de Deux, Coda, from Don Quixote
MM quarter note equals 136

Tour en l'Air: Glazunov: Var. III, from Raymonda
MM quarter note equals 69

Other Examples of Preparations

Polonaise: For a polonaise, use the following standard rhythmic motif for a preparation.

The following is a simple but adequate example of a preparation for a polonaise in E major.

Below is a good preparation that might be used for Chopin's Polonaise in F-sharp minor, op. 44. The two-measure preparation precedes the opening phrase, which begins in measure 9.

Mazurka: For a mazurka, use the following standard rhythmic motif for a preparation:

The following is a simple but adequate example of a preparation for a mazurka in F minor.

Below is a good preparation that might be used for the mazurka from Act I of Delibes's *Coppelia*.

A few other examples of suitable musical preparations are given below, for various hypothetical time and key signatures in various tempos.

Slow 4/4: E Major (chordal)
MM quarter note equals 66

Slow 3/4: B-flat Major (chordal)
MM quarter note equals 76

Polonaise: A-flat Major
MM quarter note equals 88

Petit Allegro (2/4): B Major
MM quarter note equals 92

Grand Allegro Waltz: C Major
MM dotted half note equals 66

Cadences

Graceful Endings. In surveying the musical suggestions in chapter 4 and in doing his own research, the ballet technique accompanist will discover that, in arranging music for class, he will frequently have to improvise cadences at key places in the score to coincide with the end of dance combinations. Normally, these cadences should not sound abrupt, chopped off, or unexpected—even if they come up suddenly and without warning. Cadences are generally, or potentially, required at the ends of musical phrases, after multiples of eight bars. Each example of repertory in chapter 4 provides the accompanist with instructions regarding where to cadence, and guidance regarding how to end gracefully and in some proper key.

Many types of cadences are satisfactory, as long as the accompanist is mindful of making them sound natural, musically logical, and as smooth as possible, within the context of whatever piece of music is being played. Below are several possible cadential solutions based on pieces listed in chapter 4. In the process of arranging music so that it falls acceptably into even, square phrases, the accompanist will note that the desired cadential point often occurs in an inconvenient place in the score, which places the onus on the accompanist to formulate a logical ending that addresses the issue. In studying the following examples, the accompanist is encouraged to refer back in each case to the cadential instructions given in chapter 4.

Plié: Fauré: Nocturne in E-flat Major, op. 36
MM quarter note equals 50

Fondu: Schumann: "Erinnerung," from Album for the Young, op. 68
MM quarter note equals 52

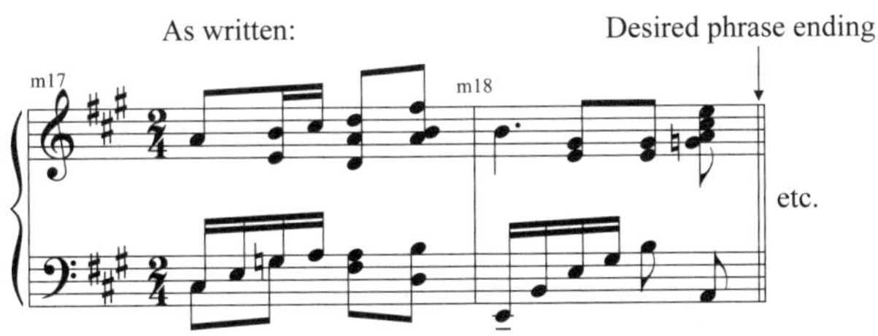

Battement sur le Cou-de-Pied: Chopin: Étude in A Minor, op. 25, no. 4
MM quarter note equals 132.

As written:

Improvised cadence:

Adagio: Chopin: Étude in E Minor, op. 25, no. 5
MM quarter note equals 138

As written:

Improvised cadence:

Petit Allegro (2/4): Czerny: The Art of Finger Dexterity, op. 740, no. 33
MM dotted quarter note equals 96

As written: Desired phrase ending

Improvised cadence: Phrase ending

Petit Allegro (3/4): Tchaikovsky: Tempo di Valse, from Weihnachten, op. 37, no. 12
MM dotted half note equals 80

As written: Desired cadence

Improvised cadence: Phrase endi

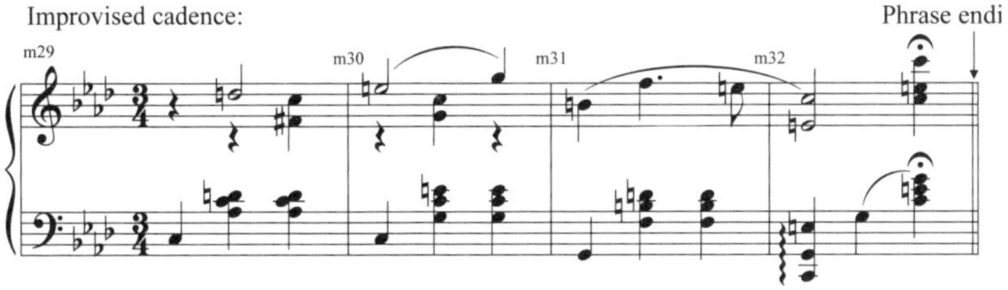

Simplifying Music

Attractive, but Too Demanding. The ballet technique accompanist will likely come across music that seems to have excellent potential for use in class, but she may become discouraged by the fact that the music is very technically demanding and therefore requires much practice and preparation. She may not have the time to work on this kind of potential repertory outside of class. If such is the case, she can often simplify, or revise, the music so that it is immediately more playable, without compromising those essential qualities that make it a good piece for dance. (Note: If the accompanist must sight-read difficult piano reductions of ballet scores on short notice, frequently she can simplify them without impairing their effectiveness. See "Repertory Class," chap. 8)

Overcoming Difficult Octaves in Brahms. A good example for illustrating this issue is Brahms's Var. XIII, Book I, of the Variation on a Theme by Paganini, op. 35, which was previously discussed in the section of chapter 5 entitled "How to Play a Musical Preparation." This variation, which has been suggested for use with grand battement, has a right-hand melodic line comprised of rapid, sixteenth-note octaves. There is no reason why the accompanist cannot make this variation more technically accessible by playing the melodic line just as single notes, rather than octaves. The music may thereby be a bit less powerful, but it is still effective if the accompanist plays the right hand strongly.

As written:

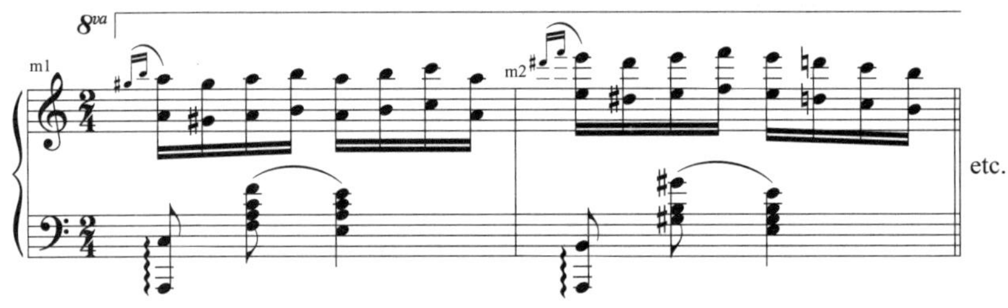

Without octaves:

Leaping Octaves in Czerny. The accompanist may also refer to The Art of Finger Dexterity, op. 740, no. 33, by Czerny (discussed in "Music for Petit Allegro (2/4)," chap. 4), an excerpt of which is highlighted in this chapter in the preceding section, "Cadences." Here again is a rapid, right-hand theme in leaping octaves, which can certainly be simplified for the purposes of ballet technique. The exercise for which the music is intended must have a light, dancy character for its use with petit allegro; a preponderance of heavy octaves, potentially played awkwardly, would not encourage the proper feeling. Of course, if the accompanist can play octaves really well and can render them lightly enough—at the required tempo—then there is no reason to omit them.

As written:

Without octaves:

Omitting the Unnecessary. There will be times during ballet class when brilliance and virtuosity are quite effective, as long as they do not interfere with the essence of the music or compromise the dance combination. Brilliant playing on a grand scale is especially inspiring in grand allegro steps and combinations. Here, a well-developed piano technique is a real asset. However—and be advised—the accompanist cannot play herself to death all the time, and where it is appropriate she should not hesitate to cut out of the music any unnecessary and encumbering material. The following musical examples contain material that may be clumsy if the tempo is, or becomes, too fast; this material may be omitted without hesitation.

Battement Tendu: Brahms: Variations on a Theme by Handel, op. 24, Var. I
MM quarter note equals 60

Note that the rapid, twelve-note grouping in the right hand may be replaced with something simpler.

Original version:

Alternate version:

Petit Allegro (2/4): Czerny: The Art of Finger Dexterity, op. 740, no. 35
MM quarter note equals 84

The rapid right-hand triplets may be readily replaced by more manageable duplets, which are easier to play at faster speeds.

Original version:

As written:

Duplet version:

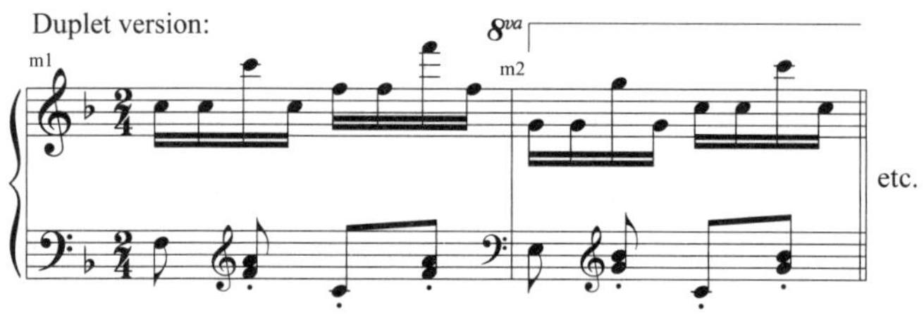

Good Judgment. The ballet accompanist should exercise her own good judgment, based on a realistic self-assessment of her own technical limits, in deciding when to omit musical material that she considers to be musically nonessential and technically overdemanding.

When Music Is Too Difficult or Too Complex

Aspirations. Sometimes the ballet accompanist will come across a piece of music—it may almost seem as if that music had found its way to him—that excites him as a possibility for use in the dance class; or, some composition that he has been familiar with for a long time suddenly takes hold of his imagination as a candidate. Such discovered or remembered music often ends up as a valuable asset in the accompanist's repertory. However, the accompanist's aspirations may be dampened or extinguished—either because the music is simply too technically challenging for him or because it defeats all of his efforts to adapt it suitably for dance technique, likely because of irregular phrasing that cannot be fixed.

Excessive Technical Challenges. Pianists come in a broad range of technical facility, from average to virtuosic. An advanced pianist may be able to get a piece of music under his fingers almost immediately, while the same level of mastery, if attainable at all, may take another pianist weeks. Therefore, in considering music for use in the ballet class, the accompanist will need to exercise judgment in selecting repertory that is sufficiently within his technical reach such that, depending on the demands on his time, he will not expend an excessive or unrealistic amount of energy in learning a piece, or chapter of a piece, that is simply not worth the time or that ends up not working at all.

It is essential to learn, early in the process of accumulating repertory for dance, to make objective assessments about the technical challenges that a composition presents. When faced with excessive technical challenges—the majority of the Chopin Études are a good example, many of which can, in principle, be appropriated and arranged, at least in part, for the ballet class—the accompanist may wish to ask himself, "Does this project, however attractive, really offer a big enough payoff? Or could time perhaps be better spent learning two or three other less technically challenging compositions that, although not as dazzling, are still appealing and that serve just as well?"

Again, the Chopin Études Opus 10 and Opus 12 offer numerous examples of music that could, if arranged appropriately, be dazzling in a ballet class, but which amount to technical quicksand for all but a virtuoso. The following are representative examples of this:

Étude, op. 10, no. 2, in A Minor
Étude, op. 10, no. 5, in G-flat Major
Étude, op. 25, no. 9, in G-flat Major

Accompanists who lack the experience or maturity to make realistic judgments about technically difficult music in this situation will end up wasting a lot of time, and they will probably include music in their ballet music binders that they avoid again and again—perhaps never playing it at all. A judicious, early retreat from a technically overwhelming score reflects maturity, as opposed to ego-driven obstinacy that will likely lead to defeat.

Simplification. A lot of difficult music can be rendered usable by simplifying it. The question then arises, "Will it require so much simplification that its appeal will be lost?" Possibly. The accompanist will have to make the decision.

An interesting observation may be made by looking again at Chopin's Étude, op. 10, no. 2, in A Minor, referenced above. As written, the chromaticism in the third, fourth, and fifth fingers of the right hand presents a challenge that is beyond the ability of many pianists. However, rearranging the accompanying chordal content that Chopin originally allocated to both the left and right hands so that all of it is addressed in the left—a cheat, indeed, but a reasonable compromise—leaves the right hand entirely free to play the upper chromatic passages with relative ease when they are refingered.

Many compositions that, for the most part, are technically accessible may be sprinkled with passages that, for example, suddenly introduce a high level of virtuosity for just a few measures—perhaps great flourishes in the right hand that then return to the original texture. In many such cases, it may be a mature and intelligent choice to eliminate finger work that, after all, is not really critical to the musical coherence of the piece, and thereby not "throw the baby out with the bathwater."

Complex and Irregular Phrasing. The accompanist will encounter musical candidates for ballet class that, upon examination, are seen to be comprised of phrasing that does not fall into regular four- or eight-bar phrases. This is common enough, and it is often satisfactorily fixed either easily or with reasonable effort. In fact, if the accompanist is competent and industrious, many compositions made up of quite irregular phrasing can survive the "surgery" necessary to render them usable—and musically palatable—for ballet technique. The technique of adapting unevenly phrased music for ballet class is discussed in greater detail elsewhere in this book.

Sometimes, the accompanist will encounter a composition that, during casual or even focused listening, appears to be an enticing candidate for the ballet class. Upon more detailed analysis, however, that same composition may reveal itself to be not just problematic, but so problematic that no amount of musical surgery will bring its phrasing into compliance with the four- or eight-bar mandate without mauling it.

The Rachmaninoff "Vocalise." An excellent example of such an irredeemably noncompliant piece of music is the "Vocalise" by Sergei Rachmaninoff, composed in 1912 as the last song in his 14 Romances, op. 34. Written for high voice (soprano is best) with piano accompaniment, this masterpiece of lyricism is free of words and is sung instead on a single vowel of the singer's choosing. It has been transposed into many keys and made into innumerable arrangements for instrumental soloists and for orchestral and other instrumental ensembles. Of special interest to the ballet accompanist, it has been transformed into a number of arrangements for solo piano, some better than others.

A passive listening to the "Vocalise"—the preferred method because of its beauty—will likely not expose a serious phrasing challenge for the ballet accompanist. The graceful, floating character of the piece will eclipse such considerations. However, upon examination of the music score, various issues arise.

Although the time signature is "C"—a general indication of 4/4 time—an occasional measure in 2/4 time occurs. This in itself, in many compositions, could be overcome with a sensitive rewrite. In the case of the "Vocalise," however, addressing this issue is problematic, in part because the vocal line is delicate and easily damaged by alteration.

The first phrase, in which the second measure only is in 2/4 time, ends in measure 7, which also includes a significant pickup to measure 8, which is the first full measure of the second phrase.

The second phrase, which is long and properly ends in measure 18, consists, therefore, of eleven measures (not including the pickup from measure 7). In addition, measure 17 is in 2/4 time.

The entire section discussed above then repeats. At the end of the repeat, measure 19 introduces the pickup to the next phrase, the first full measure of which is measure 20.

The phrase that begins in measure 20 (not including the pickup in measure 19) is thirteen measures long, ending in measure 32. The prospect of breaking up this melody or adding to it to make a square phrase is, to say the least, formidable—actually disheartening.

The section described just above also repeats. At the end of the repeat, measure 33 introduces the pickup to the next—and final—phrase, the first full measure of which is measure 34.

The final phrase of the piece, beginning with measure 34 (not including the pickup in measure 33), is eight measures long and ends in measure 41, and includes two measures in 2/4 time.

To summarize briefly, the "Vocalise" is characterized by phrases that, except for the final one (irrelevant, at any rate, because of its nonuniform-measure time signatures), are not square, and are of varying lengths. Further, it is peppered with 2/4 measures that are interspersed throughout the overall 4/4 measure format, further impacting the phrase lengths.

This might not seem especially onerous to the enthusiastic arranger of music for ballet class, since other compositions that, on the face of it, rival the characteristics and challenges of the "Vocalise" could be reshaped with some work into something usable—and respectable. The problem with the "Vocalise" is that its phrasing is especially delicate. Further, although it is very well planned and executed, it is artfully designed to create the impression of the very definition of a *vocalise*—a singing exercise employing individual syllables or vowel sounds to develop flexibility and control of pitch and tone. In fact, the "Vocalise," with its free-flowing melodic line, has an almost improvised character.

Therefore, for the ballet accompanist, the "Vocalise" embodies the kind of piece that seems to invite—almost in a sirenlike way—an arrangement for the technique class but, pursuant to such an attempt, ends up being essentially an editing nightmare doomed to disheartenment and failure.

Ballet accompanists are strongly encouraged to obtain access to the score to a piano arrangement of the "Vocalise" and, with the above discussion fresh in mind, experience firsthand the pitfalls described, by way of an object lesson. Fortunately, such alluring land mines do not float by every day, and with some experience and vigilance the accompanist will not often find himself in this kind of thorny thicket.

Choreography versus Technique Class. Finally, it should be stressed emphatically that the problem with the "Vocalise" and works like it is not that they cannot be exquisitely choreographed for ballet or other forms of dance by a talented choreographer. Part of the excitement and beauty of ballet—and modern dance—is precisely that this can be done and is done. The issue here is that such pieces can—unfortunately—be tantamount to quicksand when considered as candidates for the ballet technique class.

The Rachmaninoff "Elégie." The ballet accompanist is encouraged to review the piano score for Rachmaninoff's "Elégie" (from *Morceaux de Fantasie*, op. 3, no. 1, in E-flat Minor) and compare it to the "Vocalise." The "Elégie" is an excellent example of a Rachmaninoff piano piece that, in contradistinction to the "Vocalise," can be used easily—that is, with almost no editing of the phrases—for the ballet technique class, specifically for combinations like pliés and adagios. The "Elégie," a serious piece, is in "C" time—4/4—and is characterized by long melodic phrases that often float over the bar lines.

After the introduction in measures 1 and 2, measures 3 through 18 (sixteen measures) comprise a melodic line subdivided into two eight-bar phrases, playable exactly as they are for ballet technique. A three-beat pickup in measure 18 introduces a new melodic line in measure 19, which can be played exactly as written for the first eight bars (measures 19 through 26). To complete the piece for use in the ballet technique class, the second eight-bar phrase—not including the prominent three-beat pickup in measure 26—can be made up of measures 27 through 33, plus measure 39 (transitioned to directly from measure 33 by eliminating measures 28–32).

The piece continues, but all the music that the accompanist will ever reasonably need from this composition is included in measures 1 through 39, as edited above: that is, four eight-bar phrases with only one very minor edit required for the final measure, thereby readily yielding an edited composition of thirty-two measures.

Arranging, Enriching, and Embellishing Music

Natural and Instinctive. There will be many times—possibly most of the time—when the ballet technique accompanist will want to enrich, embellish, or otherwise arrange music that she uses for class. With experience, these practices become natural, and even instinctive and spontaneous, especially when the accompanist's improvisation skills flower and as she learns more and more what kinds of musical textures are appropriate and helpful for specific dance steps and combinations.

Arranging for All Requirements. There are plentiful occasions for which a sparseness of notes and a simple texture are not only appropriate, but also ideal—even elegant—for the dance step or combination at hand. At other times, a quality of fullness, depth, or movement in the music may be desired, and the score can be enhanced if it is embellished or given added color, or enriched with more moving notes. A sense of breadth and expansiveness may thus be imparted to pliés or to adagio music. Music for grand battement may be imbued with more weight, power, and momentum. Petit allegro and grand allegro, respectively, may, as the occasion demands, be rendered lighter and more airy, or fuller and more substantial. Bass patterns, in particular, may be energized by replacing single notes that fall on the downbeat with octaves or chords, or by playing them in a sharper, more accented, or even explosive manner than the score itself would indicate.

The Advantages of Reinvention. The outstanding advantage to being skilled in arranging—and rearranging—music freely is that the same score may be reinvented to suit many different steps and combinations. The ballet accompanist thereby gains tremendous advantage over her circumstances and is enabled to dramatically stretch and diversify her repertory. Much—actually, most—of the musical repertory in chapter 4 may, with imagination, skill, and experience, be used for a very wide variety of dance steps, often requiring little more than a tempo adjustment and a different touch in the simpler cases. In other cases, the music may successfully undergo a dramatic metamorphosis.

Discard Snobbery. The various examples provided throughout the remainder of this section of chapter 5 illustrate some of the ways in which music can be enriched, embellished, and rendered usable for many different dance combinations. Musical snobbery and puritanism should be discarded. They are impediments to inventiveness. The ballet accompanist is urged to consider the following issues: rendering the music more fully and more expansively for the dancers' ears; heightening the expressive effects that are already present, to a degree, in the music; and imbuing the music, as appropriate, with greater rhythmic vitality, clarity, and overall danceability. The accompanist should strive always to accomplish these tasks without vulgarizing or destroying the inherent aesthetic beauty and desirability of any given piece of music. Many of the examples that follow are taken from the repertory lists in chapter 4. Other examples are entirely new; some are, as originally written, unsuitable for most any ballet combination, but may be arranged to be quite effective.

Access to Freedom. This section is not in any way intended to be an exhaustive treatment of the techniques of improvisation. It is hoped, however, that what is discussed here will at least stimulate the accompanist's thinking and imagination and enable her to realize that she has a tremendous amount of freedom to use music in any way that will render it suitable for her dance accompaniment purposes. Accessing this freedom will help her locate and use musical material, avoid ruts in her musical thinking, and evolve her concepts of what music best compliments and supports the work of the dancers. (Refer also to chap. 7, "Improvisation.")

The Examples. The following examples are presented alphabetically, by composer. Although they are brief by intention, in each case they give the accompanist a clear idea as to the trend to follow. Most examples are four measures long; others are two measures, or eight, as appropriate.

Bach: Menuet II, Partita in B-flat Major
Original version:

As is the case with much traditional piano or other keyboard repertory when it is used for ballet technique class, the tempo may be, or can be, significantly altered. When the above Menuet is used for slow pliés, it will be played a good deal more slowly that the original tempo. Therefore, the following alterations are quite appropriate, since they help to sustain the music at a considerably diminished tempo.

For Plié: MM quarter note equals 88
With alterations:

Bach: Bourée II, Partita in B Minor (Overture in the French Manner)
Played as written for Battement Tendu Dégagé: MM quarter note equals 88

As written:

Played as originally written, above, this movement was listed as well suited for battement tendu dégagé. Because of its modest texture, it would not be so suitable for slower combinations. The example provided below illustrates how the material might be modified and enriched for a slower combination, such as pas de cheval.

Arranged for Pas de Cheval: MM half note equals 60

Beethoven: Third Movement, from Sonata, op. 31, no. 2
MM: dotted quarter note equals 69
As originally written:

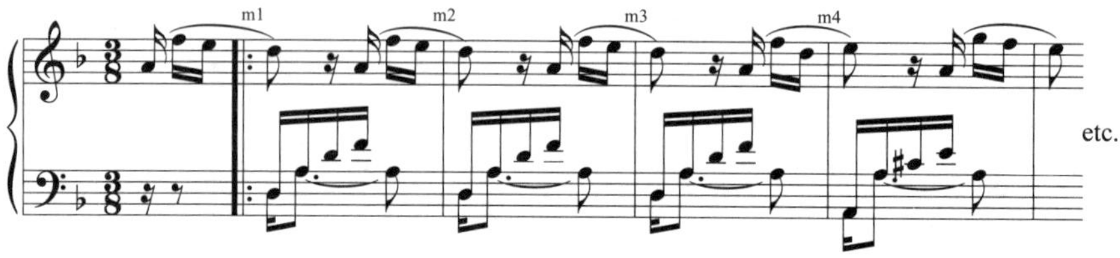

As originally written, above, the opening of this movement is a logical, sixteen-measure phrase that, when suitably arranged as below, would be quite effective for battement frappé. For this purpose, the meter is changed from 3/8 to 3/4. Sixteen measures of the original music would then equal eight measures in the arranged example.

Arranged for Battement Frappé: MM half note equals 60

Brahms: Variations on a Theme by Paganini, op. 35, Book I, Var. XI
Played as written for Fondu: MM eighth note equals 50

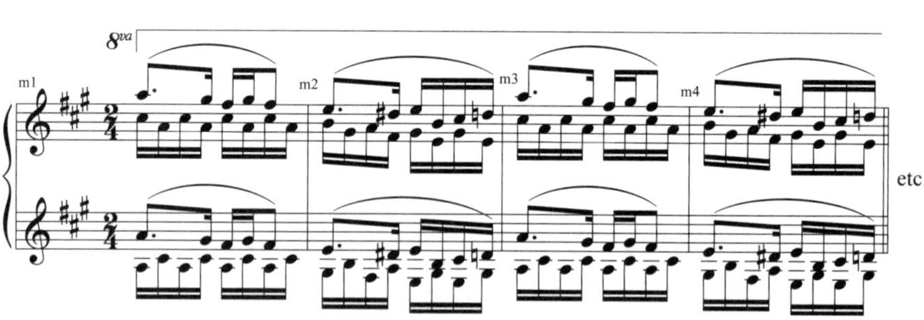

As originally written above, this music was suggested for fondus. The variation might be modified in any number of ways for other combinations. Two possibilities are suggested below, one for ronds de jambe à terre, the other for battement frappé. In the modification process, the music undergoes changes in texture, tempo, and meter.

Arranged for Ronds de Jambe à Terre: MM eighth note equals 112

Arranged for Battement Frappé: MM quarter note equals 88

Chopin: Étude, op. 25, no. 4
Played as written for Battement sur le Cou-de-Pied: MM quarter note equals 132

As originally written, above, this étude was suggested for battement sur le cou-de-pied. Below are two arranged versions. The first is for a moderate battement tendu. In this slower version, the bass is made more substantial, and the right hand is enriched with moving notes. The second arranged version is for battement en cloche. The texture is modified, and the meter is changed to a swinging, 6/8 waltz feeling.

Arranged for Moderate Battement Tendu: MM quarter note equals 60

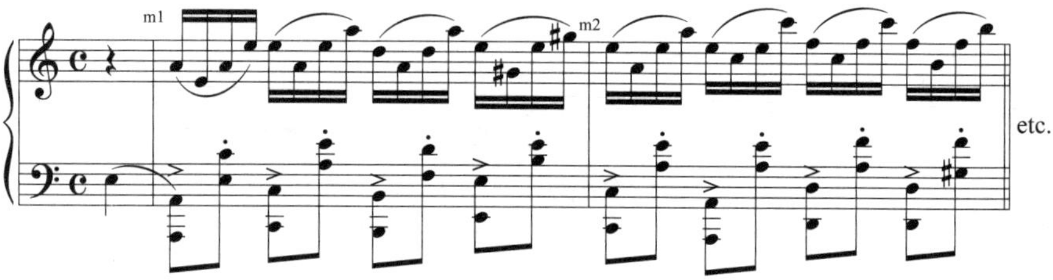

Arranged for Battement en Cloche: MM dotted quarter note equals 66

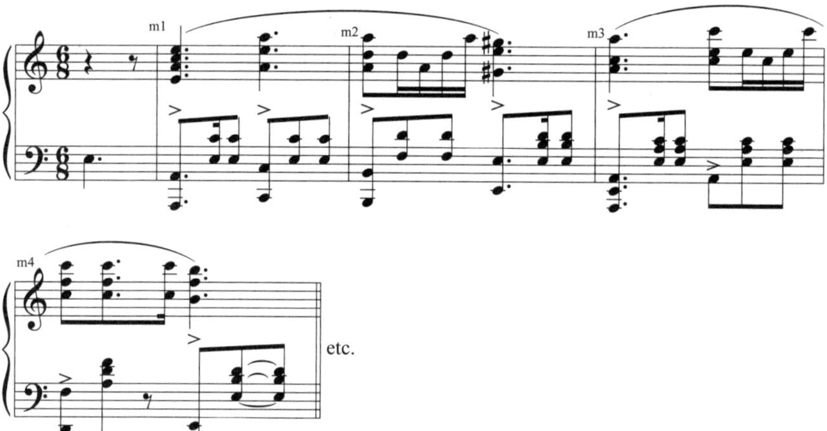

The accompanist will note that in the example just above (arrangement for battement en cloche), one measure of music is equivalent to one half measure of music in the original étude. In other words, the harmonic rhythm of the example just above is half as fast as in the original music.

Chopin: Prelude in C Major, op. 28, no. 1
Original version:

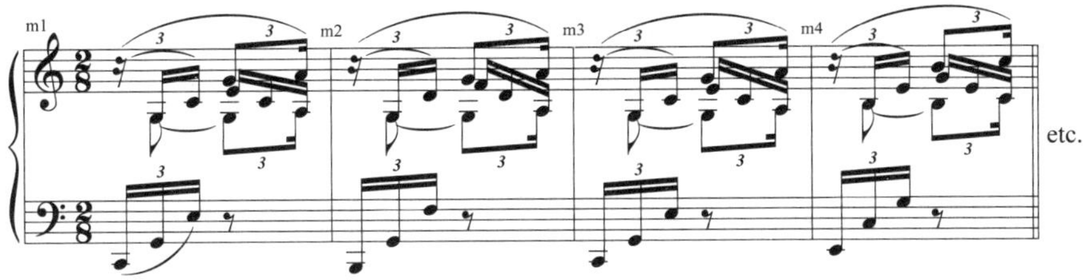

This prelude is not, as originally written above, really appropriate for any ballet technique class combination. However, the examples that follow illustrate that the music can be arranged to be excellent for at least two types of combinations.

Arranged for Battement Piqué: MM eighth note equals 132
The rhythm is made sharper and more defined by rewriting the bass in the manner of a typical left-hand accompaniment.

Arranged for Ronds de Jambe à Terre: MM quarter note equals 116
The meter is changed to a flowing 3/4, and the texture is appropriately reinvented. The harmonies remain unchanged.

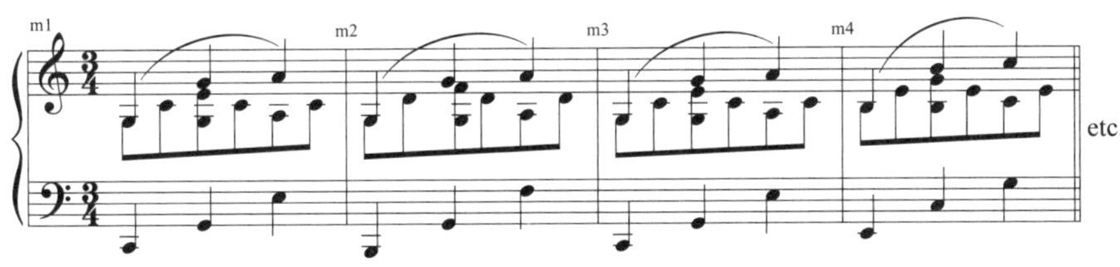

Chopin: Nocturne, op. 55, no. 1
Played as written for Fondu: MM quarter note equals 80

The combination for which this piece was originally intended was fondu, to be played as originally written, above. With minor changes, the music can be molded into good music for faster 2/4 combinations, both at the barre and in the center. The example that follows is for petit allegro 2/4.

Arranged for Petit Allegro (2/4): MM quarter note equals 88

etc.

Delibes: Mazurka, from Act I of Coppelia
Played as written for Grand Allegro (3/4): MM quarter note equals 104

etc.

This piece, shown just above as written, is listed under pas de basque (grand allegro 3/4). The example provided below suggests how the accompanist may convert this mazurka into a polonaise, by applying some minor rhythmic alterations. There are occasions in the ballet technique class when it is very advantageous to be able to convert a mazurka into a polonaise—for example, when a mazurka tempo becomes too bogged down and draggy.

Arranged for Polonaise: MM quarter note equals 84

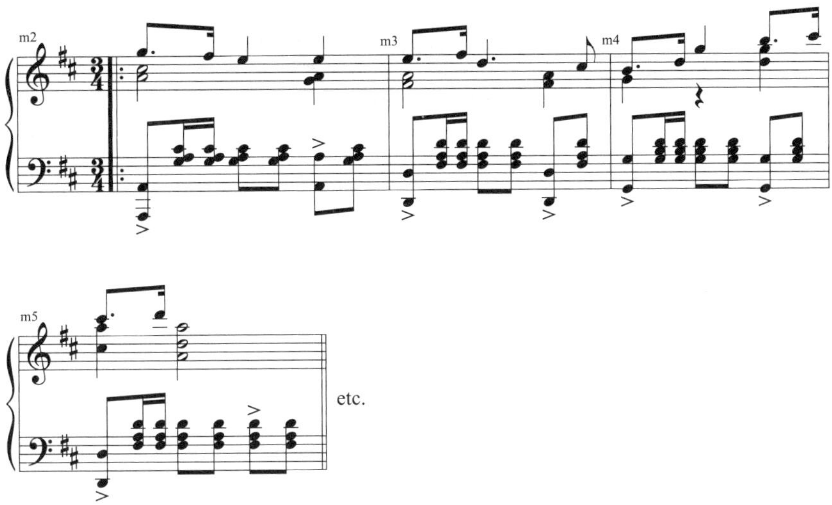

Dvořák: Slavonic Dance no. 2
Played as written for Petit Allegro (2/4): MM quarter note equals 92

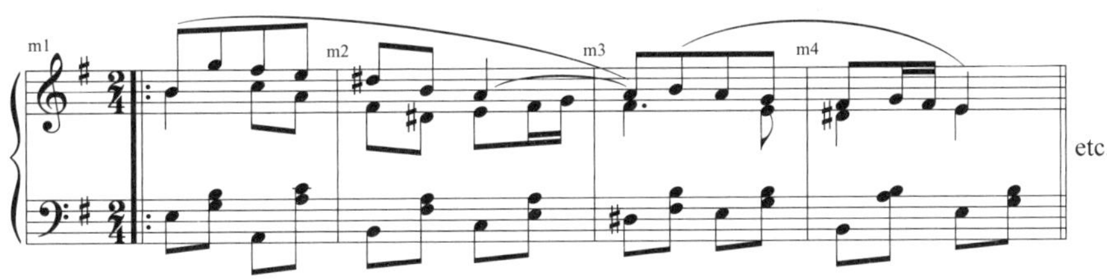

This piece, shown just above in its original form, was originally listed under petit allegro 2/4. The following example shows this piece arranged in a 6/8 meter to make it suitable for ronds de jambe à terre. The music could just as easily have been arranged in a 3/4 meter, but was done here in a 6/8 meter to keep the harmonic rhythm the same as in the original music. With a 6/8 meter, the number of measures remains the same.

Arranged for Ronds de Jambe à Terre: MM dotted quarter note equals 116

Fauré: Theme, from Theme and Variations, op. 73
Played as written for Grand Battement: MM quarter note equals 60

Played as originally written, above, this theme was suggested for grand battement. Two excellent examples follow, modified rhythmically to render them effective for a polonaise and for a développé, respectively. Notice that, in the first arrangement, for a polonaise, the harmonic rhythm in each measure is half as fast as in the original. In the second arrangement, for a slow waltz, the harmonic rhythm is even slower—only one fourth as fast as in the original music.

Arranged for Polonaise: MM dotted quarter note equals 88

Arranged for Développé: MM dotted quarter note equals 88

Granados: Valses Poeticos, no. 1
Played as written for Ronds de Jambe à Terre: MM quarter note equals 116

etc.

This waltz, suggested as originally written above for ronds de jambe à terre, would make an excellent, bright 2/4 for battement sur le cou-de-pied. It requires only minor changes, as shown below.

Arranged for Battement sur le Cou-de-Pied: MM quarter note equals 132

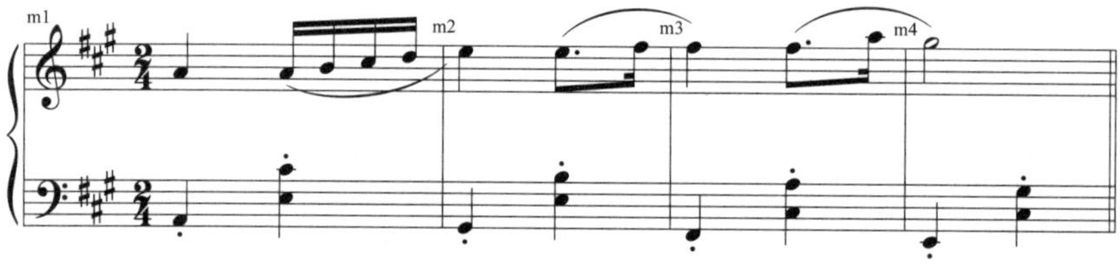

etc.

Granados: Valses Poeticos, no. 2
Played as written for Pirouettes from fourth, fifth, and second: MM quarter note equals 138

etc.

As originally written above, this waltz was suggested for slow pirouettes from fourth, fifth, and second. With skillful enrichment and embellishment, this waltz would serve as a very nice adagio piece, as demonstrated in the following example.

Arranged for Adagio: MM quarter note equals 112

Grieg: Wedding Day at Troldhaugen, op. 65, no. 6
Played as written for Grand Battement: MM half note equals 60

As written:

As originally written above, this piece was suggested for grand battement. The arranged version below is in a 6/8 meter and has a swinging quality that would be very well suited for battement en cloche.

Arranged for Battement en Cloche: MM dotted quarter note equals 63

Mozart: Second Movement, Sonata in F Major, K. 332
Played as written for Adagio: MM eighth note equals 76

As originally written above, this slow movement was suggested for adagio. It would, with skillful handling, also make a nice, bright 2/4 (for battement tendu, for example), as illustrated below.

Arranged for Battement Tendu: MM quarter note equals 60

Rachmaninoff: Variations on a Theme of Corelli, op. 42, Var. IV
Played as written for Développés: MM quarter note equals 88

This piece, as originally written above, was originally suggested for développés. It will also yield an excellent arrangement for grand battement, when rewritten into a powerful 2/4 style.

Arranged for Grand Battement: MM quarter note equals 69

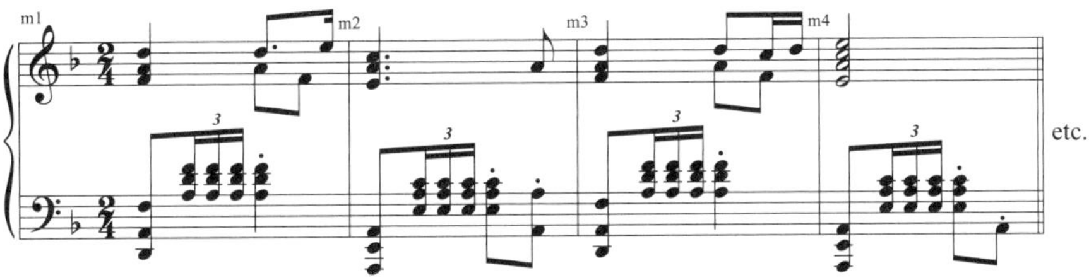

Schubert: Twelve Valses Nobles, op. 77, D. 969, no. 1
Played as written for Battement en Cloche: MM dotted half note equals 66

As originally written above, this waltz was suggested for battement en cloche. When the meter is changed to 4/4, it is suitable for tour en l'air (or grand battement). Note the example below.

Arranged for Tour en l'Air: MM half note equals 69

Schubert: Twelve Valses Nobles, op. 77, D. 969, no. 4
Played as written for Grand Allegro 3/4: MM dotted half note equals 66

As originally written above, this waltz was suggested for grand allegro 3/4. It may be easily arranged to be a most suitable piece for petit allegro 2/4 or for various tendu combinations at the barre.

Arranged for Petit Allegro 2/4: MM half note equals 84

Schumann: Promenade, from Carnaval, op. 9

Played as written for slow Pirouettes from fourth, fifth, and second: MM quarter note equals 138

This piece, as originally written above, was suggested for slow pirouettes from fourth, fifth, and second. It might be arranged, as in the following example, for battement tendu (quick).

Arranged for Battement Tendu (quick): MM quarter note equals 60

Schumann: Valse Allemande, from Carnaval, op. 9

Played as written for Grand Allegro 3/4: MM dotted half note equals 63

As originally written above, this waltz was suggested for grand allegro 3/4. Like the Schumann example above (Promenade, from *Carnaval*, op. 9), this movement would make a fine 2/4, perhaps for battement frappé.

Arranged for Battement Frappé: MM half note equals 88

Schumann: Waltz, op. 124, no. 4
Played as written for Grand Allegro 3/4: MM dotted half note equals 66

This piece, as written above, was listed under grand allegro 3/4. The example just below demonstrates how the texture may be enriched somewhat to render the music fuller and more powerful. The characteristic grand allegro waltz rhythm in the right hand of measure 4, as written, is generally more helpful in the odd-numbered measures, as was discussed earlier. Note the following example and the rhythmic alternatives offered in the starred measures.

Schumann: Novelette, op. 21, no. 2

This piece, which is not taken from the repertory lists in chapter 4, is not really suitable for any ballet technique combination as written. Appropriately arranged, however, it can be very usable in a number of contexts. The following examples illustrate this and demonstrate graphically that music should not be disregarded as unusable for ballet technique class simply because, as originally written, it is not immediately functional. The accompanist is encouraged to always examine potential ballet material with an open mind and a sharp imagination. She will thereby greatly expand and develop her dance repertory in terms of both quantity and style.

The most readily adaptable material in the Schumann Novelette is measures 1 through 16. The original tempo marking is "MM quarter note equals 152." The following three examples alter the tempo markedly, as well as altering the texture of the original composition, while preserving the overall melodic and harmonic contours. The first four measures as originally composed are reproduced just below.

Played as originally composed: MM quarter note equals 152

Arranged for Battement Tendu Dégagé: MM quarter note equals 88

Arranged for Ronds de Jambe à Terre: MM quarter note equals 116

Arranged for Grand Allegro (3/4): MM dotted half note equals 63

Like the preceding example, this arrangement has been changed into a triple meter and has been recast in the style of a grand allegro waltz.

Scriabin: Étude in E Major, op. 8, no. 5

Played as composed for Ronds de Jambe en l'Air: MM half note equals 50

This étude, as originally written above, is listed under ronds de jambe en l'air. The example provided below, consisting of the first two measures of the original composition, is sufficient to demonstrate that this material may be arranged to make a very lovely adagio. One beat of the original composition is equivalent to one 3/4 measure of the arranged adagio material.

Arranged for Adagio: MM quarter note equals 104

Since the harmonic rhythmic of the arranged adagio, above, is only one quarter as fast per measure as the original composition, the first four measures of the original material would equal sixteen measures of adagio music.

Tchaikovsky: Chanson Triste, op. 40, no. 2
Played as originally composed for Ronds de Jambe en l'Air: MM half note equals 50

As originally written, above, this piece is listed under ronds de jambe en l'air. Two examples of arrangements follow. The first example renders the material as a sharp 2/4, suitable for bright combinations like battement frappé. The second example converts the material into a smooth waltz, suitable for ronds de jambe à terre.

Arranged for Battement Frappé: MM quarter note equals 88

Arranged for Ronds de Jambe à Terre: MM quarter note equals 116

In the example just above, the harmonic rhythm of each measure is again changed. One measure of the original composition equals two measures of waltz in the arranged version.

Tchaikovsky: Schneeglöckchen, op. 37, no. 4

Played as originally composed for Ronds de Jambe à Terre: MM eighth note equals 116

This piece was originally suggested for ronds de jambe à terre, just above. The example provided below converts the original material to an adagio by enriching and embellishing it.

Arranged for Adagio: MM eighth note equals 100

6 Adapting Piano Repertory with Complex Phrasing Challenges: Four Advanced Lessons

Three Preludes from Bach's *Well-Tempered Clavier*

Bach—A Rich and Inexhaustible Resource. The music of Johann Sebastian Bach offers a rich and virtually inexhaustible resource both for dance choreography of every kind and for music repertory for the ballet technique class. The topic of adapting Bach's keyboard music to the ballet technique class could easily fill a book in itself, because so many examples could be put forth.

Three Preludes. For the purpose at hand, three of the preludes from Bach's *Well-Tempered Clavier* (WTC) are discussed as proven offerings:

Prelude no. 1, in C Major, BWV 846, WTC, Book 1
Prelude no. 2, in C Minor, BWV 847, WTC, Book 1
Prelude no. 6, in D Minor, BWV 851, WTC, Book 1

The classically trained pianist will be familiar with each of these preludes, and will likely have played at least one of them. As written, they present only modest technical challenges. And—with careful editing to render them square in terms of phrasing—they can either be played virtually as is or be modified in various ways to support many dance combinations.

The Challenge of Square Phrasing. All three of these preludes share a deceptive and challenging characteristic; that is, upon analysis, they reveal phrasing that is not as regular as the casual listener might think. This is the primary impediment to their immediate use in dance class. The amount of work required to fix them for this purpose is not insignificant. It requires skill and musical sensitivity.

These three preludes, discussed below, present increasingly complex challenges in arriving at a squarely phrased composition while preserving musicality and logic.

Prelude no. 1, in C Major, BWV 846, WTC, Book 1

This prelude, when listened to just as the beautiful piece of music it is and in a nonanalytical way, flows forth with grace and logic. Most likely, the listener is not alerted to the fact that the phrasing is not square (although not uncommon with Bach). It must be made square, though, if it is to be used in ballet class. With some careful editing, the music can be arranged into four-, eight-, twelve-, and sixteen-bar components, plus another sixteen bars, all of which work perfectly well for the purpose intended and likely without arousing any suspicions on the part of the dancers that the original composition has been changed.

The edits presented below are certainly not the only possible solution to the "square phrasing" issue. Accompanists are not only invited, but encouraged, to explore and achieve their own successful arrangements of this piece and any other composition that they would like to consider for the dance class.

Detailed Edits. After a suitable introduction by the accompanist, the first sixteen-measure phrase of the dance exercise is created as follows:

- Measures 1 through 4, as written by Bach, can be played as is, and then repeated to make the first eight-bar phrase of the dance exercise.
- Measures 5, 6, and 7 of the composition, as written by Bach, can be played as is, and then an additional, improvised measure added, in the same style, but in E minor, to make the first four measures of the second eight-bar phrase of the dance exercise.
- Measures 8 through 11 of the composition, as written by Bach, now function as the second four measures of the second eight-bar phrase of the dance exercise.

Therefore, the first eleven measures of the composition, as written by Bach, have been edited to make the first sixteen-measure phrase of the dance exercise.

To continue, the second sixteen-measure phrase of the dance exercise (if the accompanist wishes to include it) can be created as follows:

- Measures 12 through 19 of the composition, as written by Bach, can be played as is, to make the third eight-bar phrase of the dance exercise.
- Measures 20, 21, and 22 of the composition, as written by Bach, plus measure 24 (measure 23 is skipped) make the first four measures of the fourth (final) eight-bar phrase of the dance exercise.
- Measures 25, 28, and 29 of the composition, as written by Bach (measures 26 and 27 are skipped), make the first three of the last four measures of the fourth (final) eight-bar phrase of the dance exercise.
- One measure is needed to complete the exercise. Combine the first two beats of measure 30, as written by Bach, with the first two beats of measure 31, as written by Bach, to make the final (eighth) measure of the fourth (final) eight-bar phrase of the dance exercise.
- The dance exercise can then be ended with a final C-major chord.

The methodology set forth above—which starts with a thirty-five-measure composition with uneven phrasing and transforms it into a thirty-two-measure composition that is squarely phrased and suitable for dance combinations—appears complex and, to many accompanists, not worth the effort. Whether the result achieved is worth the amount of work required is for the accompanist to decide.

Summary of Edits. The edits above are summarized below:

Table 6.1

Original Composition		**Dance Exercise**
Measures 1–4; then repeated	=	Measures 1–8
Measures 5, 6, and 7 plus one measure improvised in E minor; then measures 8–11	=	Measures 9–16
Measures 12–19	=	Measures 17–24
Measures 20, 21, and 22 plus measure 24; then measures 25, 28, and 29; then measure 30, first two beats, plus measure 31, first two beats	=	Measures 25–32 (add final C-major chord)

Substantial Payoffs for Careful Editing. In the case of the Prelude in C Major, above, reducing a composition by only three measures might, on the face of it, not give the initial impression of being labor-intensive. Such an assumption is quickly deflated, however, once the necessary surgery is begun. Taking on such a challenge will end badly if it is carried out without a thorough and sensitive analysis of the music.

Again, not all accompanists will want to spend the time needed to do this. However, the occasional highly motived, challenge-loving accompanist will likely distinguish himself from other accompanists with less ambition—because he will be introducing a rich musical repertory into the dance class that, in many cases, will rarely, if ever, have been heard there. Furthermore, absolute assurance is given here that, if musical editing is done intelligently and with care, and then is practiced sufficiently prior to introduction into the class, the accompanist can perform even heavily edited works convincingly and appealingly.

Fully Notated Edits. With complex endeavors like the one for the Prelude in C Major, it is essential that the original score be printed out and clearly notated to indicate all relevant details—new measure numbers to match the dance exercise, necessary repeats, the elimination of unused measures, any alterations in chords, etc. Not to do so invites confusion on the part of the accompanist—and thereby on the part of the dancers—during performance in the dance class.

Any Composer. The kind of music editing discussed above for the Prelude in C Major, and the potential payoffs of such editing, also apply not only to the two Bach preludes discussed below, but also to an incredible variety of compositions by hundreds of composers, spanning centuries.

Other Potential Modifications to the Bach Prelude in C Major. Although the discussion above focuses on creating logical eight-bar phrases for dance

Bach, Prelude no. 1 in C Major, WTC Book 1.

m19
8
m20
9
m21
10
m22
11
m23
m24
12
m25
13
m26
m27
m28
14
m29
15
m30
16
m31
m32
m33
m34
m35
C

exercises, a few other editing options are briefly touched upon below. (The nature of these appears frequently and in more detail with regard to other compositions elsewhere in this book.) Such potential adaptations will depend largely on the dance exercise contemplated, but considerable flexibility is possible.

Triple Time. The uniform texture and straightforward harmonic progressions in this piece make its "C" (4/4) time signature especially, and easily, adaptable to improvisations in triple time—in various ways and in various tempos.

The subdivision of four sixteenth notes for each beat can be changed to triplets. At moderate tempos, this will yield a smoother-sounding 4/4.

At reduced tempos, the same configuration as described just above can give the effect of a slow, graceful "3/4" composition, so that each beat of the original composition then becomes a "3/4" measure in itself, thereby potentially quadrupling the length of the music. In this case, each "3/4" measure can, if desired, then be further subdivided into sextuplets so that, to the listener, it sounds like a "3/3" composition, with each quarter note subdivided into eight notes. Many variations to this approach are possible, and are easily improvised.

Other Enhancements. Regardless of whether the edited-for-dance version is performed with its original rhythmic configurations, with the adaptations suggested immediately above, or with those easily summoned up by the accompanist, the piece can be additionally enhanced, for example, by doubling the first note of each beat into an octave or by lowering it an octave. This will create additional rhythmic clarity and stability, and it will enrich the tonality.

Tempo. Finally, the experimentally minded accompanist can demonstrate for himself that, with the appropriate modifications possible to texture, rhythmic configuration, accents, and energy, the Prelude in C Major can be convincingly played at a very wide range of tempos that completely alter its character—making it, in effect, a new piece, and even a candidate for rapid, sharp steps in the center portion of the class.

Prelude no. 2, in C Minor, BWV 847, WTC, Book 1

Although this prelude is similar in rhythm to the Prelude in C Major discussed above ("C" time, with continuous sixteenth notes), it has a very different character. Its minor tonality, coupled with its unrelenting sixteenth notes in both hands, give it a driving, mechanistic quality that lends itself beautifully to certain dance steps. It is reasonable to suggest that this prelude, as written by Bach, would likely be performed within a range of tempos also appropriate for the Prelude in C Major.

The Prelude in C Minor, like the Prelude in C Major, is similarly deceptive to the casual listener, in that its phrasing is not square, although it begins squarely enough. In fact, one challenge for the accompanist in squaring up this piece for dance exercises is that, the more closely it is examined, the more ambiguity there seems to be with respect to where one phrase ends and another one starts. There is also the issue of the long, cadenzalike passage at the end, which offers serious resistance to "roping and branding" for the purpose intended. Nevertheless, careful work yields a suitable solution, presented below.

Detailed Edits. After a suitable introduction by the accompanist, the first sixteen-measure phrase of the dance exercise is created as follows:

- Measures 1 through 8, as written by Bach, can be played as is, to make the first eight-bar phrase of the dance exercise.
- Measures 9, 10, and 11 of the composition, as written by Bach, plus measure 13 (measure 12 is skipped) make the first four measures of the second eight-bar phrase of the dance exercise.
- The same measures 9, 10, and 11 of the composition, as written by Bach, plus measure 13 (measure 12 is skipped) are repeated, to make the second four measures of the second eight-bar phrase of the dance exercise.

Therefore, the first thirteen measures of the composition, as written by Bach, have been edited to make the first sixteen-measure phrase of the dance exercise.

To continue, the second sixteen-measure phrase of the dance exercise (if the accompanist wishes to include it), can be created as follows:

- Measures 14, 15, 17, and 18 (measure 16 is skipped) make the first four measures of the third eight-bar phrase of the dance exercise.
- Measures 19 and 20, played and then repeated, make the second four measures of the third eight-bar phrase of the dance exercise.
- Measures 21, 22, 23, and 24, as written by Bach, make the first four measures of the fourth eight-bar phrase of the dance exercise.
- Measures 25, 27, and 35 and the last half only of measure 37 plus the first half only of measure 38 make the last four measures of the fourth eight-bar phrase of the dance exercise. (Measures 26, 28–34, 36, and the first half only of measure 37 are skipped.) That is to say, the final measure (four quarter-note beats) of this eight-bar phrase is composed of the last half of measure 37 plus the first half of measure 38.
- The last half of measure 38 can be used for a final cadence, played either as is or simply as a C-major chord.

The accompanist is advised that, if he transcribes the above verbal edits for this prelude graphically onto the score, the last three measures, as written by Bach—measures 36, 37, and 38—should have the bar lines redrawn as follows, to reflect in part what has been described above:

- The original measure 36 and the first half of the original measure 37 should be lined out.
- A new, prominent bar line should be drawn halfway through the original measure 37, just before the C half note (third beat) in the bass.
- Another new, prominent bar line should be drawn halfway through the original measure 38, just before the third beat.

Bach, Prelude no. 2 in C Minor, WTC Book 1.

x 2
m19
5
7
m20
6
8
m21
9
m22
m23
m24
12
m25
13
m26
m27
14
m28
Presto
m29
m30
m31
m32
m33
m34
Adagio
m35
Allegro
15
m36
m37
16
m38
C

A measure has now been clearly redefined, consisting of the last half of the original measure 37 and the first half of the original measure 38. Thus, the original bar line at the beginning of the original measure 38 can be either ignored or lined out. (The final cadence follows, based on the last half of the original measure 38.)

The editing job above yields a square dance exercise of thirty-two measures, further subdivided into sixteen-, eight-, and four-bar sections. In order to accomplish this, a judicious and fairly complex process, sometimes challenged by ambiguity in the original phrasing, had to take place, including the repetition of certain measures, the elimination of others, and the relocation of a few bar lines. The process was rendered especially challenging, due to the cadenzalike passages in the fast fifteen measures, a good portion of which had to be eliminated in order to preserve a consistent overall character for the purpose of dance class.

As in the Prelude in C Major, the surgery performed on the Prelude in C Minor is—or at least appears to be—complex and labor-intensive, and therefore it is probably not appetizing to many accompanists. However, if the edits are incorporated and are practiced well, the new version will come off sounding natural and seamless—and many dancers and instructors who appreciate music will respond to such a unique and beautiful offering.

Table 6.2

Original Composition		Dance Exercise
Measures 1–8	=	Measures 1–8
Measures 9, 10, 11, and 13; then repeated	=	Measures 9–16
Measures 14, 15, 17, and 18, plus measures 19 and 20, which are repeated	=	Measures 17–24
Measures 21, 22, 23, and 24, plus measures 25, 27, and 35, and ending with last half of measure 37 plus first half of measure 38	=	Measures 25–32 (add final C-major chord or arpeggiated figure)

Summary of Edits. The edits above are summarized here:

Textural and Rhythmic Possibilities. The accompanist is encouraged to explore, as applicable, various rhythmic, textural, and other possibilities as they occur, in the spirit of those offered for the Prelude in C Major. The Prelude in C Minor is ideal for many sharp combinations in duple time at the barre or during the first portion of center work.

Two specific suggestions:

- The music can be played in a very steady, staccato or semi-staccato manner, with a strong accent on the first sixteenth note of each beat.
- The rhythm in the right hand (only) can be modified from four sixteenth notes per beat to a dotted sixteenth note plus a thirty-second note (then repeated) per beat, to provide an effective and powerful rhythmic counterpoint.

Prelude no. 6, in D Minor, BWV 851, WTC, Book 1

The vigorous character of the Prelude in D Minor, with a time signature of "C" (4/4), is achieved through a sparse texture of relentless sixteenth-note triplets in the right hand above driving eighth notes in the left hand, creating an unmuddied rhythmic repetition that impels the music forward.

Square Phrasing a Challenge. This prelude, like the two discussed above, requires some fixing—in this case, a significant effort—in order to bring it in line for a squarely phrased dance exercise (although it has been successfully choreographed exactly as written for ballet performance repertory). Like the two other preludes, a casual hearing of this one can easily lull the listener into the impression of repeatedly square phrasing, probably due in part to its driving, metronomic character. However, analysis reveals, once again, some ambiguity regarding exactly where one musical thought ends and the next picks up—no problem for listening, but trouble for a dance exercise.

Confusing Bar Lines. To add significantly to the problem, this prelude exhibits a peculiarity, addressed in detail below, with respect to where its bar lines were originally drawn (not an issue in the other two preludes). This peculiarity confuses the ear, and it must be overcome if the piece is to be used in the ballet class.

Anyone who had not analyzed this piece and who was listening to it without a score could reasonably be expected to hear the first two unaccompanied eighth notes in the left hand as the pickup to an *assumed* downbeat of the first measure—that is, where the sixteenth-note triplet pattern in the right hand enters. In fact, an uninformed hearing of this piece based on this expectation is reinforced as the music progresses, because the patterns of phrasing in the right-hand triplets seem to validate this perception.

To restate the above, the third eighth note in the left hand, with the first right-hand triplet above it, is convincingly heard as the downbeat to the first measure. In fact, however, the first two left-hand eighth notes are not a pickup. They are the downbeat of the first measure, which has no pickup (except a single sixteenth-note triplet in the right hand). It follows that the first sixteenth-note triplet is not the downbeat of the first measure after all. It begins on the second count.

The reality is that, unless the listener had carefully studied the score and had trained herself to "hear" the bar lines as they are actually written, it would be almost impossible to grasp the piece as it is notated. The likelihood of dancers understanding it as written while performing a combination in class is nonexistent. The solution is to *redraw the bar lines so that they match how the piece sounds*! In addition, certain measures must be skipped in order for the material to be dished out in square phrases—the *sine qua non* for combinations in the ballet class.

To arrive at a revised score that can be easily read, the accompanist must begin with a clean printout of the original score and use a heavy marking pen to draw new bar lines as indicated below, while ignoring the original bar lines.

An approach to the challenge of squaring up the Prelude in D Minor and realigning its bar lines for use in ballet class is offered below (referred to as Realigned Dance Exercise).

Detailed Edits. After a suitable introduction by the accompanist, the first sixteen counts of the Realigned Dance Exercise are as follows (a quarter note equals one count):

Realigned Dance Exercise, New Measure 1 (Counts 1–4)
- The new measure 1 bar line is redrawn to the left of the first right-hand triplet.
- New measure 1 ends after the first count of original measure 2.
- The two opening left-hand eighth notes now become the pickup to new measure 1.

Realigned Dance Exercise, New Measure 2 (Counts 5–8)
- The new measure 2 bar line is redrawn one count to the right of its original location.
- New measure 2 ends after the first count of original measure 3.

Realigned Dance Exercise, New Measure 3 (Counts 9–12)
- The new measure 3 bar line is redrawn one count to the right of its original location.
- New measure 3 ends after the first count of original measure 4.

Realigned Dance Exercise, New Measure 4 (Counts 13–16)
- The new measure 4 bar line is redrawn two counts to the left of original measure 6.
- New measure 4 ends after the first two counts of original measure 6.

Explanation: Realigned Dance Exercise, New Measure 4 (Counts 13–16). To square up phrasing, the last three counts of original measure 4 have been eliminated, as well as the first two counts of original measure 5. Therefore, the downbeat of new measure 4 is now what was formerly the third count of original measure 5. New measure 4 ends halfway through original measure 6, where a new bar line should be drawn. If the dance exercise ends here, it will be conveniently in F major. (Note: If the accompanist wishes, to make the transition from the last triplet of new measure 3 to the first triplet of new measure 4—a large, rapid leap—more accommodating technically, the first note only of the last triplet of new measure 3 may be played, and the last two notes eliminated.)

The second sixteen counts of the Realigned Dance Exercise are as follows (a quarter note equals one count):

Realigned Dance Exercise, New Measure 5 (Counts 1–4)
- The new measure 5 bar line is redrawn after the second count of original measure 6.
- New measure 5 ends after the first two counts of original measure7.

Realigned Dance Exercise, New Measure 6 (Counts 5–8)
- The new measure 6 bar line is redrawn after the second count of original measure 7.
- New measure 6 ends after the first two counts of original measure 8.

Realigned Dance Exercise, New Measure 7 (Counts 9–12)
- The new measure 7 bar line is redrawn after the second count of original measure 8.
- New measure 7 ends after the first two counts of original measure 9.

Realigned Dance Exercise, New Measure 8 (Counts 13–16)

- The new measure 8 bar line is redrawn after the second count of original measure 9.
- New measure 8 ends after the first two counts of original measure 10. If the dance exercise ends here, the new measure can end in A minor.

The third sixteen counts of the Realigned Dance Exercise are as follows (a quarter note equals one count):

Realigned Dance Exercise, New Measure 9 (Counts 1–4)

- The new measure 9 bar line is redrawn after the second count of original measure 10.
- New measure 9 ends after the first two counts of original measure 11.

Realigned Dance Exercise, New Measure 10 (Counts 5–8)

- The new measure 10 bar line is redrawn after the second count of original measure 11.
- New measure 10 ends after the first two counts of original measure 12.

Realigned Dance Exercise, New Measure 11 (Counts 9–12)

- The new measure 11 bar line is redrawn after the second count of original measure 12.
- New measure 11 ends after the first two counts of original measure 13.

Realigned Dance Exercise, New Measure 12 (Counts 13–16)

- The new measure 12 bar line is redrawn after the second count of original measure 13.
- New measure 12 ends after the first two counts of original measure 13. However, two counts must be inserted at the end of new measure 12 in order to make it complete (four counts). In order to do this, two counts in D minor are added, with the same type of sixteenth-note triplet configuration as in all previous counts.

The fourth sixteen counts of the Realigned Dance Exercise are as follows (a quarter note equals one count):

Realigned Dance Exercise, New Measure 13 (Counts 1–4)

- The new measure 13 bar line coincides with the original measure 16 bar line.
- New measure 13 ends where original measure 16 ends.

EXPLANATION: REALIGNED DANCE EXERCISE, NEW MEASURE 13 (COUNTS 1–4). To square up phrasing, all of original measures 14 and 15 have been eliminated. This being the case, the first right-hand note in new measure 13—the B-flat (above middle C) sixteenth note—should be played, and the tie-over from the now-eliminated previous measure should be ignored.

Realigned Dance Exercise, New Measure 14 (Counts 5–8)

- The new measure 14 bar line coincides with the original measure 17 bar line.
- New measure 14 ends where original measure 17 ends.

Bach, Prelude no. 6 in D Minor, WTC Book 1.

m13
8
9
+ 4 beats, D minor 16 (32 beats)
m14
m15
m16 1
Play
8
m17 9
16
m18
m19
m20
m21 1
8
m22 9
(64 beats)
16
A7
(End D major)
m23
m24
m25
m26

Realigned Dance Exercise, New Measure 15 (Counts 9–12)

- The new measure 15 bar line coincides with the original measure 21 bar line.
- New measure 15 ends where original measure 21 ends.

EXPLANATION: REALIGNED DANCE EXERCISE, NEW MEASURE 15 (COUNTS 9–12). To square up phrasing, all of original measures 18, 19, and 20 have been eliminated.

Realigned Dance Exercise, New Measure 16 (Counts 13–16)

- The new measure 16 bar line coincides with the original measure 22 bar line.
- New measure 16 ends where original measure 22 ends. The final three sixteen-note triplets in the right hand may be improvised as an A-major seventh chord, with a final cadence to D major on the following beat.

Two Important Comments. Two important comments are offered here regarding Prelude no. 6, in D Minor, BWV 851, WTC, Book 1:

1. Alteration of Bar Lines. The alteration of bar lines in the Prelude in D Minor in order to square up the music into even phrasing began by shifting them by one count (one quarter note) to the right. However, beginning with new measure 4, new bar lines are shifted to the middle of what were the original measures.

2. Counts versus Beats. The above vetting of the Prelude in D Minor is in the context of four quarter-note counts per measure, just as the piece was written. Those studying the edited score that follows should not be confused by the circled, handwritten numerals—1, 8, 9, 16, 32, and 64—that repeat themselves throughout. These numerals are not measure numbers; rather, they are intended merely as convenient aids to indicate to the performer where phrases of eight *eighth-note beats* begin and end throughout the edited piece. Therefore, the numbers indicate the following:

- The smallest phrases of eight beats (eighth notes) each,
- Larger, overarching phrases of sixteen beats (eighth notes),
- Larger, overarching phrases of thirty-two beats (eighth notes), and
- Larger, overarching phrases of sixty-four beats (eighth notes).

The pattern above is repeated in the second half of the edited exercise, yielding two equal sections of sixty-four beats each.

One Possible Rhythmic Modification. The accompanist is encouraged, as always, to explore her own modifications to original compositions. One suggestion is presented below, as an example, for the Prelude in D Minor.

- The sixteenth-note triplet rhythm in the right hand can be modified throughout to the duple rhythm of an eighth note plus two sixteenth notes.

Note Regarding Bach's Cello Suite no. 1, First Movement—Prelude. The Prelude to the Cello Suite no. 1, G Major, BWV 1007, First Movement, is a good example of a composition by Bach for an instrument other than the keyboard that can be modified for ballet technique class. While consisting of only the solo line, its elegant lyricism folds into a rich, logical harmonic plan in a manner that only Bach does so well, rendering it a beautiful piece for the piano.

This composition does require significant editing in order to square up its phrasing for a slow dance exercise, similar to the work required for the three preludes from the *WTC*, discussed above. It can be enriched through judicious pedaling to emphasize the harmony. No detailed analysis will be presented here regarding its editing or performance. The point to be made is that, if the accompanist is interested, nonkeyboard alternatives can be found and appropriately arranged.

Prokofiev's Piano Concerto no. 2, G Minor, op. 16, mvt. 1—Andantino

Editing a Piano Concerto for the Ballet Class. The first movement—Andantino—of the Concerto no. 2 in G Minor for Piano and Orchestra, op. 16, by Sergei Prokofiev, is an example of how material from a piano concerto can be adapted for the ballet class. In general, this four-movement concerto is—without exaggeration—fantastically difficult and not for any pianists except the most advanced. However, the opening material in the first movement offers a lyrical theme with gentle accompaniment that is ideal for slow combinations like pliés and adagios. This music should be particularly appealing to the ballet accompanist because the piano part—at least the portion addressed in this discussion—can be extracted from the orchestra with minimal consequences and played quite presentably as a piano solo.

Making the Phrasing Square. The chief issue in fixing up this music for a ballet technique class is making the phrasing square—in this case, a moderately difficult challenge, requiring careful attention. The graphic at the end of this section, which shows the hand edits to the score that make this possible, should be examined in parallel with the textual description immediately below.

Layout of the Edited Score

- The first few pages of the Andantino comprise sufficient material to arrive at the edited version for a ballet class combination. The rest of the movement can be discarded.
- The first piano part has been extracted from the two-piano, four-hand version for editing. The second piano part—the orchestral reduction—is nonessential and has been discarded.
- The edited material is arranged so that no page turns are required (not always possible, but convenient in this case). The two-page score can be placed on opposite sides of a binder.
- The final product is in two sections, each sixteen measures in length.
- The original measure numbers are hand-written in small characters at the bar lines; the measure numbers as identified and counted for the edited version are heavier and circled. The latter will be used in the Detailed Edits presented just below.

Prokofiev, Concerto no. 2 in G Minor for Piano and Orchestra, op. 16, mvt. 1—Andantino (excerpt).

m18
3
4
m19
mp
m20
5
p
m21
6
m22
7
m23
8
m27 - Last Beat
m28
9
13 un poco cresc.
m29
10
14
m30
8va
11
15
m31
12
mf
16
C
2nd x
Omit

Detailed Edits. The first sixteen-measure section should be revised as follows:

- The original version of this composition has four measures of introduction—two for the orchestra followed by two for the piano. Only the second of the two measures for piano shows in the edited version, due to the layout of measures on the page. However, the left-hand accompaniment is identical in both measures; therefore, the accompanist can simply repeat the introductory measure in the left hand in the edited score to allow for more dance preparation.
- In the edited version, measures 1 through 8 (circled numbers) can be played as originally written to make the first eight-bar phrase of the dance exercise.

Although measures 9, 10, and 11 (circled numbers) work beautifully in the original composition, they constitute an incomplete fragment that must be fixed for the dance class.

- Measures 9, 10, and 11 are played as is, and measure 11 is repeated, yielding measures 9 through 12. This entire process is repeated, yielding measures 13 through 16. This makes the second eight-bar phrase of the dance exercise.

For the second sixteen-measure section, the measure numbering restarts with a circled "1."

- Measures 1 through 7 (circled numbers) are played as is, followed by the first three counts of measure 8 (circled number). These measures correspond to measures 16 through 22 of the original composition, followed by the first three counts of measure 23 of the original composition.

Fixing the Phrasing. At this point, because of phrasing issues that must be addressed—always the overriding consideration—the fourth count of measure 23 of the original composition is omitted, as well as measures 24, 25, and 26, and the first three counts of measure 27 of the original composition. Note: These omissions are not expressly shown in the graphic at the end of this section. These original measures are simply not there, because this allows the complete, edited version of the material to be laid out on two pages.

- The last count for measure 8 (circled number—was measure 23 of the original composition) is supplied, as shown in the graphic, by the fourth count of the original measure 27, which has been pasted into the attached graphic and serves as the pickup to measure 9 (circled number). This makes the third eight-bar phrase of the dance exercise.
- Measures 9, 10, and 11 (circled numbers), and the first three counts of measure 12 (circled number) are played as is (the fourth count is omitted), *plus the fourth count of the newly edited measure 8 (circled number), which is returned to here and which serves for the second time as the pickup to measure 9 (circled number).* Measures 9, 10, and 11 (circled numbers), and the first three counts of measure 12 (circled number) are then repeated, and an improvised fourth count added in C major, in

a style like the previous configurations, to complete the phrase. This makes the fourth (final) eight-bar phrase of the dance exercise.

Complex, but Smooth with Practice. Although the somewhat complex procedure set forth immediately above for massaging the musical material into four eight-bar phrases is proven, it is understandable that it might be a bit overwhelming to at least some potential users. For this reason, the musical score, including all graphic depictions of the edits, is included below for reference and comparison with the above text. If the edited score is practiced sufficiently, so that the changes proceed smoothly and musically, the material will sound seamless. Only a pianist who knows the original score well would realize that something has been changed.

Summary of Edits. The edits above are summarized below:

Table 6.3

Original Composition		**Dance Exercise (Circled Numbers)**
First Sixteen-Measure Section		
Measures 5–12	=	Measures 1–8
Measures 13 and 14, plus measure 15 played twice. Then repeat.	=	Measures 9–16
Second Sixteen-Measure Section		
Measures 16–22, plus first three counts of measure 23; add fourth count of measure 27.	=	Measures 1–8
Measures 28–30, plus first three counts of measure 31; add fourth count of new measure 27 (second time) as pickup to repeated measures 28–30, plus first three counts of measure 31, with fourth count of measure 31 omitted and replaced with improvised configuration in C major.	=	Measures 9–16

As with any editing exercises set forth in this book to make original compositions usable for ballet classes, the methodology above is certainly not the only solution. Accompanists are always encouraged to explore other possibilities.

7 Improvisation

Improvisation, Lack of Training, Common Illusions

Lack of Improvisation in Classical Training. Ballet accompanists and pianists who aspire to become ballet accompanists will learn or have learned that some degree of skill at improvisation is extremely valuable. The reality, however, is that most classical pianists who have been trained in university or conservatory environments—that is to say, those who have received a degree, or even an advanced degree, in music, including programs aimed at performance—may have had no training whatever in improvisation. This is despite the fact that, in some previous centuries, improvisation has played a significant role in certain classical music performance traditions.

In relatively modern times, solo cadenzas for piano concertos are not left to the soloist to improvise. Cadenzas, along with the rest of the piece, are conceived by composers and are published in finished form. The soloist—regardless of his instrument—practices, memorizes, and performs the cadenza exactly as it was written by the composer. There is the occasional soloist who composes his own cadenza, but this is not an improvisation.

The Avant-Garde. Improvisation, guided or otherwise, is not uncommon in modern music, and it often appears in what has been designated as the "avant-garde." In this context, however, the improvisation called for—a chief component of which may be chance, or play—may require no knowledge whatever of traditional music theory or harmony. A striking example is "Paper Piece" by Benjamin Patterson, written in 1960 for five performers, which involves nothing but sounds of paper being crumpled, torn, rubbed, and twisted, and paper bags filled full of air and popped in accordance with a written score that, by the very nature of the concept, involves a kind of improvisation.

Improvisation for Modern Dance. For modern dance accompanists, improvisation is an absolutely indispensable tool. Ideally, it includes a broad knowledge of music and musical styles, including the use of modes, jazz, dissonance, and atonality; and, at least at times, it utilizes the piano as the percussion instrument that it is, in that sounds traditionally produced on the piano are accomplished by hammers striking strings. The modern dance accompanist should be extremely comfortable with varied and complex rhythms and untraditional phrasing. In the modern dance class, the piano can be employed in many nontraditional ways: for example, by playing the instrument after the insertion of paper, paper clips, or other materials into the strings, or by plucking the strings, or by producing various rapping sounds that cause the instrument to resonate.

Pianists are used not infrequently for modern dance accompaniment. However, there is a broad opinion that the best instrumentation for modern dance accompaniment is percussion: for example, a bongo, or a complete drum set, possibly with a marimba or a xylophone.

The Ballet Class—Improvisation versus Musical Scores. Broadly speaking, one encounters two types—or extremes—of accompanists in the ballet class: those who use printed music and those who do not. Some accompanists come into class with binders full of music. A session or two spent listening to this type of accompanist generally indicates that very little, if any, improvisation is going on—even with a score as the basis, which is almost always rendered more or less literally. The opposite extreme is the accompanist who never, or at least very rarely, comes to class with any printed music. This means either that he has all or most of his music memorized, or that he is doing a great deal of improvising. Both extremes—being score-bound and score-free—limit the repertory, production capacity, and creativity of the ballet pianist. A synthesis of these extremes—extremes that can, in fact, be highly complementary to each other—yields virtually unlimited possibilities for musical ideas and material.

Common Illusions. There are some common illusions, or misconceptions, about the extremes of improvisation and playing from printed music that bear deconstructing. One illusion is that ballet accompanists who improvise all or most of the time are always fresh and creative. This is completely untrue, because accompanists who improvise all of the time generally fall into ruts.

Just like other pianists, accompanists who rely solely on improvisation have, with rare exceptions, their own artistic and technical limitations. Therefore, without constant self-vigilance and a serious desire to expand musically, they end up sounding pretty much the same in every class—replaying the same patterns and ideas over and over, and even falling into the habit of playing in only one or two keys. Even the limitation to a couple of key signatures can, in time, wear on the dancers and dull them, whether they realize it or not.

This question might be raised: *When does improvisation cease to be improvisation?* The answer is that, when improvised patterns or ideas are repeated over and over—and cemented through this repetition—they cease to be improvisation, largely, and become memorization. The point is that, just because an accompanist does not have a printed score in front of him, it does not mean that he is improvising in the pure sense of the word, even if the musical ideas were originally his.

The other illusion—or assumption—is that accompanists who carry around a lot of music do not or cannot improvise; in other words, that they are dependent solely on their manuscripts. Although this is frequently true, pianists do often combine, at least to some degree, scores and improvisation. In fact, the pianist who works from printed scores and has the ability to modify and reinvent this material may be less vulnerable to repetition than the pianist one who never uses printed music.

Improvisation in the Ballet Class. With regard to improvisation for the ballet class, although it is true that classical musicians who are trained at college levels receive teaching in music theory and harmony, there is no likely mandate or pressure, or even occasion, to use this knowledge in a practical way—for example, to learn to improvise. The exception is the jazz student and musician, for whom improvisation is generally the basis of the art.

Improvisation on Printed Music

Practice. Improvisation, like any other skill, must be practiced. For the ballet accompanist, developing the ability to improvise can be accomplished in a variety of ways. One of these is to wade gradually into improvisation by modifying and embellishing the printed music that he uses for class. Conservative first steps can lead to more emboldened experiments. Embellishing—or improvising on—printed music can and should include these efforts:

- Taking the opportunity to present musical introductions in a variety of ways
- Changing single bass (left-hand) notes to octaves, as appropriate
- Changing melodies in the right hand from single notes to octaves (or broken octaves), or vice versa
- Changing chords to arpeggios
- Embellishing single-note melodies with thirds or sixths
- Adding passing tones to melodic patterns, including appoggiaturas (accented passing tones)
- Adding trills or other decorative flourishes
- As appropriate, changing legato patterns to staccato, and vice versa
- Changing key signature from major to minor, and vice versa
- Enriching or altering rhythmic patterns in the bass (An excellent example would be taking almost any piece in duple meter and making a tango out of it: a dotted eighth note plus a sixteenth note, followed by two eighth notes; or a sixteenth note plus an eighth note plus a sixteenth note, followed by two eighth notes. Ragtime would be another candidate.)
- Changing duple meters to triple meters, and vice versa, to accommodate various dance steps and combinations
- Altering—that is to say, elongating—the musical content between each set of bar lines to render one 4/4 or 3/4 measure as two (a great way to stretch, that is, double, musical material, especially where it is limited, and especially applicable for slow dance combinations like pliés and adagios).

Artistic License. An experienced ballet accompanist should be capable of taking most of his repertory of printed music and making three or more on-the-spot arrangements—or improvisations—out of it in order to accommodate various dance steps and combinations. The ballet accompanist needs to own the mindset that improvising on, or otherwise embellishing or arranging, a musical score is almost always a justifiable and worthwhile practice, as long as the effort is done with intelligence and skill. Stated succinctly and with a slightly different perspective, almost anything goes—as long as the instructor likes it.

The ballet accompanist should not be intimidated by experimentation if it is informed by awareness of the context, by skill, and by experience. A false or unwarranted sense of musical purity will generally serve only to hobble the accompanist. Appropriately altering or transforming compositions to fit dance steps—either through improvisation or through formal arrangement—is no different from what countless classical composers have done for centuries, in musical forms like the symphony or sonata, or theme and variations, or what the composer of a sound track for a film does when he molds and manipulates thematic material in various ways to fit various situations or moods in the film.

Printed Music as a Harmonic Foundation for Improvisation. Innumerable compositions and, in this case, their harmonic structures, specifically, can and should be used as a basis for improvisation in the ballet class. Competent, comfortable, spontaneous harmonic modulation, unsupported by printed music, takes practice and experience and can be a challenge. Thus, it is strongly recommended that the accompanist complement other strategies in his exploration of improvisation by engaging with many of his music manuscripts solely on the basis of their harmonic structure, as a final step in improvising on printed scores as described in paragraphs above. That is so say, the accompanist should challenge himself from time to time—and often, if possible—to use the printed score solely as if it were a chart of chord progressions.

It follows that the accompanist, depending on his adventurousness, may begin this endeavor with scores that are relatively straightforward, even simple, harmonically speaking. However, the concepts apply to music of significant harmonic complexity as well. In general (but, as always, subject to many case-by-case exceptions), it is suggested that music with a simpler harmonic content is suitable for virtually any dance step or combination, while the more highly complex harmonies characteristic of the twentieth century may be more readily applied to slower combinations like pliés, adagios, and stretches—at least until the accompanist becomes relatively comfortable with improvising for faster combinations.

At any rate, limiting himself, as above, to the map of harmonic progressions before him, the accompanist should, as appropriate to the dance combinations being supported, improvise every other aspect of his musical offering—meter, rhythm, melody, and supporting or embellishing configurations. Flexing his wings in this way, the accompanist can prepare himself as much as possible for the leap into pure improvisation. In addition, he will, in effect, be increasing his repertory enormously.

The Fertile Ground of Twentieth-Century Harmonies. Music from the twentieth century is an especially rich source of music for improvisation. Slow, lyrical combinations involving pliés, adagios, stretches, or a port de bras or slow rond de jambe are an open door for the ballet accompanist to render beautiful, largely intuitive, supporting music. The accompanist can take harmonies even from just a measure or two of a score by, for example, Debussy, Ravel, or Poulenc, and expand them into brief, on-the-spot improvisations. The rich harmonies of composers like these can be woven one or two at a time into coherent yet richly ambiguous textures, underpinned by an appropriate rhythmic framework and melodic fragments.

Polytonality. Polytonality is a special niche of twentieth-century music that lends itself readily to attention-getting and exciting improvisations for dance music, and the accompanist definitely should exploit it as an occasional spice for ballet technique classes. Polytonality uses more than one key or tonality simultaneously. (If only two keys or tonalities are used at the same time, the applicable term is *bitonality.*) Polytonality has been used by composers such as Stravinsky (*Petrushka*), Prokofiev (*Sarcasms for Piano*), and Darius Milhaud (*Saudades do Brasil*); the work by Milhaud is explored a bit further just below.

Saudades do Brasil. *Saudades do Brasil*, op. 67—famous for its polytonality—is a suite of twelve dances for piano, a work of nostalgia and longing, composed in 1920 (later transcribed by Milhaud for orchestra) after the composer's visit to Brazil in 1917–1918. Each dance, named after a place or neighborhood in Rio de Janeiro, is based on a duple tango or samba rhythm:

Sorocaba (Dedicated to Madame Regis de Oliveira)
Botafogo (Dedicated to Oswald Guerra)
Leme (Dedicated to Nininha Velloso-Guerra)
Copacabana (Dedicated to Godofredo Leão Velloso)
Ipanema (Dedicated to Arthur Rubinstein)
Gávea (Dedicated to Madame Henrique Oswald)
Corcovado (Dedicated to Madame Henri Hoppenot)
Tijuca (Dedicated to Ricardo Viñes)
Sumaré (Dedicated to Henri Hoppenot)
Paineiras (Dedicated to La Baronne Frachon)
Laranjeiras (Dedicated to Audrey Parr)
Paysandu (Dedicated to Paul Claudel)

Saudades do Brasil is specifically mentioned here because it is a rich source of polytonality, combined with rhythms that are perfect for many dance combinations in duple meter, both at the barre and during the first portion of center work. Ballet accompanists are encouraged to explore this work both as a composition in itself (and which is amenable to modification and variation) and as a source of tonal and rhythmic inspiration for pure improvisation.

Improvisation without Printed Music

Suggestions and Guidelines. Improvising without printed music is a subject that, in itself, could fill several books. Here the discussion is limited to some basic suggestions and guidelines for the ballet accompanist. When implemented and practiced along with the techniques based on printed scores as set forth above, improvisation can help open the door to the development of some facility in this area. Ballet accompanists seeking additional material on improvisation will find extensive sources on the internet, especially relating to jazz and jazz harmonies—some material will be downloadable at no charge and others for a cost.

Although a number of in-depth books on jazz are available, written by prominent figures, they are not easy to follow. The authors of these books are highly accomplished professionals, but the way the books are organized may make absorption of the material highly challenging. At any rate, the field of jazz requires a great deal of application and practice and, ideally, direct contact with those in the field in order for the accompanist to progress. However, even if the ballet accompanist gleans only a few ideas from one or two of these books, that payoff may be worth it.

Exercises for Improvisation. The following basic exercises—and others like them that the accompanist can develop on his own—will help the accompanist to develop a degree of confidence, flexibility, and freedom in improvisation.

- Practice basic cadences, in various inversions, for all major and minor keys (following the circle of fifths), such as V–I, IV–V–I, and ii–V–I for major keys, and V–i, iv–V–i, and ii–V–i for minor keys.
- Practice modulating from a major key to its relative minor key, and vice versa.
- Practice embellishing basic chords with various color tones by adding the sixth, seventh, ninth, and thirteenth.
- Practice playing various seventh chords and alternating among them—that is, the dominant seventh, major seventh, and minor seventh, or the half-diminished seventh and the fully diminished seventh.
- For all of the above, play scales and improvise melodies in the right hand while playing chords and other accompaniments with the left hand.

"Sink or Swim." An interesting and challenging exercise to practice at the keyboard (but primarily outside the ballet class, or at least until some facility has been developed) is an approach that might be aptly dubbed "sink or swim." Without any deliberation, the pianist quickly and randomly places his hands on the keys; wherever they land, the pianist's challenge is to work his way to a logical harmonic resolution in three or four moves. Once the exercise is accomplished, it can be repeated as many times as desired.

The Tightrope and the Net. Imposing improvisational challenges on oneself can be done at the keyboard when one is alone or in the context of the ballet class. However, although the accompanist will want to acquire some facility at improvisation before trying out anything in the dance studio, there is something to be said for taking chances, at some point, in the presence of the dancers. In this context, things may happen, ideas may occur, and the accompanist may find resolutions almost instantaneously that are far less accessible—or, frankly, are not available at all—when there is no pressure. In this kind of "tightrope walk" approach, the accompanist must improvise, on the spot, the "net" that will save him, literally without a second's hesitation, from disrupting or interrupting the combination—something to be avoided at all costs. Although doing this can be a bit frightening, it can also be exhilarating, and it becomes easier and more natural with time. Additionally, developing this kind of skill and flexibility will be an extremely valuable tool if the ballet accompanist ever decides to try playing for modern dance.

Theory versus Intuition. The best improvisation embraces an ever-shifting interplay of knowledge and intuition—or, to use another word, inspiration. Possessing a firm knowledge of music theory and harmony is not an impediment to inspiration, but rather the basis for it. Cerebral work and diligent practice are required to develop the base—the working technique—that serves as a springboard to the flight of intuition. Freedom comes from informed discipline. The time and energy that the accompanist devotes both to objective knowledge of harmony and to the practice of stepping off into the open space of improvisation will pay off.

Observing Other Accompanists. Aspiring or beginning accompanists, and those who have had a few months of experience, are strongly encouraged to find opportunities, if possible, to observe other accompanists playing for ballet classes. The goal is to see how they operate, how they organize themselves, if at all, and what mix of improvised and printed music they draw upon. Refer to the section of chapter 2 entitled "Observing Other Accompanists."

8 Ballet-Related Accompanying Outside the Ballet Technique Class

Other Ballet-Related Accompanying

Other Accompanying Opportunities. The pianist who plays for ballet technique classes will, in some cases, and depending on the type and sophistication of the institutions or academies where he works, have the opportunity to do other ballet-related accompanying. This work may include accompanying for pointe classes, for ballet repertory classes (and rehearsals), for adagio (partnering) classes, or for national character dance classes. Each type of class deals with a special aspect of ballet, and a professional ballet dancer will likely be thoroughly trained in each area. In doing the accompanying work referenced above, the accompanist may want to make some special preparations. Each area of accompanying is discussed below.

Pointe Class

Demanding and Athletic. Pointe work, which is done while wearing hard-toed pointe shoes that enable the dancer to balance over the ends of the toes, traditionally involves only female dancers, in order to make them appear weightless or airy. Although men occasionally perform in pointe, generally it is done for a special or even comedic effect. Men do sometimes take pointe classes, because proper training in pointe builds up core body strength and can improve body alignment and balance.

Pointe work is a serious athletic discipline. It is difficult and demanding, and it requires years of proper training and conditioning in order to be done without some degree of discomfort or injury to the dancer. Beginning pointe classes are especially demanding and can be very painful, especially for the legs and feet. Other issues are that pointe shoes need to be specially fitted and demand serious attention and responsibility to maintain. Dancers may wear their pointe shoes during all or part of their regular ballet technique classes.

Of central importance in pointe work are to train dancers to balance properly and also to strengthen their feet and ankles. The accompanist will observe that correctness of approach is heavily stressed and that the rising steps (relevé and sous-sus) discussed in chapter 3 of this book are basic to pointe work (and, indeed, to all dancing).

General Structure of the Pointe Class. In the pointe class, which generally lasts about an hour, there may or may not be some barre work to warm up the dancers' feet. It is usually better for the dancer to become thoroughly warmed up before attempting pointe work. An ideal way to ensure this is for the dancer to take a technique class before the pointe class. After the barre work (which may include many of the traditional combinations used in barre work for technique class, such as pliés and ronds de jambe), the dancers proceed to the center work. The material covered in the pointe class may seem less established and organized than what is covered in the technique class, and it will vary from session to session. After playing for pointe class a few times, the accompanist will have a better grasp of the situation and will be more confident about what to expect.

Music for Pointe. Much of the music literature that the accompanist uses for technique class may be used in the pointe class—if the accompanist keeps certain considerations in mind. A good deal of the music for pointe class demands an especially light, uplifting quality. Music that is heavy, weighty, or lugubrious is generally not suitable. The majority of music in 2/4 time should be played with a strong upbeat and should have a bright, staccato quality in order to underscore the sharp, precise movements of the dancers. Music for pirouettes will also be in demand. For bourrées and other steps, the accompanist should have available a number of waltzes with a light, running character. In other words, the accompanist's approach to pointe work should be characterized by a quality of lightness and clarity, supported by a rhythmical pulse that is bright and well accented.

Adagio (Partnering) Class

Pas de Deux, Codas. In adagio (or partnering) classes, dance students are trained to work with other dancers. Although more than two dancers sometimes work together, adagio work is usually done with one partner. Each female dancer is paired with a male dancer, and their work together trains them in the various aspects of pas de deux. The French term *pas de deux* literally means "step of two," and it includes both the singular form and the plural form. In ballet, *pas de deux* can be thought of as a dance sequence for two dancers. Not all of the work in pas de deux is of an adagio nature, by any means, although much of it is. In adagio work, the partners will learn how to waltz together, how to perform mazurkas and polonaises, and how to execute a wide variety of other combinations and styles—including codas. *Coda*, in ballet, refers to the finale of a group of dancers and, generally, the finale of a pas de deux. Typically, the coda is the fourth section of the pas de deux. The structure of a classical grand pas de deux is touched upon briefly just below.

Grand Pas de Deux. A grand pas de deux, usually performed by principal dancers (ballerina and danseur), generally comprises four parts: the entrée (introduction), the adagio, the variations (two,—one solo for each dancer), and the coda (conclusion). These elements share a theme—love, for example—and are regarded collectively as the virtuosic highlight of the ballet.

- *Entrée.* This is a short introduction, or prelude, to the pas de deux. The dancers enter with great show (at the same time or one after the other), acknowledge each other, and position themselves for the adagio.
- *Adagio.* This is a slow, graceful, elaborate partnering sequence in which the ballerina performs elegant, sustained movements while the danseur supports her, often with lifts.
- *Variations.* The dancers separate and, in turn (generally, the danseur first), perform dance solos that feature the dancers' virtuosity and athleticism.
- *Coda.* The coda (or tail) is the final element of the grand pas de deux. Generally, it is a kind of summation of the entire dance sequence, incorporating features of the adagio, the variations, or both, and ending with a great climax.

Pas de Quatre, Swan Lake. As a relevant side note, most ballet accompanists, a large portion of the public audience, and all trained or aspiring ballet dancers will be familiar with both the choreography and the music (instantly locatable on YouTube) to the famous pas de quatre—"The Four Little Swans"—from Act II of Tchaikovsky's *Swan Lake.* However, examples abound in ballet of other pas de quatre choreographies.

The Accompanist's Role. The accompanist will use a wide range of musical offerings and styles for adagio classes. If she comes to class equipped with a scope and quality of music comparable or identical to what she would be using for standard ballet technique classes, she should generally find herself well prepared. In particular, she should have a plentiful repertory of adagios and waltzes of all varieties, and some bright, energetic 4/4 or 2/4 pieces suitable for turns.

Specific Scores. Sometimes, adagio work requires specific music from the classical ballet repertory; in these cases, the accompanist will be confronted with piano reductions from various ballet scores, which range in readability and difficulty from moderate to nearly impossible. Thus, the accompanist should, if possible, obtain scores (piano reductions) ahead of time and do some preparation—or she should be very skilled at sight-reading. Pianists are advised here that many piano reductions of orchestral music can be extremely *unpianistic* and may lay very awkwardly—even impossibly—under the hands. Accompanists should not hesitate to simplify these scores so that they are reasonably playable without hours of practice.

Outside of occasional sight-reading or advance preparation, however, the accompanist should not encounter any special difficulties in playing for adagio classes. In general, this work will demand the same standards of alertness and musicality that are necessary for ballet technique class accompaniment.

Men's Classes. Some dance schools include men's classes in their curriculum. It is not necessary to address men's classes in a separate part of this book, since the requirements of the ballet accompanist for such classes will not be unique in terms of music. As in adagio classes, traditional ballet music may come into play. The main purpose of men's classes is to build technique and strength in general—but especially to condition and prepare male dancers for the special challenges of partnering with women: providing the necessary physical support, developing sensitivity to the needs of female partners, and ensuring the very critical ability to properly and safely execute lifts and catches.

Repertory Class

Corps de Ballet Work. The purpose of repertory classes is to teach dancers the various choreographies of established ballet repertory. Corps de ballet work is emphasized. The dancers perform together in groups of varying size, learning dance steps and focusing on working as an organized, closely coordinated unit, while developing a knowledge of traditional ballet works.

Sight-Reading. For repertory classes, it is highly desirable that the accompanist have strong sight-reading skills. As noted in the previous section, "Adagio (Partnering) Class," many piano reductions of orchestral ballet scores are extremely difficult to read on sight—especially relatively modern ballet scores, like those of Stravinsky and Bartók, for example. Sight-reading some works from the nineteenth century is relatively less challenging, since it is often possible to anticipate where the harmony is going. Nevertheless, many "reductions" of orchestral scores hardly seem like reductions at all, and one might feel that the arranger has tried to cram in everything possible—whether playable or not—from the original orchestra score. Of course, the reading is somewhat easier to handle if the accompanist has at least some familiarity with the musical material—making it easier to fake.

Capturing the Essential. Whether the ballet accompanist does some outside preparation (advisable for inexperienced and less-skilled sight-readers) or sight-reads the score during class, she will often find it helpful, perhaps even necessary, to determine what material in the score is of primary importance and what can be considered nonessential. She should focus first on capturing the essential melodic, harmonic, and rhythmic content of the score, and from that point she may add whatever else she can manage. Once the accompanist has grasped the essence of the music, she will find it easier to add other embellishing and enriching material.

Coordinating the Score with the Dancers. Often, the accompanist will discover that the score does not include tempo variations and changes that the dancers—or more specifically, the choreographer—may require. In such cases, various musical accommodations may be asked of her. She is advised to note them down or at least to bear them in mind from rehearsal to rehearsal. If the accompanist can also retain a general idea—the more specific, the better—of what choreography goes with what music, the choreographer will not have to wade through all of the music to show the accompanist where the dancers are starting.

Live Performances. Many choreographers and dancers have frightening stories about ballet conductors letting the music either run away or lag during a live performance—nearly causing disaster. It follows, of course, that if the accompanist is going to be involved during live performances—which is not uncommon—it is a sine qua non that she reproduce accurate, dependable tempos and know exactly what the dancers are doing at every point in the music—actually watching them as much as possible.

The Accompanist as a General Asset. The dancers, the choreographer, and the ballet master/mistress depend on the accompanist's ability to accurately reproduce the music in all of its aspects from one rehearsal to another and during performances. The accompanist who can absorb the necessary information discussed above and reflect it back will be an invaluable help to everyone involved. At times, the accompanist will have opportunities to remind the dancers and others of various counts and measure numbers that coincide with various dance steps; the accompanist can also offer significant support in accurately retaining, reproducing, and indicating correct tempos, pauses, *the all-important entrances*, and other performance data. These abilities, which a good dance accompanist should possess, develop gradually with time, as she becomes involved with more dance repertory and rehearsal work.

Character Class

Importance of Character Work. In character class, the dancers learn the various steps that comprise the national character and folk dances of different countries. Thorough training in character work is essential to the aspiring professional dancer, since much corps work is made up of character dances—the mazurka, tarantella, czardas, and many others (see the Character Dance Chart). Many dancers start out professionally in the corps de ballet of dance companies, and if they expect to make it through auditions and retain their jobs, they need to be proficient in character dance.

The Accompanist's Role. As in repertory work, some of the material that the accompanist will be required to play for character work will come from traditional ballet scores, since they include a plentiful assortment of character music. A significant portion of character class time, however, will be used to teach and drill the dancers in basic character steps at the barre and in the center. The accompanist who plays for character classes will gradually acquire some knowledge of the essential nature of various character steps. She should work to acquire an adequate collection of character music in many styles; and with some experience, she likely will be able to improvise in different styles (a very desirable skill) that approximate the various character idioms. Many dancer instructors, schools, and companies own printed collections of character music, which they usually will make available for the accompanist's use. Collections of such music appear to be difficult to find online.

Character Dance Chart. Outside of the basic repertory differences, an experienced dance accompanist should not have any particular problem playing for character classes. The character dances in the chart are representative of some of the major countries and might be taught in character class. This listing is by no means complete, but it will familiarize the accompanist with the tempo and quality of some of the major character dances.

Character Dance Chart

DANCE	TEMPO AND QUALITY
AUSTRIA	
Schuhplattler	Moderate 3/4
Ländler	Moderate 3/4
CZECHOSLOVAKIA	
Janoschka	Slow 2/4
Kalamajka	Light 2/4
ENGLAND	
Morris dance	Steady 4/4
Sailor's hornpipe	Bright 2/4
FRANCE	
Bourée	Slow 3/4
Farandole	Quick 6/8
Gavotte	Bright 4/4
Quadrille	Moderate 2/4
GREECE	
Syrtos	Slow 4/4, followed by fast 2/4
HUNGARY	
Czardas	Slow 4/4, followed by fast 2/4
IRELAND	
Jig	Quick 6/8
ITALY	
Tarantella	Fast 6/8
POLAND	
Krakowiak (or Krakoviak)	Fast 4/4
Mazurka	Moderate 3/4
Polonaise	Stately 3/4
RUSSIA	
Gopak	Fast 2/4
Khorovod	Stately 2/4
Troika	Fast 2/4
SCOTLAND	
Fling	Steady 4/4
Reel	Quick 4/4
Sword dance	Steady 4/4
SPAIN	
Jota	Quick 3/8
Tango	Moderate 2/4
SWEDEN	
Daldans	Moderate 3/4
YUGOSLAVIA	
Kolo	Moderate 2/4

Index of Steps

GERALD R. LISHKA plays for ballet across the Los Angeles basin. His affiliations include California School of the Arts—San Gabriel Valley, University of Southern California—Glorya Kaufman School of Dance, Westside School of Ballet, and C. Round Ballet Works. He has worked at, among others, Interlochen Arts Academy; the American Dance Festival; Indiana University–Bloomington; Wayne State University–Detroit; National Academy of Arts in Champaign, Illinois; Louisville Ballet; and Pasadena Dance Theatre. Mr. Lishka holds Bachelor of Music and Master of Music degrees in piano from the University of Illinois at Urbana-Champaign, and he did postgraduate work there and at Indiana University–Bloomington. He is the author of *A Handbook for the Ballet Accompanist* (Indiana University Press).